Palgrave Game

MW00354064

### Series Editors
Neil Randall
The Games Institute
University of Waterloo
Waterloo, ON, Canada

Steve Wilcox
Game Design and Development
Wilfrid Laurier University
Brantford, ON, Canada

Games are pervasive in contemporary life, intersecting with leisure, work, health, culture, history, technology, politics, industry, and beyond. These contexts span topics, cross disciplines, and bridge professions.

*Palgrave Games in Context* situates games and play within such interdisciplinary and interprofessional contexts, resulting in accessible, applicable, and practical scholarship for students, researchers, game designers, and industry professionals. What does it mean to study, critique, and create games in context? This series eschews conventional classifications—such as academic discipline or game genre—and instead looks to practical, real-world situations to shape analysis and ground discussion. A single text might bring together professionals working in the field, critics, scholars, researchers, and designers. The result is a broad range of voices from a variety of disciplinary and professional backgrounds contributing to an accessible, practical series on the various and varied roles of games and play.

More information about this series at
http://www.palgrave.com/gp/series/16027

Kishonna L. Gray
Gerald Voorhees • Emma Vossen
Editors

# Feminism in Play

Gerald Voorhees
Managing Editor

*Editors*
Kishonna L. Gray
Department of Gender and Women's Studies
and Communication
University of Illinois at Chicago
Chicago, IL, USA

Gerald Voorhees
Department of Communication Arts
University of Waterloo
Waterloo, ON, Canada

Emma Vossen
Department of English Language
and Literature
University of Waterloo
Waterloo, ON, Canada

Palgrave Games in Context
ISBN 978-3-319-90538-9        ISBN 978-3-319-90539-6   (eBook)
https://doi.org/10.1007/978-3-319-90539-6

Library of Congress Control Number: 2018956252

Cover credit: Keith Mclean
Cover design by Fatima Jamadar

This Palgrave Macmillan imprint is published by the registered company Springer Nature Switzerland AG
The registered company address is: Gewerbestrasse 11, 6330 Cham, Switzerland

# Acknowledgements

It is a commonplace, but a true one, to start by saying that this book would not have been possible without the efforts of a great many people. We owe thanks to the generous colleagues who donated their time and intellectual energies to help review manuscripts for this volume: Jennifer Whitson, Steve Wilcox, Betsy Brey, Kim Nguyen, and Rachel Miles.

We would also like to thank our fellow editors who did magnificent work on the other two volumes in this trilogy. Of course, this book can and does stand on its own, but it has been enriched by our collaboration with Todd Harper, Meghan Blythe Adams, and Nick Taylor on the *Queerness in Play* and *Masculinities in Play* anthologies.

We would be remiss to overlook the editorial team at Palgrave Macmillan, notably Shaun Vigil, whose support made this ambitious project possible, and Glenn Ramirez for laying out clearly how to make it actual.

Kishonna would like to thank the courageous women inside and around gaming for their daily sacrifices and for sharing their stories with us. The world needs to know how dope you are.

Emma would like to thank everyone from First Person Scholar including faculty advisors Neil Randall, Gerald Voorhees, and Jennifer Whitson. Special thanks go to my fellow FPS editors and friends Elise Vist, Alexandra Orlando, Judy Ehrentraut, Betsy Brey, Meghan Adams, Chris Lawrence, Phil Miletic, Rob Parker, Jason Hawreliak, Michael Hancock, and especially Steve Wilcox—without all of you I wouldn't be studying games. I would also like to thank all my family and friends including my favorite gamer, my brother Edward. Extra special thanks to my partner Keith and my mother Nancy who do the daily labour of listening to me complain while making sure I'm safe, fed, and happy.

Gerald would also like to thank colleagues who provided advice, encouragement, criticism, and even resources to help make this project happen. Vershawn Young, Jennifer Simpson, Jennifer Roberts-Smith, Kim Nguyen, Neil Randall, Jennifer Jenson, and Suzanne de Castell all deserve thanks, as do any others I may have neglected to list here. I reserve my most special gratitude for Kim and Quinn for their support during this project, but more importantly for their sustained encouragement to better practice feminism in my everyday life.

# Contents

# Notes on Contributors

**Angela R. Cox** received her PhD in English Rhetoric and Composition from the University of Arkansas, USA in 2016. She grew up playing Nintendo and Sierra games, unaware that these were "for boys." Her scholarly interest in games started while studying at Ohio State University, USA, with some research in fantasy that quickly grew into research in feminism. She teaches English at Ball State University, USA.

**Milena Droumeva** is Assistant Professor of Communication and Sound Studies at Simon Fraser University, Canada, specializing in mobile technologies, sound and multimodal ethnography. She has a background in acoustic ecology and works across the fields of urban soundscape research, sonification for public engagement, as well as gender and sound in video games. Milena is co-investigator for ReFiG, a SSHRC partnership grant exploring women's participation in the games industries and game culture.

**Simone Evangelista** is a PhD candidate in the Post-graduate Program in Communication at Federal Fluminense University, Brazil, and a member of the Laboratory in Experiences of Engagement and Transformation of Audiences (LEETA).

**Reynaldo Gonçalves** is a Master's student in the Post-graduate Program in Communication at Federal Fluminense University and a member of the Laboratory in Experiences of Engagement and Transformation os Audiência (LEETA).

**Kishonna L. Gray** is an assistant professor in the Department of Gender and Women's Studies and Communication at the University of Illinois at Chicago, USA. She is also a faculty associate at the Berkman Klein Center for Internet and Society at Harvard University, USA. Gray previously served as a MLK Scholar and Visiting Professor in Women and Gender Studies and Comparative Media Studies at the Massachusetts Institute of Technology, USA.

**Robyn Hope** is a Master's student in Media Studies at Concordia University, USA, finishing her thesis under the supervision of Mia Consalvo. Prior to studying at Concordia, Robyn obtained an undergraduate degree in English and Cinema Studies at the University of Toronto, Canada. Her academic interests include digital games, game narratives, and play performance. In her spare time, she practices digital art and enjoys tabletop role-playing games.

**Elyse Janish** is a PhD candidate in the Department of Communication at the University of Colorado Boulder, USA. She researches issues related to gender and sexuality in digital contexts, focusing lately on the spaces and communities that arise around video games.

**Stephanie C. Jennings** is a PhD candidate in the Department of Communication and Media at Rensselaer Polytechnic Institute, USA. Her research focuses on feminist theory, play, horror films and video games, and histories of witch trials. She also occasionally dabbles in pedagogical theory and games-based learning.

**Marie-Josée Legault** has taught labor relations at TÉLUQ, Université du Québec à Montréal (UQAM), Canada, since 1991, where she is also responsible for a graduate program in HRM in project-based context. She is also an associate professor at the Laval Faculty of Law and UQAM's Department of Sociology. She is pursuing research on regulation of work in project-based environments, among software designers and video game developers in Canada. She has been responsible for four formally funded research teams and projects and has a current industry partnership with the International Game Developers Association to conduct their annual Developer Satisfaction Survey. She is a member of the Interuniversity Research Centre on Globalization and Work (CRIMT).

**Barbara LeSavoy, PhD** is Director of Women and Gender Studies (WGST) at The College at Brockport, SUNY, USA. She teaches Feminist Theory; Global Perspectives on WGST; Gender, Race, and Class; and Senior Seminar in WGST. Her research/publication areas include women's global human rights, sex and gender in literature and popular culture, intersectionality and educational equity, and women's stories as feminist standpoint. LeSavoy serves as lead faculty for a COIL global classroom linking students at the College at Brockport in NY and Novgorod State University in Russia and has taught several WGST seminars at the NY Institute of Linguistics, Cognition, and Culture in St. Petersburg, Russia.

**Alessandra Maia** acts as Innovation Researcher of the Laboratory of Digital Media (LMD-PPGCom/Uerj), with a Qualitec Research Scholarship of InovUerj. With a degree in Game Designer (2017) from Senac Rio, and PhD (2018) and MA (2014) in Communication from the Post-graduate Program in Communication of the State University of Rio de Janeiro, Brazil (PPGCOM/Uerj), Alessandra conducts research investigating entertainment, especially video games, and the potential for learning and development of cognitive skills for different areas of social interaction.

**James Malazita** is Assistant Professor of Science & Technology Studies and of Games & Simulation Arts & Sciences at Rensselaer Polytechnic Institute, USA, where he is the Founder and Director of Rensselaer's Tactical Humanities Lab. Malazita's research interests include the epistemic infrastructures of computer science, design, and the humanities; digital fabrication; the politics of the digital humanities; game studies; and the synthesizing of humanities and technical education. His research has been supported by the National Endowment for the Humanities, the Popular Culture Association, The New Jersey Historical Commission, and Red Hat Inc.

**Robert Mejia** is an assistant professor in the Department of Communication at North Dakota State University, USA. His research focuses on the relationship between culture, economics, politics, and technology, and addresses how these factors affect the operation of race, propaganda, entrepreneurialism, philanthropy, and video game play. His research has been published in journals and edited collections, such as *Communication and Critical/Cultural Studies, Explorations in Media Ecology, Journal of Virtual Worlds Research*, and *The Intersectional Internet: Race, Sex, Class, and Culture Online*. He is co-editor with Jaime Banks (West Virginia University, USA) and Aubrie Adams (California Polytechnic State University, USA) of the *100 Greatest Video Game Characters* and *100 Greatest Video Game Franchises*.

**Tsugumi Okabe** is a PhD candidate at the University of Alberta, Canada, where she is conducting her SSHRC funded research on detective manga in the Department of Modern Languages and Cultural Studies. She is co-translator of *Game Freaks Who Play with Bugs – In Praise of the Video Game Xevious* and the translator for the PC game *Nagasaki Kitty* (http://nagasaki-kitty.ca). Her research on women's participation in the Japanese game industry is ongoing. For more information, please visit her personal website: http://mimiokabe.com.

**Thaiane Oliveira** is a professor at Federal Fluminense University, Brazil, in the Post-graduate Program in Communication and coordinator of the Laboratory of Investigation in Science, Innovation, Technology and Education (Cite-Lab), which develops practice research on engagement experiences in the Laboratory in Experiences of Engagement and Transformation of Audiences (LEETA).

**Julia Silveira** holds a PhD in Communication from Federal Fluminense University, Brazil, where she teaches in the Post-graduate Program in Communication and conducts research on gender in digital environments.

**Lena Uszkoreit** is a postdoctoral fellow in the UXR lab at the University of Ontario, Canada's Institute of Technology. She received her PhD in Communication from the University of Southern California, USA's Annenberg School for Communication and Journalism. Her dissertation explored the relationship between viewing and objectifying female Twitch streamers and the perception of female gamers and women in general. Her favorite games include *Portal 2, World of Warcraft, The Sims*, and *Overwatch*.

**Gerald Voorhees** is an assistant professor in the Department of Communication Arts at the University of Waterloo, Canada. His research is on games and new media as sites for the construction and contestation of identity and culture. In addition to editing books on gender and digital games, role-playing games, and first-person shooter games, Gerald is co-editor of Bloomsbury's Approaches to Game Studies book series.

**Emma Vossen** is an award-winning public speaker and writer with a PhD from the University of Waterloo, Canada. Her research about gender and games was selected as the focus of a 50-minute documentary made by CBC Radio and broadcast across Canada in 2016. Her dissertation examines the sexism girls and women face when participating in games culture. She is the former Editor-in-Chief of game studies publication *First Person Scholar*.

**Emma Westecott** is Assistant Professor in Game Design and Director of the game:play lab at the Ontario College of Art & Design (OCAD), University in Toronto, Canada. She has worked in the game industry for over 20 years in development, research, and the academy. She achieved international recognition for working closely with Douglas Adams as game designer then producer for the best-selling CD-ROM adventure game, *Starship Titanic* (1998). Since then, Emma has built up a worldwide reputation for developing original as well as popular game projects.

**Johanna Weststar** is Associate Professor of Industrial Relations and Labour Studies in the DAN Department of Management and Organizational Studies at Western University, Canada. A primary research topic is project-based workplaces with a focus on working conditions, worker representation, and workplace regulation in game development. She also studies pension board governance. Johanna is a member of the CRIMT research network and a past president of the Canadian Industrial Relations Association (CIRA).

**Emma Witkowski** is a senior lecturer at RMIT University, Australia's School of Media and Communication. As a socio-phenomenologically informed ethnographer, her research explores esports cultures, high performance play, gender, and networked play. She is a board member on the Australian Esports Association and in 2017; she was a postdoctoral researcher with Locating Media, University of Siegen, Germany, studying pro-esports teams, coaching, spectatorship, and mega-events. Her current research explores esports in Australia, and grassroots cultures of involvement.

# List of Figures

# 1

# Introduction: Reframing Hegemonic Conceptions of Women and Feminism in Gaming Culture

Kishonna L. Gray, Gerald Voorhees, and Emma Vossen

Despite the disciplinary norms and institutional investments of games studies that malign and marginalize critical perspectives (Jensen and de Castell 2009), recent history has proven feminist lenses to be an essential facet in examining games, gamers, and gaming culture. As Nina Huntemann (2013) argues, feminist game studies examines how gender, and its intersections with race, class, sexuality, and so on, is produced, represented, consumed, and practiced in and through digital games. This volume continues and extends the project of feminist game studies, examining the varied representations, practices, and institutions of games and game cultures from a feminist perspective, exploring personal experiences, individual narratives, and institutional phenomenon inherent in the hegemonic, often patriarchal, structures of gaming.

Though current events make it all the more pressing, in fact there is a rich, far-reaching history of feminist theory and games criticism that the essays in this book build upon. Media scholars have long examined the presumption that games depict women in a manner that is both polarizing and marginalizing: as either sexual objects or damsels in distress (Gailey 1993; Dietz 1998).

K. L. Gray (✉)
University of Illinois, Chicago, IL, USA

G. Voorhees • E. Vossen
University of Waterloo, Waterloo, ON, Canada

© The Author(s) 2018
K. L. Gray et al. (eds.), *Feminism in Play*, Palgrave Games in Context,
https://doi.org/10.1007/978-3-319-90539-6_1

**1**

The continued under-representation (and erasure) of female game characters has been documented (Williams et al. 2009), as has the tendency to depict women in a sexualized manner with either less clothing (Beasley and Standley 2002; Taylor 2006), absurd or idealized body proportions (Schröder 2008; Martins et al. 2009), or narrative and discursive positioning as sexually promiscuous (MacCallum-Stewart 2009). Nevertheless, some studies examining the depiction of women in digital games have drawn attention to an increasingly diverse set of portrayals of female gender identity. One of the first game characters to warrant this attention is Lara Croft, the titular character of the *Tomb Raider* series. There is a small but significant body of feminist media criticism that argues that Croft functions (alternatively or simultaneously depending on the author) as an object of sexual desire, a femme fatale, a model of empowered womanhood, or a masculine style of femininity (Schleiner 2001; Kennedy 2002; Mikula 2003; Jansz and Martis 2007). Stang (2017) and Voorhees (2016) each finds an extremely capable and heroic figure in Ellie, the teenage girl from *The Last of Us*, who is nevertheless disempowered not through sexualization but rather by the game's positioning of her as a daughter-figure to Joel, the other, and primary, playable character. Still, despite the proliferation of increasingly capable heroines, Summers and Miller's (2014) recent study of game advertising demonstrates that while the more traditional depiction of the virtuous damsel in distress is less common in games, female game characters are simultaneously increasing sexualized.

As feminist game studies has developed, a number of focal points have emerged, notably: women and marginalized peoples' erasure or unfavorable representation in games, exclusion and harassment in game cultures and communities, and participation in the game industry and other sites of production. More recently, it has become increasingly clear that the intersecting facets of these problems (which we discuss in detail in the next section) and the intersectional identities of the people who experience the greatest precarity in games and game cultures are vital sites of inquiry.

This volume aims to continue to propel feminist theory and criticism of games forward in the midst of the social, political, and material reality that is #Gamergate, Black Lives Matter, the Trump administration, and the general social trend toward a more reactionary, conservative politics of exclusion. As the chapters within this volume reveal, these conditions may shift the grounds of the complex conversations we continue to have about women within games, women and girls as gamers, and women within the industry, but they do not fundamentally redefine it.

# Patriarchy and Power in Games

Whether visible in the persistent color line that shapes the production, dissemination, and legitimization of dominant stereotypes within the industry itself, or in the dehumanizing and hypersexual representations commonplace within virtual spaces, video games encode the injustices that pervade society as a whole. According to Williams, Martins, Consalvo, and Ivory (2009), gaming is a space defined by the "systematic over-representation of males, white and adults and a systematic under-representation of females, Hispanics, Native Americans, children and the elderly." Similarly, rape culture, inscriptions of toxic masculinity, and homophobia are ubiquitous to gaming; the criminalization of black and brown bodies and the profiling of black and brown gamers is foundational to gaming culture; and the injustices that predominate in gaming culture also sit at the core of the political, social, and communal arrangements of mainstream US culture. In this way, games provide both training grounds for the consumption of narratives and stereotypes and opportunities to become instruments of hegemony. As many of the essays argue in Nick Taylor and Gerald Voorhees' edited volume, *Masculinities in Play*, they offer spaces of white male play and pleasures, and create a virtual and lived reality where white maleness is empowered to police and criminalize the Other. Games provide opportunity to both share and learn the language of racism, sexism, and the grammar of empire, all while perpetuating cultures of violence and privilege (Gray 2012, 2014; Nakamura 2009; Leonard 2003, 2006, 2009, 2014).

No contemporary example of this hegemony is more salient than #Gamergate. #Gamergate gained media attention through misogynist and racist attacks on women gamers, critics, and developers. Followers of #gamergate attempted to justify their campaign as a move to restore ethics in video game journalism, resulting in hostile and violent environments for women, queer folk, and people of color. This is exceptional, given the way that "gaming capital" has been distributed, historically, in a manner that overwhelmingly centers heteronormative, white, masculinity, equating this perspective and identity as the default player (Consalvo 2008). However, it is not new. For women, the sexually marginalized, and people of color, this treatment reaches far back beyond this moment, and stems from certain elements fundamental to games and game cultures.

While #GamerGater may have been the "straw that broke the camel's back," it certainly does not represent the origins of harassment experienced by the marginalized in gaming communities. Kishonna Gray's foundational work explores harassment campaigns and hostile environments experienced by women in console gaming since these spaces first went live (Gray 2012). She also explored the experiences of racial and ethnic minorities within gaming communities for failing to conform to the White male norm (Gray 2014). Additional work is emerging showcasing the disturbing realities for women, people of color, and queer gamers within streaming communities (Gray 2016). These examples rightfully demonstrate that #Gamergate did not create a culture of toxicity; rather, this reality is central to gaming contexts.

Prior to #Gamergate, harassment in gaming has been excused, minimized, and outright overlooked as a matter of boys and men too immature to understand the consequences of their vitriol. But now that the average age of a gamer is 31 (Shaw 2012), there is an increased urgency to acknowledge that the normalizing of this behavior is inherent to the patriarchal culture of digital games. This culture extends beyond the gamers; the devaluation of marginalized bodies is present in the games that we play, the developers who create them, and the culture and institutions that sustain them—making them all complicit in the continued oppression of the marginalized.

The attention generated by another recent controversy also highlights that women in games have always experienced marginalization and erasure. During the design and development of *Assassin's Creed: Unity*, Ubisoft developers revealed that they viewed the task of creating a female playable character for the game's multiplayer mode with customizable avatars to be an unreasonable burden. Their comments are illustrative of their stance:

> It would have doubled the work on those things. And I mean it's something the team really wanted, but we had to make a decision… It's unfortunate, but it's a reality of game development. (Williams 2014)

Concerned gamers immediately took to Twitter to critique the legitimacy of the notion that creating a female character was double the work using the hashtag #WomenAreTooHardToAnimate. One commenter rightfully stated that, "unless you are killing her, buying her or selling her, @Ubisoft can't animate a woman you can actually play #womenaretoohardtoanimate." In short, this "inability" to animate women is a part of a larger culture of exclusion in which women gamers have always found themselves situated.

This blatant sexism has become a highly visible antagonist in an increasingly dominant narrative about the importance of diversity in the content and even production of games. But it bears repeating that #Gamergate doesn't reflect some aberration or new subculture within gaming—this is the culture in gaming. This is our society. As Lisa Nakamura (2012) states, masculinity is performed by the display of technical knowledge, and gaming is the most recent iteration of this form of social display. Gaming itself becomes a mark of privilege within symbolic discourse. Following Adrienne Shaw (2012), through this project we endeavor to continue the work of dispelling the myth and imagery of the "dominant White, heterosexual, male, teen gamer image" (29). Arguments for the practical and economic necessity of this inclusion aside, we embrace the ethical, political imperative of this act: the inclusion of women and other marginalized people in games and game cultures is fundamentally about justice, parity, and access to the common (media) experiences that connect us.

It is in this context that we view, with some uncertainty and even concern, the growing trend of development studios claiming to be willing to respond to calls for creating more diverse content, diversifying teams, and creating a more diverse industry. For an industry that actively and intentionally centers men, such efforts will no doubt be troubled by entanglements with entrenched cultural values masquerading as objective, neutral practices. History is replete with instances where the rhetoric and ideals of inclusion are contradicted by the very policies and practices intended to instantiate them. One such effort to challenge the preeminence of masculinity in the game industry and carve out women's spaces in games, which peaked in the 1990s and early 2000s, is the "pink games" movement. While still pursued by some, in addition to fostering greater uptake and involvement by women, "pink games" also re-entrench a number of essentialist stereotypes about women and girls (Cassell and Jenkins 1998). Aside from this, this collective history of games is largely the story of women as passive, casual, or non-essential participants within a culture dominated by endless narratives of men and hegemonic masculinity. Thus, one of the imperatives of this book is highlight how women have been and continue to be vital to the making of games, the building of community around them, and constructing cultures of play.

Despite efforts to involve more women in games, the promotion and marketing discourses employed by the gaming industry are also complicit in reinforcing the assumption that women are intermittent, casual participants while men are perpetual hardcore players (Chess 2010). During a press release for the Xbox 360 at E3 in 2005, the new console was pitched to appeal to the casual gamer (Plunkett 2011, para. 1). This included a comparison between two fictitious users, one named Striker and the other Velocity Girl. Velocity Girl is described as someone for whom gaming is not a "central part of her existence":

now, she might never pick up a controller, never take a run in the halfpipe but she'll be able to design and sell stickers, shirts, boards, sound tracks and even design her own skate park for those hardcore gamers like Striker. (Plunkett 2011, para. 3)

Aside from feminizing and gendering the gamertag associated with womanhood, the story highlights how gendered cultural scripts are embedded in the codes of media artifacts. The framing of Velocity Girl serves as an example of how powerful and pervasive the narrative of subservient, passive women is within mediated contexts. The female gamer is there to support the experience and recreation of the male gamer through her labor, with her creations. According to Wood (1994) media are "one of the most pervasive and powerful" influences on how we view people because they are "woven throughout our daily lives" and "insinuate their messages into our consciousness at every turn" (p. 31). The media rely on stereotypes to frame messages and narratives. As Potter and Kappeler (2012) posit, "the end result of these media portrayals is a reinforcement of ethnic, gender, and class stereotypes, cobbled together in brief, dramatic, and disturbing images and words" (p. 9). The framing of Velocity Girl as a passerby within the world of gaming serves to distort women's contributions and construct a reality of men and masculinity as the central and normal entity within gaming. The term framing can be understood as a "point of view" on a given issue or event used to interpret and present "reality," magnifying or shrinking aspects of that issue or event to make it more or less salient (Hardin and Whiteside, p. 313). There is both a conscious and unconscious process occurring with the framing of Velocity Girl. While the creators intended for her framing to serve as a catalyst to encourage passive, casual gamers (i.e. girls) to become a part of the Xbox community, the ultimate effect was reify the stereotype that women as not real gamers.

Because frames are usually based on cultural understandings, they are easy for media professionals to access (Hertog and McLeod 2001; Ryan et al. 2001; Entman 1993). And the framing of women through this lens becomes even more powerful when aggregated across time and space and we begin to see the pattern of continual diminishing of women's participation in gaming. Indeed, the gendering of play has received much attention from feminist media scholars such as Shira Chess (2010) who focuses on how labor and leisure within gaming contexts have become gendered. She argues that "the playful is political" and calls for feminism to adopt play as a form of activism whereby seemingly frivolous activities can serve to unite women, especially younger feminists, and subvert the dominance of play practices defined by masculinity (Fron et al. 2007). Chess (2010) specifically refers to online worlds and games as "creating limitless possibilities for potential forms of playful activism" (13). In a way, it is co-opting a potentially negative framing of women's engagements, appropriating the hegemonic narrative of women, leisure, and casual play.

Much of feminist games scholarship pushes back against the pernicious conception of women as accessories to games and game play, and so it is imperative that this volume seeks to decenter the presumption of the male player as default, and to amend the narrative of women in gaming so as to highlight vital contributions by women in game development and culture. As Laine Nooney (2013) rightfully asserts, historical recallings of video game history are largely imagined as a "patrilineal timeline." She further explains that when women emerge as participants in the game industry, they are typically portrayed as outliers, exceptions, or early exemplars of "diversity" in the game industry.

We join with others who are cultivating an emerging groundswell of efforts to decenter masculine perspectives within games and gaming. Kaifai, Richards, and Tynes' *Diversifying Barbie and Mortal Kombat* (2016) is one of the first efforts to not only critique to masculine bias is games and game studies but to also displace it by focusing on intersectional voices. Jennifer Malkowski and TreaAndrea M. Russworm's compelling volume, *Gaming Representation* (2017), participates in this movement to displace representations that have historically, and consistently, reflected the narratives, worldviews, and desires of cis-heterosexual white men. The volume reveals the ways that folks marginalized on the basis of their gender, sexuality, race, and nationality—a rich diversity of creators and characters—are variously valorized, demonized, and otherwise domesticated (for the presumed cis-male white player) in games and gaming contexts. The powerful volume, *Queer Game Studies*, edited by Bonnie Ruberg and Adrienne Shaw (2017) reflects the efforts of queer scholars and intersectional feminists within the gaming community to rethink and make visible the queerness inherent to games. Their volume goes beyond traditional explorations of representations within games to also think about mechanics and community norms as queer, challenging traditional dichotomies within game studies (i.e. narratology/ludology) that restrict innovation ways of experiencing and studying games. Unsurprisingly, these queer mechanics and norms are most explicit in independently published, or indie, games. The volume *Queerness in Gaming* edited by Todd Harper, Meghan Adams, and Nick Taylor also participates in this project to decenter men and masculinity from discussions about games. It does so by looking unapologetically and intensely at queer games and game mechanics, queer players, and queer practices.

In this light, another imperative of feminist game studies is to continue highlighting the innovative games being created at the margins. Take for example the interactive game "Hair Nah" created by Momo Pixel. This game allows players to customize an avatar who can "smack away as many white hands" as possible within a certain time frame as they approach locs, twists, braids, or relaxed hair (Callahan 2017). The game quickly went viral. It captured a convergence of powerful contemporary racial and gendered dynamics and histories, from Black hair politics to the history of white supremacy as it relates to the hyper policing and surveillance of Black women's bodies to the daily toll of racial microaggressions Black women face. From its conception to reception, *Hair Nah* exemplifies the yearning for disruptive and transformative games. It also demonstrates the ways that games, online technology, and game culture have the potential to disrupt the hegemonic structure of gaming and address physical inequalities using digital tools.

These spaces for change are where we exist—at the intersection of possibility and potential for effecting significant change. Within the sites where games are produced, technology, communities of gamers, and virtual reality are important and potentially powerful tools for broader fights for social justice. The works of Anna Anthropy, a transgender video game designer, serve as a powerful example of using tools to fight for social and material justice. Fed up with the limited character development options and clichéd story lines in AAA games, she challenged conventional game development and design principles. Using Game Maker, a novice friendly computer program, she began creating her own games. This and other accessible game design tools enable communities traditionally excluded from power structures in gaming to participate and create innovative games. Anthropy's games include *Keep Me Occupied*, a collaborative two-player arcade game featuring Occupy protesters in Oakland being subject to tear gas and grenades, as well as *Dys4ia*, a game based on the creator's experiences with hormone replacement therapy (Lipinski 2012). As more people work their way in from the margins of games and game cultures using these and other tools, games become an increasingly viable platform for feminist activism and the struggle for social justice. It is clear that women in games and gaming push back and contest patriarchy in as many ways as they are challenged and ensnared by it; that there are as many misconceptions about the history of women within gaming culture as there are actual issues facing women in games. Women are harassed and terrorized when they play games, and so in this book we explore how graphic engines, genres, and design decisions perpetuate this. But this is the backdrop within which women also dominate by demonstrating highly skilled play, do the work of building communities around games, and generate their own experiences and meanings from play. Women are marginalized in an industry that thrives on masculine norms and expectations, so in this volume we continue to direct attention to sexism in the profession and pipeline. But in spite of and sometimes because of this, women nevertheless persist to make games and to challenge conventions rooted in bias. And because women continue to be portrayed in games in demeaning ways that diminish their worth, in this book we explore how graphic engines, genres, and design decisions perpetuate this. But women and feminists have cultivated a growing number of progressive representations, feminist histories, and ways of perceiving and experiencing games which need to be highlighted and carried forward.

Beyond these timeless yet timely problems, it is our hope that the scholarship in this book can help to address the deeply rooted, mythical assumption that women are new additions to the games industry and games culture and instead demonstrates their integral shaping of games and games culture throughout history *despite* continued attempts to exclude and alienate them from it.

\* \* \*

Like the other books in this trilogy, this volume is organized by its examination of how gender is represented in games, how gender is constructed in and through the cultural and material apparatuses that constitute game cultures, and the future directions for research and for feminist intervention in and around games. In the first section of the book, "Neither Virgin Nor Vixen: Representations of Women," we assembled five chapters that scrutinize how women are depicted in games. These essays highlight that, both historically and presently, narrative and visual representations of women in digital games are more complicated, as is their relationship to patriarchy, than we typically give them credit for. And while they are all anchored in textual (or content) analysis, these chapters also take great pains to consider how norms of production, practices of consumption, and technological systems impact the representation of women typical of contemporary digital games.

The first chapter, Angela Cox's study of the representation of women in the Sierra games designed by women, challenges the assumption that more women in game development automatically equate to more positive or progressive portrayals of women. Looking closely at Roberta Williams's *King's Quest* series and *Phantasmagoria*, Lori Cole's *Quest For Glory: So You Wanna Be a Hero?*, and Jane Jenson's *Gabriel Knight: Sins of the Fathers*, Cox argues that having women in lead roles in the game development process is necessary but not sufficient to break out of androcentric conventions. We shift granularity from a studio to a specific series with Robyn Hope's chapter on feminist history in Her Interactive's *Nancy Drew* series. Hope (mostly) lauds the series' representation of Nancy Drew, but argues that, ultimately, the series captures the fraught relationship that present-day women experience in relation to female histories.

Milena Droumeva's chapter continues and extends the examination of the representation of women in games but focuses specifically on the aural dimension, on the voices of the characters. Droumeva notes that most women are represented in action sequences through higher pitched vocalizations, including a variety of "breathy exhalations, grunts, and moans," and by examining specific female characters, as well as positive and negative player reactions to character voices, offers a set of tropes that identify conventional representational norms. Droumeva's reading of voice in games is grounded in sonic studies and is keenly aware of the role of technology in the generation of patterns of representation, like the subsequent chapters in this section.

The final two chapters in this first section focus on more contemporaneous developments regarding the representation of women in games, looking at a modern game series and studying how advances in technology impact representation. James Malazita's critique of "magical feminism" in *Bioshock Infinite* (2013) focuses on the character of Elizabeth and argues that over time she transforms from a resilient "magical feminist" sidekick into a fearful playable character whose primary agency is to sneak and hide. Malazita discusses developer interviews alongside the contrasting depictions of Elizabeth in both *Bioshock Infinite* and its downloadable content (DLC) *Burial at Sea* (2014), but also emphasizes the discursive and material impact of the game engine. His analysis illustrates the political implications of the representation of Elizabeth's character while also taking note of technical and economic constraints that both the game and the DLC were created in. Robert Mejia and Barbara LeSavoy's chapter shares a concern for how game technologies, and discourses about them, have impacted the sexual politics of video game graphics. Focusing on the *Final Fantasy* and *Tomb Raider* franchises from the Playstation 1 to Playstation 3 eras, Mejia and LaSavoy critique the "photorealistic imperative" typical of the video game industry as a direct contributor to chauvinist and misogynist sexual politics of the industry. A fitting end to this section on representation, both of these chapter chart the evolution of representations of women in games in order to remind us how the technical and the sociocultural work together to create design choices.

The second section of this volume, "All Made Up: Gendering Assemblages," features four chapters that each center a different phenomenon or experience that is typically treated as marginal. Instead of centering games, they center the sites where games are produced and the communities where players organize and around games. Together, these chapters illustrate how women in the game industry and game cultures navigate the vast material and discursive contexts in which games are situated, and remind us that not all gameplay occurs on or in front of a screen.

The first two chapters look at women in the global game development industry. Johanna Weststar and Marie-Josée Legault's chapter examines the "pipeline" to careers in game development, asking the question: can women take the dominant career path into game development or do they have to forge their own alternative paths? Weststar and Legault comb through the International Game Developers Association's 2014 and 2015 Developers Satisfaction Survey," in order to outline what it means to be a woman in contemporary game development. Highlighting statistical evidence that suggests that women experience "blocks and leakages" when they attempt to access the dominant pipeline, Weststar and Legault identify a set of persistent cultural and institutional factors that, ultimately, suggests that an alternative, indie pipeline may be a more viable option for women. Complementing the previous chapter's focus on how women enter the game industry, Tsugumi Okabe provides a detailed examination of why there are so few women in the Japanese games industry that moves deftly between national labor policies and interviews with women working at game development studios. The chapter takes into account the cultural context of Japanese labor and what Okabe has called "gendered work practices." In Japan only 12% of game developers are women and only 5% of women developers stay in the industry for longer than five years, in her chapter Okabe interviews women working in the Japanese games industry and discusses the various causes for these low numbers. In addition to illuminating how culture and policy intersect in a very specific domain of women's experiences, the chapter also contributes to the emerging body of work in regional and global game studies, helping counter the often Western and Eurocentric perspectives of game studies.

The next set of chapters turn their focus on women's experiences in the mediated spaces in which communities of players associate. Thaiane Oliveira and Reynaldo Gonçalves' chapters bring us, again, outside of the typically Eurocentric scope of game studies. They focus their analysis on the Brazilian website *WoW Girl*, which is managed by women and features content produced solely by women, and supplement it with a survey of users of the *WoW Girl* website. In doing so, Oliveira and Gonçalves build a strong case for understanding how Brazilian women gamers resist marginalization and "machismo." Lena Uszkoreit's chapter also examines the lived experience of female gamers, studying how streamers are using Twitch as a platform on which they perform their identity as both gamers and women. Uszkoreit identifies the conventions—aesthetic and performative—that are relatively unique to women streamers, all grounded in case studies of the practices of three women streamers. Uszkoreit's chapter also draws our attention to the dialectic of feminized, arguably exploitative, performances by certain streamers and efforts to displace this construction of women in games, ultimately reminding scholars and players alike that feminism can be messy, even unruly, in practice.

In the last section of the book, "Beyond Feminization: Gaming and Social Futures," we turn our attention to future directions for research and for feminist intervention in and around games. While the chapters in this section share the same concerns about the (re)production of current oppressions, the works gathered here all have strong bearings on the possible futures for women in games and feminist intervention in game cultures.

The first two chapters in this section are concerned with understanding what it means to be a "gamer girl." Picking up similar themes as Uzskoriet, Emma Witkowski's chapter looks at the different personas and performance of female gamers who are "high performance players" in the e-sport community. Witkowski tackles the complexity of the term gamer girl and, through a series of in-depth interviews, identifies the struggles of players to establish themselves as "real gamer girls" as opposed to "fake gamer girls" in e-sports, and the ways that the very notion of the "gamer girl" is formed, policed, lived, produced, and fought against. This chapter offers a much-needed counterweight to the prevailing idea in game studies, that women do not see themselves as gamers, instead providing an insightful historical account of the contexts in which they do. Emma Vossen's chapter offers a more personal and highly vulnerable perspective on the "gamer girl" by bringing her own experiences with consent as a young female gamer into conversation with theorizations of Huizinga's "magic circle." Vossen starts off the chapter with the provocative question: "why was I more afraid to pick up a controller than take off my clothes?" She then attempts to answer this question by interrogating how consent is practiced (and often ignored) between and among gamers, arguing that troubling conceptions of the magic circle contribute to the contemporary context. By drawing from sexuality studies, Vossen attempts to build a model for thinking about and practicing critical consent with other players when playing games.

Elyse Janish's chapter proceeds similarly, methodologically, in its effort to illustrate how self-doubt structures women's gameplay. Beginning from an autoethnographic study of her own experiences, Janish leads the reader through her own experiences of doubt playing and studying online games as well as her experiences of doubt as a feminist scholar presenting this research and studying games post-gamergate. Ultimately, Janish employs a feminist epistemology to interrogate both how games are played by women and how games are studied, arguing that women bring "doubt" from their everyday lives into games and games research. She proposes, and the chapter performs, a "narrative autoethnography" that is structured to enable to reader to experience and think through doubt.

The final two chapters in this section, and the book, are most explicitly aimed at feminists praxis and intervention in games and game cultures. Stephanie Jennings' chapter theorizes a "feminine gaze" in video games, a set of aesthetic and affective orientations that make space for player agency, subjectivity, and intersectional identity. Jennings engages with both the history of the male gaze in film theory and game studies, grounding her critique through a detailed examination of Ada Wong, from the *Resident Evil* series, as both a character being represented and an avatar being performed. Her reading contends with the complex interplay of sexualization, identification, and agency as they manifest in the practice of the male gaze, demonstrating how a contrasting "feminine gaze" enables feminist gameplay. Lastly, Emma Westecott's chapter asks how do we make, identify, and recognize feminist games and feminist performance in games? Westecott looks at various games, mods, and machinima alongside theater and performance art, to establish a model of gameplay as a form of performance. Building from theories of performativity and precedents in other media forms, Westecott brings the volume to a close by outlining a rubric for how women, and players generally, can enact the feminist performances of gameplay.

*   *   *

It is important that we continue to highlight the contributions of women and other marginalized groups who have always been present in games despite being marginalized and ignored. While we cannot hope that this book will remove the many obstacles women face when they play games or attempt to navigate the game industry and game culture, we are confident that the book does contribute to several ends. By further developing and advancing feminist games criticism, players may better recognize how the games they play implicate them in relations of power. By centering the women who make, play, and discourse about games, we decenter the presumed male subject of games. And by focusing on the attitudes and norms of practice characteristic of women in games, we hope to provide a sense (if not a roadmap) for players, critics, and developers to continue the struggle for radical inclusiveness in games.

Lastly, this book, which was conceived of, composed, and edited in a post-Gamergate age, can be seen as an affirmation of feminist games scholars and their scholarship, and an unequivocal rejoinder to the continued attempts to silence the voices of those of us researching and writing about gender and games. While Gamergate may have made it more perilous for already marginalized folks to do game studies, it has by no means stopped the production of knowledge about gender and games, and in fact has encouraged increased attention to these areas of inquiry. The chapters in this volume do not exist to respond to those who criticize and harass us, instead they demonstrate that despite these attempts to silence us we will go deeper, we will speak more loudly, and we will continue to build on the legacy of work that feminists have been developing since the genesis of game studies. We may do this by examining the representations of women in games from unique and novel angles (like Droumeva, Malazita, Mejia, & LaSavoy, and Hope), by showcasing our own experiences and vulnerabilities as women gamers and games scholars (like Janish and Vossen), by helping elevate the voices of women pro-gamers, streamers, and industry professionals (as do Cox, Oliveira & Gonçalves, Okabe, Uszkoreit, Weststar & Legault, and Witkowski) or by creating our own ways of framing our experiences and creations (like Jennings and Westecott). These essays don't only speak to the problems of games culture, they showcase crucial experiences and perspective, they look toward solutions, and they work toward a space and time where games culture belongs to all of us.

# Bibliography

Beasley, Berrin, and Tracy Collins Standley. 2002. Shirts versus Skins: Clothing as an Indicator of Gender Role Stereotyping in Video Games. *Mass Communication & Society* 5 (3): 279–293.

Callahan, Yesha. 2017. If You're a Black Woman Who's Tired of White People Touching Your Hair, There's a Game for That. Accessed November 19, 2017. https://thegrapevine.theroot.com/if-youre-a-black-woman-whos-tired-of-white-people-askin-1820505693.

Cassell, Justine, and Henry Jenkins, eds. 1998. *From Barbie to Mortal Kombat: Gender and Computer Games*. Cambridge, MA: The MIT Press.

Chess, Shira. 2010. How to Play a Feminist. *Thirdspace: A Journal of Feminist Theory Culture 9.1*. http://journals.sfu.ca/thirdspace/index.php/journal/article/view/273.

Consalvo, Mia. 2008. Crunched by Passion: Women Game Developers and Workplace Challenges. In *Beyond Barbie and Mortal Kombat: New Perspectives on Gender and Gaming*, ed. Yasmin B. Kafai, Carrie Heeter, Jill Denner, and Jennifer Y. Sun, 177–192. Cambridge, London: The MIT Press.

Dietz, Tracy L. 1998. An Examination of Violence and Gender Role Portrayals in Video Games: Implications for Gender Socialization and Aggressive Behavior. *Sex Roles* 38: 425–442.

Entman, Robert M. 1993. Framing: Toward Clarification of a Fractured Paradigm. *Journal of Communication* 43 (4): 51–58.

Fron, Janine, Tracy Fullerton, Jacqueline F. Morie, and Celia Pearce. 2007. The Hegemony of Play. *Situated Play, Proceedings of DiGRA 2007 Conference*.

Gailey, Christina W. 1993. Mediated Messages: Gender, Class, and Cosmos in Home Video Games. *Journal of Popular Culture* 27 (1): 81–98.

Gray, Kishonna L. 2012. Deviant Bodies, Stigmatized Identities, and Racist Acts: Examining the Experiences of African-American Gamers in Xbox Live. *New Review of Hypermedia and Multimedia* 18 (4): 261–276.

———. 2014. *Race, Gender, and Deviance in Xbox Live: Theoretical Perspectives from the Virtual Margins*. London: Routledge.

———. 2016. "They're Just Too Urban": Black Gamers Streaming on Twitch. In *Digital Sociologies*, ed. K. Gregory, T. McMillan Cottom, and J. Daniels, 351–364. Bristol: Policy Press.

Hertog, James K., and Douglas M. McLeod. 2001. A Multiperspectival Approach to Framing Analysis: A Field Guide. In *Framing Public Life: Perspectives on Media and Our Understanding of the Social World*, ed. S.D. Reese, O.H. Gandy, and A.E. Grant Mahwah, 139–161. New Jersey: Lawrence Erlbaum Associates.

Huntemann, Nina. 2013. Introduction: Feminist Discourses in Games/Game Studies. *Ada: A Journal of Gender, New Media, and Technology* 2. http://adanewmedia.org/2013/06/issue2-huntemann/.

Jansz, Jeroen, and Raynel G. Martis. 2007. The Lara Phenomenon: Powerful Female Characters in Video Games. *Sex Roles* 56: 141–148.

Jenson, Jennifer, and Suzanne de Castell. 2009. Gender, Simulation, and Gaming: Research Review and Redirections. *Simulation & Gaming* 41 (1): 51–71.

Kennedy, Helen. 2002. Lara Croft. Feminist Icon or Cyber-bimbo? The Limits of Textual Analysis. *Game Studies* 2 (2). http://www.gamestudies.org/0202/kennedy/.

Kiafia, Yasmin, Gabrielle Richards, and B. Tynes, eds. 2016. *Diversifying Barbie and Mortal Kombat: Intersectional Perspectives and Inclusive Designs in Gaming*. Pittsburg, PA: ETC Press.

Leonard, David J. 2003. Live in Your World, Play in Ours: Race, Video Games, and Consuming the Other. *Studies in Media & Information Literacy Education* 3 (4): 1–9.

———. 2006. Not a Hater, Just Keepin' It Real: The Importance of Race- and Gender-based Game Studies. *Games and Culture* 1 (1): 83–88.

———. 2009. Young, Black (& Brown) and Don't Give a Fuck: Virtual Gangstas in the Era of State Violence. *Cultural Studies? Critical Methodologies* 9 (2): 248–272.

———. 2014. Dismantling the Master's (Virtual) House: One Avatar At a Time. In *Race, Gender, and Deviance in Xbox Live: Theoretical Perspectives from the Virtual Margins*, ed. K. Grey, xi–xvi. London: Routledge.

Lipinski, Jed. 2012. Video-game Designer Anna Anthropy Describes the Life of a Radical, Queer, Transgender Gamer. *Politico.* https://www.politico.com/states/new-york/city-hall/story/2012/04/video-game-designer-anna-anthropy-describes-the-life-of-a-radical-queer-transgender-gamer-067223.

MacCallum-Stewart, Ester. 2009. 'The Street Smarts of a Cartoon Princess': New Roles for Women in Games. *Digital Creativity* 20 (4): 225–237.

Malkowski, Jennifer, and TreaAndrea M. Russworm. 2017. *Gaming Representation: Race, Gender, and Sexuality in Video Games.* Indiana University Press.

Martins, Nichole, Demitri Williams, Kristen Harrison, and Rabindra A. Ratan. 2009. A Content Analysis of Female Body Imagery in Video Games. *Sex Roles* 61 (11–12): 824–836.

Mikula, Maja. 2003. Gender and Videogames: The Political Valency of Lara Croft. *Continuum: Journal of Media & Cultural Studies* 17 (1): 79–87.

Nakamura, Lisa. 2009. Don't Hate the Player, Hate the Game: The Racialization of Labor in *World of Warcraft. Critical Studies in Media Communication* 26 (2): 128–144.

———. 2012. Queer Female of Color: The Highest Difficulty Setting There Is? Gaming Rhetoric as Gender Capital. *Ada: A Journal of Gender, New Media, and Technology* 1 (1). http://adanewmedia.org/2012/11/issue1-nakamura/.

Nooney, Laine. 2013. A Pedestal, a Table, a Love Letter: Archaeologies of Gender in Videogame History. *Game Studies* 13 (2). http://gamestudies.org/1302/articles/nooney.

Plunkett, Luke. 2011. Microsoft, Why Did You Lie to Velocity Girl? *Kotaku.* https://kotaku.com/5763772/microsoft-why-did-you-lie-to-velocity-girl.

Potter, Garry, and Victor Kappeler. 2012. Introduction: Media, Crime and Hegemony. In *The Harms of Crime Media. Essays on the Perpetuation of Racism, Sexism and Class Stereotypes*, ed. D. Bissler, 3–15. Jefferson, NC: MacFarland.

Ruberg, Bonnie, and Adrienne Shaw. 2017. *Queer Game Studies.* Minneapolis, MN: University of Minnesota Press.

Ryan, Charlotte, Kevin M. Carragee, and William Meinhofer. 2001. Theory into Practice: Framing, the News Media, and Collective Action. *Journal of Broadcasting & Electronic Media* 45 (1): 175–182.

Schleiner, Anne-Marie. 2001. Does Lara Croft Wear Fake Polygons? Gender and Gender-Role Subversion in Computer Adventure Games. *Leonardo* 34 (3): 221–226.

Schröder, Arne. 2008. 'We Don't Want It Changed, Do We?' Gender and Sexuality in Role-Playing Games. *Eludamos* 2 (2): 241–256.

Shaw, Adrienne. 2012. Do You Identify as a Gamer? Gender, Race, Sexuality, and Gamer Identity. *New Media & Society* 14 (1): 28–44.

Stang, Sarah. 2017. Big Daddies and Broken Men: Father-Daughter Relationships in Video Games. *Loading...* 10 (6): 162–174.

Summers, Alicia, and M.K. Miller. 2014. From Damsels in Distress to Sexy Superheroes. *Feminist Media Studies* 14 (6): 1028–1041.

Taylor, T.L. 2006. *Play Between Worlds: Exploring Online Game Culture*. Cambridge, MA: MIT Press.

Voorhees, Gerald. 2016. Daddy Issues: Constructions of Fatherhood in *The Last of Us* and *BioShock Infinite*. *Ada: A Journal of Gender, New Media and Technology* 9 (2).

Williams, Lauren. 2014. Gamers Revolt After Video Game Developers Says Creating Female Character Would Be "Double the Work". *Think Progress* 13. https://think-progress.org/gamers-revolt-after-video-game-developer-says-creating-female-character-would-be-double-the-work-63d74a93d17f/.

Williams, Demitri, Nichole Martins, Mia Consalvo, and James D. Ivory. 2009. The Virtual Census: Representations of Gender, Race and Age in Video Games. *New Media & Society* 11 (5): 815–834.

Wood, Julia T. 1994. *Gendered Lives: Communication, Gender and Culture*. Boston, MA: Cengage.

# Part I

## Neither Virgin Nor Vixen: Representations of Women

# 2

# Women by Women: A Gender Analysis of Sierra Titles by Women Designers

Angela R. Cox

Women in game design and games targeted to women are generally assumed to be a newer phenomenon, but women have been involved in digital game design from at least as early as the 1980s. This chapter will examine the feminist expression and representation of women in selected games designed by three prominent designers whose work was published by Sierra On-Line: Roberta Williams's *King's Quest* series and *Phantasmagoria*, Lori Cole's *Quest For Glory: So You Wanna Be a Hero?*, and Jane Jenson's *Gabriel Knight: Sins of the Fathers*. The retro-gaming trend has increased both the availability and relevancy of older games, including resurgence in interest in Sierra's legacy, in part owing to the company having recently resurrected to distribute indie developer games, including the 2015–2016 *King's Quest* serial by Odd Gentlemen. Thus, these influential games occupy a significant place in the formation of video games and the development of the roles of women in games. In her historical overview of gender inclusivity in game design, Sheri Graner Ray (2004) acknowledges the role of Sierra (and in particular, Williams's and Jensen's contributions), but goes into very little detail beyond acknowledging their games as significant titles that were designed by women.

A. R. Cox (✉)
Ball State University, Muncie, IN, USA

© The Author(s) 2018
K. L. Gray et al. (eds.), *Feminism in Play*, Palgrave Games in Context,
https://doi.org/10.1007/978-3-319-90539-6_2

## Background and Definitions

Feminist studies discussing video games have tended to focus on two features: representation and audience. Critics are often concerned that the conventionally anticipated male audience of games has underestimated the potential appeal of games to girls,[1] and has therefore focused on how to make games also appeal to girls, or to be "gender-inclusive." Ray (2004) has proposed that "gender-inclusive game design"[2] be focused on narrative, nonviolent gameplay, avatar personalization, and interpersonal relationship development; by this standard, all of the games by Williams, Cole, and Jensen are gender inclusive (except for avatar personalization), but these attributes also generally describe the adventure game genre in which these designers worked. Meanwhile, other feminist inquiry has focused on the physical representation of female characters, especially in cases such as Lara Croft of the *Tomb Raider* series, who has been lauded both as a role model and decried as eye candy for the male players, depending on which aspects of the games the analysts focus on.[3] Representation is a serious concern in gender inclusivity, as misogynist portrayals of women are often alienating to potential female (or feminist) players. Ray (2004, 29) argues that there are, historically, "two ways game designers deal with female representation in games … as a sexual object … [or] as an object to be retrieved or rescued." Other research generally affirms Ray's description of dual objectification, as in Pamela Takayoshi's 2007 study of gamer responses to games. Takayoshi (2007) finds that video games tend to exclude, sexualize, and objectify women; that there is discrimination against women among players; and that the majority of female representation in games is understood as appeals to heterosexual men.

In the case of Williams, Cole, and Jensen, the representation of women in their games is complicated, even in this apparently binary framework. As this chapter will demonstrate, their games are at once an example *and* a rebuttal of assumptions about representation of women in games. While women in these games are often objectified, the later games also tend to explicitly address that objectification. Each designer notably has her own approach, but also the Sierra titles overall developed over time to become more explicitly feminist as the company grew and employed more female designers. These three designers, especially in their earlier work, have tended to comply with androcentric[4] tropes, even when doing so somewhat critically. In the remainder of this chapter, I will address Jane Jensen's *Gabriel Knight*, Lori Cole's *Quest for Glory I* (QFGI), and Roberta Williams's *King's Quest* series and *Phantasmagoria* as case studies in how female designers have presented female characters in video games in the past and how increased support for female designers tends to produce more feminist work.

# Jane Jensen's *Gabriel Knight*: Saying Is Not Doing

Jane Jensen was a fairly late addition to Sierra's notable designers but no less influential; she worked with Sierra from 1991 to 1999, and continues to design games.[5] She contributed to other designers' work, notably helping with later games in Roberta Williams's *King's Quest* series, which was a common early assignment for Sierra employees. Her most prominent game for Sierra, however, was *Gabriel Knight: Sins of the Fathers*, a 1993 point-and-click adventure utilizing the live-action film capture technology that would reach its apex two years later with *Phantasmagoria*. *Gabriel Knight* could be said to be gender inclusive according to Ray's definition, save again for avatar personalization, as the game progresses primarily on character interactions and interpersonal relationships and is generally nonviolent. It could also be said to be feminist because it ends with an explicit discussion of gendered power dynamics (if the player takes the path that results in the titular character Gabriel surviving the game; there is an alternate ending in which the discussion does not take place). In this conversation, Gabriel's assistant Grace says that the "real tragedy" is that a family line of "strong women" was dominated by one personality that supernaturally possessed each one. This appears to criticize patriarchal institutions—that singular spirit may well represent patriarchy, and the women in the game, such as Malia Gedde, who has wealth and independence, might have complete agency if they were not restricted to patriarchal space with evil supernatural forces on the side of misogyny. Indeed, Grace's monologue conforms to the late 1980s/early 1990s trends in feminist popular media: obvious reversals of androcentric tropes and an emphasis on "strong female characters." And there can be no doubt that in the design process, Jensen had plenty of example and support from other female game designers at Sierra, including Cole and Williams, as well as others such as Lorelei Shannon. Indeed, there seems to have been little criticism of Jensen with regard to her gender, and certainly not the sort of misogynist attacks that now plague female game designers and critics; in fact, most contemporary reviews of *Gabriel Knight* seem to have been favorable.

However, at the same time, games were increasingly being seen as an exclusively masculine space, and there are significant problems with *Gabriel Knight* if we are to read it as a feminist text. Despite the overtly feminist summary at the end given to Grace as the surviving "strong female character," the game itself is generally androcentric, and tends to reward Gabriel's casual objectification of women. Indeed, the climax of the game quickly devolves into the familiar "rescue the princess" pattern that has been present in the video game medium nearly since its inception. Indeed, most of the significant interaction in *Gabriel Knight* takes place between men, and Malia's apparent agency and independence are entirely undercut by a supernatural entity that forces her to participate in a sacrificial ritual. In this way, *Gabriel Knight* is a prime example of a case in which game design attempts to be feminist in its writing and imagery, but fails at the crucial level of gameplay and procedural rhetoric.[6] Although the characters are given feminist themes to speak in dialogue, and the game was designed by a woman who was emboldened by publisher and colleague support, the gameplay itself remains firmly androcentric—no doubt a fact that accounts at least in part for its easy acceptance by a wide audience in an increasingly patriarchal medium.

It is, of course, possible that Grace's monologue deliberately represents a significant tension for female game designers: there is desire to produce feminist and gender-inclusive games, but convention and market pressures often dictate otherwise. Thus, the "strong women" of the game industry are controlled by one spirit—that of patriarchal industry pressure—which prevents them from fully coming into their own. Here it seems that it is not sufficient even to have prestige granted to female game designers, since games like *Gabriel Knight* persist in androcentric tropes despite overall support for their female designers.

## Lori Cole's *Quest for Glory I:* Restoring the Patriarchy

*Gabriel Knight*, however, was not without precedent. Indeed, Lori Cole's *Quest for Glory I: So You Wanna Be a Hero* (originally titled *Hero's Quest*) (1989) is incredibly similar in gender structures: the player controls a male avatar, but the plot hinges around a powerful, strong woman whose agency is magically overcome, requiring her to be rescued by the male hero. Designed for the Sierra Creative Interpreter (SCI) engine, and thus limited to 16 colors, Musical Instrument Digital Interface (MIDI) sound options, and other techno-historic limitations,[7] *Quest for Glory I* relies heavily on cookie-cutter-like fantasy tropes, but like many Sierra games, it plays these tropes up for laughs and delights in subverting them; the manual, for instance, is formatted as a correspondence course pamphlet from the "Famous Adventurers' Correspondence School for Heroes," which portrays the main character as bumbling and unqualified before the player even begins the game. *Quest for Glory I* had a significant number of women on the creative team, and the central plot of the game relies on the agency of women and paints the patriarchy as incompetent—but nevertheless, the patriarchal order is restored at the end of the game, and the player/hero amply rewarded for his part in aiding that restoration.

*Quest for Glory* is essentially androcentric in the usual fantasy-setting ways; the central problem of the plot involves an evil witch's curse on the local baron in an overreach of female power in a male space (i.e., a patriarchal, hereditary manorial system), which must be solved by a heroic young man. Likewise, the initial goal appears to be to rescue a damsel in distress, the baron's daughter Elsa; however, there is also the baron's son Bernard to rescue as well, presenting two gendered goals that diverge significantly. The other problem besetting the realm is the incurrence of a band of brigands and their powerful leader. The twist, however—which makes this game curiously feminist—is that the damsel in distress Elsa *is* the brigand leader, although due to the curse she is not fully aware of her identity.

At the surface level, the women in *QFGI* seem to take conventional female roles: healer, wife, little old lady, and so on, but with something a little more powerful about them. The little old lady, for instance, has an affectionate cat, as one might expect—except the cat turns out to be a *very* affectionate transforming attack panther. The healer is one of the more capable characters in the game, who directs many, although this is little amelioration for the general lack of active women in the game and the somewhat disturbingly servile representation of the orientalist-style Katta wife. Still, it is significant that—especially for a late 1980s fantasy game—these gendered tropes are often presented as humorous and invite criticism of these androcentric fantasy tropes. Indeed, even the hero is presented as fairly incompetent, largely for the sake of humor, but also to show the character's increased mastery of skills (as in any role-playing game [RPG]).

Most notably, the representations of Elsa and Bernard make Elsa better in every way than her brother. With her noblewoman identity effectively erased, she is able to take care of herself and lead the brigands into whose hands the curse delivered her. Moreover, she displays not only the ruthlessness necessary to keep the brigands in order, but also a sense of honor and morality in having spared the lives of several of the residents of the town of Spielburg. In contrast, the curse has changed her brother Bernard into a chained bear who can only be swayed by basic animal desire comforts, and when he is rescued he regards the main character haughtily and rudely, with only perfunctory gratitude, despite his father's remonstrance. Although the Baron is pleased to have his son back, it is Elsa's return that actually wins the game.

However, the overall structure of the game is ultimately *not* a feminist structure: it is, in fact, a restoration of the patriarchy. Despite Elsa's competence, Baba Yaga's power, and the healer's support, the ultimate goal of the hero is to return Elsa into her former place as merely the daughter of the local nobleman, stripping her of her earned power among the brigands. In essence, the valley is in danger and chaos when ruled by women—Baba Yaga and Elsa's brigands; peace is only restored when a man puts these women back into their places in the patriarchy and restores control to the hereditary male ruler. Moreover, the women must resort to violence, curses, and other forms of rebellion and coercion to have power, while men receive it without question. In essence, even though the development team for *Quest for Glory* was fairly diverse in terms of gender, the conventions of the genre and pressures of the market nevertheless cause a game with a female designer to still represent women in stereotypical ways and generate an androcentric, patriarchal narrative.

## Roberta Williams's *Kings Quest:* Learning to Be Feminist

In some ways, Roberta Williams is almost synonymous with Sierra On-Line; she and her husband Ken Williams founded the company as a way of distributing her titles, later expanding it to a large development studio. Justine Cassell and Henry Jenkins (1998) note that, "Roberta Williams [was] one of the first women in the computer games field. By 1989 … she started incorporating female protagonists into her games—although she admits that she was worried that she would lose her male audience in doing so." Indeed, it has been argued that Williams's character Princess Rosella was the first playable female character in computer games.

However, Williams's games did not begin as feminist or even gender inclusive. The predecessor to her most famous series, *King's Quest*, was *Hi-Res Adventure #2: The Wizard and the Princess* (1980). Its premise was simple and stereotypical: the player must rescue a princess who has been kidnapped by a wizard. The princess is simply the object to be rescued. The player is presumed to be male by convention; however, this identity is never confirmed, since the reward for rescuing the princess is half the kingdom, rather than the conventional princess's hand in marriage, and the manual only describes the character of the player as a "happy wanderer" who "love[s] adventure,"[8] so a female player is welcome to imagine the main character as herself if she chooses (*The Wizard and the Princess* 2016). The lack of gendering for the player was, however, common at the time, as the player was typically not given an on-screen avatar and was generally referred to in the second-person, so this holds true for the other Hi-Res Adventures as well; it also suggests that designers such as Williams tended to anticipate a more general audience than was expected later in the medium's development. There is one key subversion of the rescue-the-princess plot here: if the player chooses to play again at the end of the game (a common option in that period), then the wizard is shown to have magical control over time and thus undoes the player's efforts, so that the princess is rendered unreachable and unable to be rescued, denying any agency to either the princess or the player. Thus, although the game offers no explicit critique, it does offer a small ludic critique in highlighting the endless repetition of the rescue-the-princess trope into pointlessness, not unlike the famous subversion in 1985s *Super Mario Bros*, in which "the princess is in another castle."

Likewise, the first three *King's Quest* games, which established Williams's fame and prestige, follow androcentric fantasy tropes fairly uncritically, providing the player an explicitly male avatar, even though the marketing materials for the *King's Quest* series consistently claim that the games are intended for the whole family. In fact, the manuals are somewhat strange in their addresses to the player, suggesting that the player is somehow the avatar's companion, likely a holdover from previous adventure game. However, the game addresses the player as the hero himself, requiring the player to assume a heterosexual male role.

The first *King's Quest*, *Quest for the Crown*, has only three female characters: a beneficent fairy, a woodcutter's wife, and a witch. These more or less represent stereotypical women in fantasy. Moreover, the plot is entirely stereotypical, a quest for three objects in order to win the king's favor and crown, and any in-depth characterization is sparse. If there is any indication of gender-inclusive interest in the design of the game, it lies solely in the assumed domesticity of fairy tales as a genre.

However, *King's Quest II: Romancing the Throne*, which is able to go a little deeper into characterization, owing to a larger development team and some improvements to the Adventure Game Interpreter (AGI) engine, is deeply problematic and even misogynistic. At the surface, the romantic love-at-first-sight plot seems gender inclusive enough (though firmly hetero- and androcentric), but the primary female character in the game, Valanice, is regarded as little more than an object of desire and a reward for a quest in both manual and game (Childs 1985). She agrees to marry Graham almost immediately upon his successful entry into her tower prison and says very little, while almost all description of her is concerned with her attractiveness and helplessness: "her long auburn hair tumbles in luscious waves down her back. She has the bluest eyes you've ever seen and soft, creamy skin."

At the level of scripting in the engine, *King's Quest II* becomes even more problematic, demonstrating that it is not sufficient to simply have a woman in charge of a game to prevent misogyny in game development. The parser, which dictates what words and structures are understood by the game's text-based interface, lists words such as "bitch" and "cunt" as *synonyms* for "woman," so that the player can go through the entire game, in which the goal is to rescue and court a woman, deriding every woman and using misogynist language with no change in the game's responses.[9] Perhaps more tellingly, the code contains a secret response, which cannot be activated in the game while playing as distributed, but can be easily inserted in place of the above description of Valanice with a single key stroke in the engine's editor, which makes Valanice's sexual objectification in the eyes of the development team clearer: "Her long auburn hair tumbles down to cover her large firm breasts. Her erect nipples are one of the indications that her warm thighs would welcome your tender kisses."[10] Artifacts such as these indicate that the development team found humor in the sexualization of the women in the game and likely tested the game in this state; moreover, although this latter description is particularly explicit, it is nevertheless consistent with the game's treatment of Valanice overall as a willing quest reward. There seems, however, to be no publicly available commentary concerning these code artifacts among the developers or fans, despite the ready availability of the now open-source AGI engine.

*King's Quest III* offers a slight advantage over the previous game, and Roberta Williams has said in interviews that here is where she started to twist androcentric and patriarchal tropes and see the women in the game as having more agency and role in the overall plot of the series. This game again presents the typical damsel-in-distress premise, except is that the damsel Rosella is actually the hero Alexander's hitherto unknown sister, ideally removing the sexualization of the damsel in distress. However, that removal is not complete, as the description of Princess Rosella while she is bound to the stake as dragon-fodder describes her in this way: "Princess Rosella is gorgeous! Why, you'd be interested in her if she weren't your own sister! [...] Her skin is creamy white. And her BODY ... well! Embarrassed, you clear your throat and avert your eyes." Still, while the treatment of Rosella seems little better than the treatment of Valanice in the previous game, it seems that Williams and her team made *some* improvements, as the parser now lists misogynist language as synonymous with "bad word" rather than "woman," and as a result the narrator now chastises the player for using misogynist language, which yields no productive responses. And while most of *King's Quest III* offers little in the way of critique of traditional patriarchal and androcentric conventions, the *ending* suggests that Rosella, despite having been rendered helpless and nearly fed to a dragon, is in every way equal to her brother and has as much chance of inheriting the throne: Graham gives a speech and then tosses his hat into the air, so that whichever sibling catches it might assume the mantle of adventurer in his stead. The game ends with the hat in the air and both brother and sister reaching for it in a peculiar but poignant image of gender equity.

This image leads directly into *King's Quest IV: The Perils of Rosella* (1988), in which Roberta Williams's body of work takes a decidedly feminist turn, and likewise the design of her games becomes more gender inclusive (notably, she is also joined by designer Lorelei Shannon). It is, of course, speculation as to how much Williams's working with other female designers may have influenced her increased focus on feminist issues in game design, but there is no denying that these things coincide. Additionally, the introduction of the SCI engine gave Williams more creative power, so not only are her female-led games deeper in story and characterization but more complex in gameplay and technical ability. In *King's Quest IV*, former damsel in distress Princess Rosella must save her erstwhile adventuring father from an illness and a magical realm from ruin; in order to do so, she must enter into a conflict between two powerful female fairies. In fact, the space is almost entirely governed by women, with men now relegated to the unagented roles formerly occupied by women in the series—support, objects to be rescued, hindrances, and so on. Although the game frequently puts Rosella into stereotypically feminine situations, it often subverts them—while she kisses a frog to transform him into a prince, he rejects her and she him; Edgar, whom she has rescued, proposes marriage to her at the end of the game, and she freely declines his proposal without penalty even while acknowledging that he is conventionally suitable for her.

For a fantasy text published in 1988, having a princess rescue her family and reject (multiple) princes is a conventional feminist move, a response to stereotypical fairy tale princess roles that is seen in the work of novelists at the time such as Patricia Wrede and Mercedes Lackey. However, it sets up a dichotomy in Roberta Williams's work: for men, marriage is a reward for success that carries no impediment; but for women, marriage is an imposing, threatening impediment to success. In a way, though, this seems to reflect the reality of living in a patriarchal world, in which institutions such as marriage are likely to benefit men more than women, and as such critiques those institutions.

Furthermore, as the *King's Quest* series continues, there seems to be more the representation of women and female experiences. Although *King's Quest V: Absence Makes the Heart Go Yonder* and *King's Quest VI: Heir Today, Gone*

*Tomorrow* both feature the male playable characters from previous games, Graham and Alexander respectively, they also complicate the role of women in these spaces far more than in previous games. In *King's Quest V*, the player twice experiences being imprisoned and robbed of agency like the previous damsels in distress, dependent on rescue by outside forces—a mouse and Princess Cassima, who herself is also a damsel in distress, but not devoid of agency the way that previous damsels in distress in the series were. Like Rosella, Cassima is given agency, but unlike Rosella she has it from the beginning. She appears again in *King's Quest VI*, in which rescuing her is the primary goal, but again she is not without agency, even though the player plays as her male rescuer and suitor, Alexander; this time, Cassima is able to transmit messages and, depending on the ending that the player's actions trigger, ultimately stabs her captor herself while Alexander is too weak a wield the sword in that final combat. This is, tellingly, the ending that results in the most points awarded to the player, suggesting that *by design* the best solution is the one in which the princess is a key agent in her own freedom.

Williams's feminist game design in the *King's Quest* series reaches its apex with the seventh game, in which the player alternates between playing as Valanice and Rosella; like *King's Quest IV*, the conflict is driven by an evil supernatural woman taking more power than is her right. However, unlike the previous games, this one focuses primarily on the relationship between mother and daughter; indeed, Alexander and Graham are not even mentioned. Although the characters are all rendered in an exaggerated Disney-like animation style (in contrast to the push toward realism in previous games) the women are nevertheless given unprecedented agency, and the "damsel-in-distress" is, in fact, Edgar, whom Rosella also rescued in *King's Quest IV*.

It is notable that, although there are now several *King's Quest* games that follow these, those designed by Roberta Williams are the *only* ones with this increasing trend toward feminism, and even gender inclusivity, despite gender inclusivity being nearly inherent in the adventure game genre. *Mask of Eternity* was designed primarily by Mark Siebert and not only features a stereotypically heroic male avatar, but also incorporates a combat engine for the first time and focuses on advancing through the game largely through combat in order to restore a mystic temple that is a male-only space that (apparently) holds the world together, even though this temple and its central cultic object (the titular mask) have never been mentioned in another *King's Quest* game. Likewise, The Odd Gentlemen's 2015–2016 games focus on Graham's adventures, and although they feature his granddaughter as a key figure, the gameplay is primarily masculinized. Thus, it seems that, for the present at least, it is necessary to have a significant number of women on a development team in order to achieve gender-inclusive design, much less feminist design, in games. Indeed, while there have been some significant advances in representation in the industry, there is also an increased push against feminist game design, which suggests that there is overall very little progress since the 1980s in gender-inclusive game design.

## Roberta Williams's *Phantasmagoria:* A Feminist Allegory

The best evidence, however, of increased power and access to female colleagues changing a game designer's work to be more feminist is probably *Phantasmagoria*, a game in which Roberta Williams was allowed an unprecedented budget and artistic control, and which plays out as a feminist allegory concerned with the nature of domestic abuse and its impact on women. Released in 1995, *Phantasmagoria* falls between *King's Quest VI* and *King's Quest VII*, apparently pioneering the one-button interface used in *King's Quest VII*, and utilizes an advanced version of the video-capture technology used in Jane Jensen's *Gabriel Knight*.

By Ray's definition of gender-inclusive design, *Phantasmagoria* meets most of the requirements: a female playable character, female designers, focus on plot and relationships, generally nonviolent play; this does not, however, mean that the game is nonviolent—indeed, it was censored in many areas because of its violent content, but very little of the violence is perpetrated by the player, who generally plays a witness role in events. However, Ray (2004) praises *Phantasmagoria*, writing "Adrienne [the playable character] is an attractive, average woman—someone you might expect to see in the grocery store. Her clothing is simple and unprovocative. And, in a theme Roberta Williams does well, we are presented with a princess who is out to save her prince and her home." Ray's analysis is oversimplistic, though, and her final description of Adrienne would better fit Rosella from *King's Quest* than Adrienne, who ultimately is unable to save either her "prince" (husband) or her home.

Although Ray is correct about Adrienne's basic representation, which reduces her potential as an object of the male gaze from the *player*, the motivation for her black and orange outfit seems to have been primarily a result of technological limitations of the blue-screen technology used to create the game. And although the player is not invited to sexualize Adrienne, Ray's analysis fails to acknowledge that many of the most significant moments of the game involve Adrienne's sexualization by other entities in the game. The player is introduced to Adrienne in a voyeuristic opening video with her naked and engaging in sex with her husband Don; the most controversial and pivotal scene in the game is one in which Adrienne is raped by her husband in the bathroom.[11] Furthermore, her image becomes the explicit target of the male gaze—not from the player, but from Don—as seen in Don's "art," which consists of numerous beheaded photographs of Adrienne's body arranged obsessively in the dark room, of which Don says "a woman's body is a beautiful thing, but the head is useless!" (*Phantasmagoria*, disc 7). Additionally, Adrienne's agency is severely limited by the mechanics of the game—the primary way the game advances is through Adrienne *witnessing* horrific events over which she has no power, generally through psychometric episodes, and she makes very few real choices throughout the game. There is no way to win the game without killing Don, nor can Adrienne do anything but save herself by leaving her home, alone and silent, more indicative of her trauma than of any other trait.

None of this is to say that *Phantasmagoria* fails as a feminist game because it fails to imagine a space in which women have complete agency; quite the opposite, in fact. Instead, *Phantasmagoria* functions as a fantastical representation of the female experience of mundane misogyny and domestic abuse, in which the demon that possesses the key men in the game (Don in the present, Carno in the past) is a supernatural, literal manifestation of misogyny, causing men to become controlling and to react violently to any perceived threat to their authority over the women in their lives. Read this way, Adrienne's helplessness as she witnesses Carno's past violence against his wives and her own husband's transformation is not weakness on her part, though many players have seen it as such,[12] but rather debilitating fear that accompanies domestic abuse and misogyny.

All this is to say that *Phantasmagoria* treads a territory that was unexpected in video games in 1995, when the androcentric tropes were accepted without criticism from even the female designers who had been complicit with them: *Phantasmagoria* is an allegorical, procedural experience of the mundane misogyny all women experience, and the extremes to which many women are subjected. It is said that *Phantasmagoria*'s production caused significant marital tension between Roberta and Ken Williams, since Roberta wanted ever more resources for its production, and Ken was in charge of Sierra's business interests; however, *Phantasmagoria* is the sort of feminist statement that seems to be possible when women are given authority, resources, and female colleagues that embolden them to consider and express issues particular to the female experience that have been otherwise erased in mainstream culture.

# Conclusions

Because Sierra stopped producing games shortly before game studies really came into its own as a field, many of the contributions of Sierra's notable female game designers have been understudied. However, a careful corpus analysis of these texts shows a trend toward increased gender inclusivity and feminist discourse as more women joined the team and female designers were given more resources. This historical model suggests that if diversity *in representation* is a goal, as it seems many members of the video game industry have made it, there must first be diversity and support for that diversity *in the workplace* that generates that representation. It is necessary for game companies to do as Sierra did at its height, and empower and promote female game designers' work, including putting the names of the designers foremost in the promotional materials (a practice seldom followed now, but common in the 1980s and 1990s). It seems natural that, initially, female designers will be complicit with androcentric tropes, as Roberta Williams was at the start of her career; convention demands this conformity, and often it goes unnoticed and uncriticized in a team with minimal diversity; but provided creative exchange with other female designers, as when Lorelei Shannon joined Roberta Williams for *King's Quest IV*—and given developer support, as Williams, Cole, and Jensen clearly were—female designers can be emboldened to create games that explicitly discuss the female experience or create a gender-inclusive space for players.

# Notes

1. That these studies almost always discuss girls, rather than women, indicates problematic juvenilization of video games beyond the scope of this chapter, but worth examination elsewhere.
2. For several examples in one volume, see Cynthia L. Selfe and Gail E. Hawisher, *Gaming Lives in the Twenty-First Century* (New York: Palgrave Macmillan, 2007).
3. For a discussion of the inability to resolve Lara Croft's representational issues, see Helen Kennedy, "Lara Croft: Feminist Icon or Cyberbimbo? On the Limits of Textual Analysis," *Game Studies* 2, no. 2 (2002).
4. I will tend to use the term "androcentric" (from the Greek andro, for male) rather than "patriarchal," as patriarchal implies a more explicit power structure and more strongly misogynist representation, while andocentric merely labels a work as focused on the male experience without necessarily being misogynist or patriarchal in nature.

5. Biographical data has been verified via *sierragamers.com*.
6. To use Ian Bogost's term.
7. The term "techno-historic limitations" is from Andrew Hutchison, "Making the Water Move: Techno-Historic Limits in the Game Aesthetics of *Myst* and *Doom*," *Game Studies* 8, no. 1 (2008).
8. Facsimile of the manual is available online at "*The Wizard and the Princess*." *Sierra Gamers*. Sierragamers.com.
9. Ibid., accessed via the AGIstudio developer studio.
10. Ibid., also accessed via AGIstudio.
11. Roberta Williams herself actually seems to have trivialized the significance of the scene: the *Sydney Morning Herald* quotes her as having said "even though the woman was 'violated' in this scene, her husband got his comeuppance—she wound up having to kill him. So, poor guy, she won, he lost." However, this interview still suggests that Williams is working toward a certain justice in this game, a sense that misogyny is punishable even by death—a woman can be "violated" but the equivalent (or possibly trump) is to kill the man. See Stuart Clarke, "A Girl's Own Adventure," *Sydney Morning Herald (Australia)*, March 27, 1999, Lexis Nexis (accessed February 11, 2011).
12. The fact that players see Adrienne as weak is actually symptomatic of victim-blaming culture at large.

# Bibliography

Cassell, Justine, and Henry Jenkins, eds. 1998. *From Barbie to Mortal Kombat: Gender and Computer Games*. Cambridge, MA: MIT Press.

Childs, Annette. 1985. *King's Quest II: Romancing the Throne*. Manual. In *King's Quest 1+2+3*, video game via. Gog.com. PDF file. Accessed February 24, 2016.

Clarke, Stuart. 1999. A Girl's Own Adventure. *Sydney Morning Herald (Australia)*, March 27, 1999. Lexis Nexis, accessed February 11, 2011.

Hutchison, Andrew. 2008. Making the Water Move: Techno-Historic Limits in the Game Aesthetics of *Myst* and *Doom*. *Game Studies* 8.1.

Kennedy, Helen W. 2002. Lara Croft: Feminist Icon or Cyberbimbo? On the Limits of Textual Analysis. *Game Studies* 2.2.

Ray, Sheri Graner. 2004. *Gender Inclusive Game Design*. Hingham: Charles River Media.

Selfe, Cynthia L., and Gail E. Hawisher. 2007. *Gaming Lives in the Twenty-First Century*. New York: Palgrave Macmillan.

Sierra On-Line. *Gabriel Knight 1: Sins of the Fathers*, game via Gog.com. Digital Download.

Sierra On-Line. *King's Quest 1+2+3*, game via Gog.com. Digital download.

Sierra On-Line. *King's Quest 4+5+6*, games via Gog.com. Digital download.

Sierra On-Line. *King's Quest 7+8*, games via Gog.com. Digital download.

Sierra On-Line. *Phantasmagoria*, game via Gog.com. Digital download.

Sierra On-Line. *Quest for Glory 1–5*, games via Gog.com. Digital download.

Takayoshi, Pamela. 2007. Gender Matters: Literacy, Learning and Gaming in One American Family. In *Gaming Lives in the Twenty-First Century*, ed. Cynthia L. Selfe and Gail E. Hawisher, 229–249. New York: Palgrave Macmillan.

"*The Wizard and the Princess.*" 2016. *Sierra Gamers*. Sierragamers.com. Web. 24 February.

# 3

# The Material Undermining of Magical Feminism in *BioShock Infinite: Burial at Sea*

James Malazita

*If we were to just put Booker in a dress, then that would be the most awful*
*betrayal of what we're doing for Liz.*
*Amanda Jeffrey, level designer for* BioShock Infinite, Burial at Sea: Episode 2
*(Goldfarb 2013)*

*Burial at Sea: Episode 2* (BaS) (Irrational Games 2014) the last in a series of post-game downloadable content (DLC) for *BioShock Infinite* (Irrational Games 2013) casts the player in the role of Elizabeth, a major non-playable character in the game's previous installments. In earlier episodes, Elizabeth, a 19-year-old woman with the ability to move between quantum realities, magically navigates the gameworld in a manner radically different from the game's gun-toting playable character, Booker DeWitt. While Booker shoots his way through the gameworld, Elizabeth phases through time and space, confounding enemies by revealing multiple configurations of parallel worlds to them, and unraveling the mysteries of the game's plot by exploring alternative world histories and events. During interviews with *Burial at Sea*'s development staff, designers emphasized their desire for players controlling Elizabeth to have a gameplay experience that was authentic to her character, rather than playing as "Booker in a dress." Unfortunately, the resulting game featured an Elizabeth stripped of her quantum powers, whose major gameplay mechanic was hiding from enemies.

J. Malazita (✉)
Rensselaer Polytechnic Institute, Troy, NY, USA

© The Author(s) 2018
K. L. Gray et al. (eds.), *Feminism in Play*, Palgrave Games in Context,
https://doi.org/10.1007/978-3-319-90539-6_3

This chapter argues that Elizabeth's postcolonial, "magical feminist" (Hart 1989) character design, which can be read as an alternative, non-positivist, anti-imperialist framing of power, became undermined by the *material-discursive* (Barad 2007) agencies of game engines. Physics engines control objects in the gameworld via rationalist, rule-based, hierarchical logics. These logics better afford game mechanics that rely on Newtonian calculations of power and force, such as gun-based combat. While magical feminist characters in written literature serve to countermand these embedded masculinist (Nardi 2010), imperialist values, the *material-discursive* and historical processes performed by game engines actively resist the implementation of real-time, postcolonial gameplay. In order to preserve "physical realism" and to satisfy the demands of gaming architecture, designers shape playable women characters like Elizabeth as weakened men, leading to the material and performative propagation of misogynist media tropes. Thus, this chapter will argue that critically oriented games must not only strive for feminist, postcolonial narrative representations of characters, but also take into account the ways in which the affordances and histories of game design architecture can warp progressive narrative elements.

## Elizabeth the Magical Feminist

Though the player's initial encounter with Elizabeth frames her as a "damsel in distress" trope that she never quite fully escapes (the player *rescues her from a tower*, after all), the narrative of *BioShock Infinite* (BI) quickly recasts Elizabeth's position of power in the gameworld. Elizabeth has the ability to open "tears" in the fabric of spacetime, allowing her to transverse parallel "quantum" realities and timelines. As the story proceeds, Elizabeth's explorations of these tears afford her near-omnipotence; she is able to see the possible futures that may occur given actions taken by other characters, and ultimately exposes the mysterious origins of *BI*'s antagonist and his steampunk-esque floating city of Columbia by re-experiencing past events and viewing alternative forks in time.

Thus, unlike most sidekicks in first person adventure games, Elizabeth is substantially more powerful and influential in the gameworld than the player character. Her supernatural abilities are not just background flavor, they have substantial impact upon the player's experience of the game. During a short sequence where Elizabeth is running away from player-character Booker, she summons freight trains, marching bands, and parade balloons from other quantum worlds to slow him down, and eventually slips into another dimension herself. In real-time combat, Elizabeth assists the player by summoning weapons, ammunition, health items, and environmental hazards and cover.

Though her abilities are framed in pseudo-scientific terms—Elizabeth's powers (for vague reasons) are possible because of a multiverse of "quantum uncertainties"—Elizabeth's characterization and role in the narrative of *BioShock Infinite* recall the aesthetic of magical realism. Magical realism, a literary style most closely associated with Latin American postcolonial writing, incorporates "magical" or "mystical" persons and events into mundane settings, while also treating those mystical happenings as mundane. The interspersion of magic in an otherwise rationalist world serves to both highlight the oppressed ideologies of the colonized peoples—the ways in which the ontologies of the colonized, the foundational ways in which the world is thought to work, are delegitimized and erased—and to re-orient the reader's own ontological assumptions about the world; to show, as Salman Rushdie puts it, the ways in which impossible events "happen constantly, and quite plausibly, out in the open under the midday sun" (Rushdie 1991, 302).

Magical realist texts, while part of a diverse and often hard-to-define genre, share the active positioning of the reader into a state of "ontological vertigo" (Alter 1975, 223). The reader must suspend assumptions about the fundamental ordering of the world, and any attempts to impose causal, rationalistic, systems-based rule sets upon the material logics of the narrative necessarily end in frustration. Stephen Slemon identifies this intersection of colonial and postcolonial ontologies in magical realist worlds as creating a "battle between two oppositional systems ... each working toward the creation of a different kind of fictional world from the other. Since the ground rules of these two worlds are incompatible, neither one can fully come into being, and each remains suspended, locked in a continuous disjunction..." (Slemon 1995, 409). Successfully navigating a magical realist story, then, "requires a faculty for boundary-skipping between worlds" (Wilson 1995, 210).

Elizabeth's strength derives from her literal ability to boundary-skip between worlds; worlds with significantly different histories and actors. While *Infinite* tends to narrow the ways in which Elizabeth folds quantum worlds together in her combat roles, the game's narrative arc allows her more freedom. Elizabeth is ultimately cast as the hero of the game when, after joining with alternative versions of herself from forking timelines, she travels backward in time and kills the main character before he can set events into motion that create the major antagonist of the game.

Elizabeth's imprisonment by an authoritarian fatherly figure, as well as her use of the magical destabilization of reality to disrupt and overcome that figure, orient her within the magical realist subgenre of magical feminism—which Kimberly Ann Wells characterizes via the centrality of a magical "witch" character who disrupts a male-dominated world order (Wells 2007). Elizabeth's pseudomagical powers eventually lead to the downfall of a misogynistic, xenophobic political order, exemplifying both her postcolonial and radical feminist literary influences.

Though it would be difficult to argue that the developers of *BI* were consciously writing under a postcolonial, magical feminist orientation (particularly given the game's problematic representation of race relations) (Lizardi 2014), *BioShock's* developers do make clear attempts to heighten the level of socio-political discourse in mainstream gaming. During a pre-release press interview, Ken Levine, the lead developer of the *BioShock* series and something of an *auteur* figure in the gaming world, outlines the social and literary influences of *BioShock Infinite*:

> I don't think people give gamers enough credit and assume that they only want explosive, visceral experiences … I read a lot about history and I got interested in the late 19th century by the book *Devil in the White City* by Erik Larson, which is set around the 1893 World Fair. For me, that time is the most transformative in history because you had all these technologies coming into play, like radio, movies, electricity, cars—mass production in general. Alongside that, you had social transformations with suffrage, labour movements, the beginning of the civil rights movement—all these amazing uprisings bringing a sense that the colony is starting to buckle and break free. (Gallagher 2011)

The interweaving of the technological and the social that Levine traces in Larson's book becomes a focal point of *Infinite*: Elizabeth's traveling among quantum possibilities is used as both a means of evading capture by authoritarian leaders of Columbia, who hope to use Elizabeth's powers to extend their own, and as a means of exploration and learning, as Elizabeth and the player grow to understand more of *BI's* plot through the navigation of tears. Along their travels, Elizabeth and Booker encounter the diverse outcomes made possible by an underground civil rights/labor movement operating in the floating city.

Despite the explorations of these social tensions, it would be difficult to label *BioShock Infinite* an activist game. Though the game narrative shows a diverse array of characters, ideological frameworks, and socio-political structures, the game writers radicalize these frameworks in an effort to avoid the appearance of ideological bias. As Levine explains:

The real conflict of [the 1890s]—and, you could argue, what is happening today—is this left and right schism of extreme nationalism on one side, and an anti-capitalist, internationalist movement on the other. With our games we're never looking to advocate a political position and we try to ask questions more than we try to answer them. We show the extreme ends of the spectrum. (Gallagher 2011)

As the game's narrative progresses, Elizabeth and Booker discover that Columbia's authoritarian leader, Comstock, and the anticapitalist organizer, Daisy Fitzroy, each exhibit violently Machiavellian streaks, with Comstock willing to purge nonwhites and non-Christians from the city for the benefit of "social order," while Fitzroy encourages indiscriminate terrorist attacks throughout the city during her bloody revolution. The developers of *BioShock* are hardly alone in their reticence to engage in explicit social critique; the strategy of "explore the social, but don't take sides (or take blame for sides)" is a common one throughout the mainstream digital gaming industry (Bogost 2013).

By the release of *Burial at Sea*, however, *BioShock* developers were more willing to endorse specific values, particularly when it comes to the magical feminist orientation of Elizabeth. In addition to the epigraphic quote of this chapter, where she expresses a distaste for the possibility of the player's experience playing as Elizabeth being a carbon copy of playing as Booker ("Booker in a dress"), *BaS* level designer Amanda Jeffrey makes clear that the game mechanics of the DLC should change to be faithful to Elizabeth's character:

> We're still trying to work out exactly how extensive Liz's tear abilities will be in the playable Liz sequence… She has an understanding of this universe and the various universes that she can visit, and she knows, once again, constants and variables. (Goldfarb 2013)

Booker's use of vigors, a form of chemical techno-magic in the main installment of *BI*, complement his use of guns and other projectile weaponry: almost all of Booker's abilities are heavily combat oriented. Elizabeth's tear abilities, in contrast, are generally non-combative. Elizabeth's strength is her ability to explore, not her ability to kill. Again, Jeffrey notes during pre-release interviews of the team's goal to design the gameplay experience as one that reflects Elizabeth's orientation to the world:

> There's all of these different kinds of ways of being more thoughtful, and—I hesitate to say it—almost more feminine way of approaching a problem, where there's all of these people and, to be very brutally honest about it, they have the advantage in strength. But Elizabeth has the advantage in smarts. (Goldfarb 2013)

Despite the admittedly clumsy rhetoric, there does seem to be a sincere drive by the *BaS* development staff to avoid recreating what Anita Sarkeesian has identified as the "Ms. Male" trope, or the creation of a playable woman character whose major characteristics are derived from an already-well established male character—for example, Ms. Pac Man (Sarkeesian 2013). A well-designed Elizabeth player character would create a gameplay experience that allows players to experience gameplay styles that offer alternative, more "feminine" play than is often afforded in mainstream, AAA titles. During development time, then, there was a sense that *BaS* may have been a much-needed step in the variation of gameplay design in the industry, inspired, at least in part, by critical discourse.

Unfortunately, the reality of *Burial at Sea: Episode 2* did not live up to the hopeful promises of the development interviews. Instead of featuring gameplay mechanics that took advantage of Elizabeth's tear abilities, the development team instead put in a hastily scripted narrative workaround, and removed Elizabeth's powers at the start of the game. Elizabeth, instead of being featured as a character with knowledge of infinite possible branching timelines, was cast as a semi-amnesiac surrounded by enemies that, if encountered, could easily kill her. Elizabeth uses guns, vigors, and crossbows to kill or knock out unsuspecting enemies from behind, but has access to little enough ammunition that hiding and running away are generally better tactics. The gameplay in *Burial at Sea*, then, represents not a radical shift in problem solving or exploratory game design from *BioShock Infinite*, but rather a minor shift between two subcategories of the First-Person Shooter genre: action-adventure to survival horror. Rather than being a mystically powered woman, Elizabeth plays as a weakened Booker.

While game designers often make blackboxed political decisions about game mechanics in the interest of "playability" and "fun," *BioShock* developer interviews point toward another causal factor. Even while trying to build consumer excitement for the variety of play that Elizabeth will offer, we see hints from Jeffrey that the material and economic realities of AAA game development may impinge upon the possibility for alternative play designs:

> Some things for the playable Liz will have to be the same. We don't have enough time to make an entirely new game. We're building on an existing set of systems and all the rest of it…. However, I will say that, more than anything, we are trying to focus on making sure that the feel of playing as Elizabeth and just moving through the environment is a very different experience, both in the way that the player interacts with their control pad or the mouse and keyboard, and in the way that the player's thinking about the environment. (Goldfarb 2013)

The goal of the *Burial at Sea* design team, then, was to implement a radically different play style for Elizabeth while leveraging the assets and game architecture used to develop Booker's gameplay. The monetary and time constraints, combined with the political agencies of the integrated development software and computational logics used to build *BioShock Infinite* would have a *re-colonializing* effect on Elizabeth's narrative, leading to the undermining of her magical feminist origins.

This re-colonization effect occurs in two ways. First, the feminist and postcolonial explorations of alternative ontologies, possibilities, and worlds afforded by the empowering of a mystical nonmale character become boxed into a more traditional, realist, masculine play experience. Second, that very play experience—the leveraging of First-Person Shooter tropes to violently solve structural and interpersonal problems—itself recreates colonial political logics. Rather than create ontologically diverse worlds, Elizabeth is tasked with using violence to "clean levels," or to ensure that the other inhabitants in the gameworld perceived to be threats are pacified, controlled, or otherwise placed out of the way of her goals. Such level cleaning dovetails with John Romero's "Tidiness Theory" of games (Romero 2009), which posits that a core emotional drive for players is the desire to bring order to the chaos of game spaces, a theory that Cara Ellison and Brendan Keogh have used to explain the enjoyment of violent acts in games (Ellison and Keogh 2015). Of course, the edict to bring rationality and order to chaos has been an axiomatic political frame for western Empire since the Enlightenment, and, as this chapter will argue, a political frame that has been embedded in the logics of the tools of game production.

## Agonistic Engines and Logics

The economics of contemporary AAA game development are underpinned by licensed game engines: integrated software packages containing development environments, physics engines, and graphics rendering tools. While early digital games were largely self-contained programming projects, game development companies have heavily relied upon third-party development tools since the mid-2000s. The licensing of game engines offloads the labor hours required to develop core mechanical and behavioral code for new game properties, while at the same time ensuring that the toolsets available to developers are both compatible with and take advantage of new hardware and processor architectures. While most AAA studios spend considerable time and money building proprietary modifications and extensions for licensed engines, the underlying programming logics and features of the engine have a heavy influence upon the final build of the game. Game engines, then, represent a modularization and "offshoring" of digital game authorship; an authorial agency that echoes throughout all stages of the game development process.

*BioShock Infinite* was built using a modified version of the Unreal Engine 3, an industry standard development environment of the mid-2000s. Although the software gained popularity as a third-party development kit, the Unreal Engine was originally developed as a rapid prototyping tool for the game (and the engine's namesake) *Unreal*, released in 1998 for the personal computer (PC). *Unreal* was a critically acclaimed First-Person Shooter (FPS) that featured state-of-the-art graphics and unprecedented levels of mod-ability, both results of the capabilities and flexibilities of the Unreal Engine. Tim Sweeney, founder of Epic Games and author of both *Unreal* and the Unreal Engine, envisioned Unreal as a modular (Manovich 2001) building environment that provided enough built-in features to allow developers to create new games without needing to program additional development tools, but which was also extendable enough for design teams to modify the engine to fit their needs (McDonald 1998).

Though the Unreal Engine was designed to be flexible, extensions to the engine build upon—not replace—the core behavioral and physics software packaged with the Engine. As such, the built-in software features and source code of the Unreal Engine still exert authorial power upon the development processes—and results—of games that are constructed via the Engine. Although it is possible to build a diverse array of game genres within Unreal 3, the physics engines, control schema, and pre-coded functionality are heavily derived from First-Person Shooters.

As Mark Sample contends, it is important for humanists and social scientists to delve into the source code of digital texts, as the code itself reveals ideological and political assumptions held by the programmer (Sample 2013). While Sample traces explicit political decisions made by programmers, such as *Micropolis's* authoritarian, deterministic approach toward crime (populated areas always have a high crime rate unless police presence is heavily increased), software need not explicitly deal with *politics* to be engaging in *the political* (Mouffe 1993). *The political*, Chantal Mouffe argues, is the antagonistic relational sphere that exists as a fundamental aspect of all human societies, independent of whatever parties, structures, and discourses comprise a society's *politics*. All human societies, no matter their political process, feature constantly negotiated and combating ideological frameworks, if for no other reason than the diverse ontological *umwelts* (von Uexküll 2010) that arise from the divergent experiences of differing publics. As noted above, magical realism as a genre is a reflection of these competing, incommensurable ideological worlds.

Software and algorithms, both because of their authorial history and the material properties of electronic media upon which they run, constrain, and afford different ideological frameworks in different ways. Algorithms are more than artifacts with embedded politics (Winner 1986); they in fact *make* political arguments every time they are run. As Kate Crawford points out, algorithms and software packages, then, are not value-neutral or agnostic, but rather are *agonistic* (Crawford 2016). They are spaces of ideological contestation.

Given the authorial affordances of software packages, it should not be surprising that the majority of games developed using the Unreal Engine are shooters (Wikipedia 2016). Given the political agonism embedded in those affordances, it may also be unsurprising that the upgraded version of the original Unreal Engine, Unreal Engine 2, came packaged with *America's Army*, the US government-developed military simulation game *qua* recruitment tool. Unreal Engine 2 thus does double ideological work—not only do commercial and independent developers gain access to the Engine via downloading a military recruitment tool, many future game designers and developers first begin experimenting with game design by using Unreal 2 to modify and extend *America's Army* (Gee 2007), both increasing the replayability of the game as well as training new developers to create games that are easily afforded by the ideological and algorithmic politics embedded in *AA*.

To return to Elizabeth: as DLC, *Burial at Sea* expands upon *BioShock Infinite's* game architecture, developed using Unreal Engine 3. As Amanda Jeffrey confesses in an above quote, the economic realities of AAA game development, to say nothing of the technical requirements of downloadable content, necessitate that new content developed for *Infinite* post-release must be created using the same core software and toolsets as *Infinite* itself. While Unreal's First-Person Shooter toolset made an ideal fit for Booker's gameplay in the action-adventure-oriented *Infinite*, it makes an odd fit for Elizabeth's character. Not only is Elizabeth an exploration-based "investigator" character archetype, but her negotiation of the challenges of the gameworld are not physical nor violent, but rather inter-dimensional.

Unreal de-privileges each of these playstyles. Both graphical rendering and physics engines that are bundled in Unreal 3 are better equipped for running-and-gunning down hallways and constrained spaces—it took extensive modification by *Infinite* developers to make the game's sprawling outdoor vistas functionally viable, and even those areas are full of invisible walls and other "hidden suggestions" to keep the player within a bounded space (VanOrd 2013). That these kinds of exploratory constraints were necessary in a single digital space speaks to the unfeasibility of programming real-time versions of Elizabeth's ability to instantly navigate parallel worlds (i.e., managing multiple game environments simultaneously).

Further, the Unreal Engine treats most environmental interactions as physical interactions, the results of which are governed by streamlined versions of Newtonian physics. The application of physical force and the detection of interpenetrating geometries underpin most of *BioShock Infinite's* game behavior—again, an ideal set of design affordances for a shooter. The narrative work that these physics engines do augments Booker's character—one of Booker's strengths is his uncanny ability to overwhelm any obstacle with violence. With the architecture of Unreal as applied to *BioShock Infinite* as a constraint, playable Elizabeth's differentiating quality manifests as her *inability* to apply violence as effectively as Booker, while still being required to navigate the gameworld violently. The design solution to these affordances was to remove Elizabeth's tear abilities, introduce stealth mechanics, and have Elizabeth kill enemies from behind. Elizabeth's character is thus reduced to a weaker, sneakier (and therefore "smarter") Booker.

While these design decisions have political implications—Elizabeth becomes another in a list of woman game characters forced to less-effectively navigate game systems designed for violent characters and masculinist problem-solving strategies—the undermining of Elizabeth's *magical feminist* orientation stems from deeper computational logics that underpin even the embedded politics in Unreal's FPS architecture: the propositional logic of Empire.

Digital computer systems apply rationalistic, Boolean-based propositional logic, an embedded ideological system that traces back to the early ontological influences of mathematicians like Alan Turing and Allen Newell upon computer science and artificial intelligence (Davis 1995). Propositional logic (and its associated commands, like "and," "or," and "else") demands that all values and comparative statements lead to "true" or "false" statements. Propositional algorithms are decision-making, not problematizing. Questions whose responses do not afford a true or false, 0 or 1 answer are defined by Turing as inherently non-computable (Turing 1937).

Magical realism, in contrast, demands that sense-making logic is suspended, that the reader is left in a state of ontological and epistemological vertigo. While this kind of vertigo can be simulated in cutscenes and scripted events due to the relative lack of algorithmic processing in pre-rendered and scripted scenes, real-time processing, such as the kind required during player-driven interactions, requires systems that quickly make conclusive decisions. Elizabeth's interactions with the gameworld, then, must necessarily be as simple to calculate as possible, while also returning definitive Boolean values; exactly the kind of determinism that magical realism rejects.

Postcolonial gameplay that strives for agonistic plurality—the acceptance and celebration of incommensurable ontologies simultaneously existing—is not afforded by the logical architecture of computing. Boolean logic is fundamentally rationalist—it assumes the presence of a correct, determinable, universal answer; any problem must be able to return true or false. Or, to return to John Romero's Tidiness Theory, all problems must be able to be "cleaned." Computing itself argues for imperialist ideology. The ontological weight of the Enlightenment continues to materially stretch through time, agonistically asserting its rationalist and imperial logics with every manipulation of a game controller.

## Conclusion

Games, like all artistic and technological systems, influence and are influenced by the cultural milieu from which they emerge; that this edited volume exists attests to the recognition of the meaningful ways in which games act as negotiating agents in public and personal constructions of the world. And as social movements like those spearheaded by Anita Sarkeesian and Zoe Quinn show, there is a growing, vocal sentiment in the public sphere for digital game designers to take seriously the ways in which the content of their games consciously and unconsciously influences players. The rhetoric used by these feminist movements is vital, as they seek to apply academic and social critique to game design, and thereby are not only engaging in important public critique, but also are calling for the production of diverse, varied, and more conscious game development.

As activist game designer and theorist Mary Flanagan (2009) notes, most critical and activist game design projects focus on the use of narrative elements to critically engage players. Games such as *Darfur is Dying*, *Depression Quest*, and *Regicide: The Tale of the Forgotten Thief* call attention to diverse gendered, racial, and socio-political issues via plot points and diverse character representation. The use of critical narrative in games is a fundamental tool for the pursuit of social justice, as negative, stereotyped, or lack of representation of women and minorities in popular media abounds.

However, as seen in the transformation of Elizabeth from resilient magical feminist sidekick to fearful, sneaky playable character, the tactics of narrative representation that function well in linear media formats, like books and film, can be undermined by the material affordances of digital code. *Burial at Sea* represents an unfortunate side effect of the tendency to remediate narrative and grammatical strategies from older media formats into newer ones: translations are always transformations (Bolter and Grusin 1999). Magical realism—and its feminist variant—works well in a textual format because of the author's ability to privilege and de-privilege different senses and ontological orientations; the freedom to leave physical and causal events and mechanics undefined allows for a greater flexibility in maintaining co-existing, yet incommensurable worlds. In real-time computing, however, physical and causal mechanics must be explicitly defined, and all game architecture must be compatible with one another to avoid system crashes. Ontological plurality is thus impossible in real time, requiring that even developers with activist or postcolonial orientations massage their own ideological orientations to meet the agonistic political affordances of computing architecture.

This is not to argue that the developers of *BioShock Infinite* were feminist activists, nor that the Unreal Engine 3 can never be used to develop games with feminist or postcolonial orientations; indeed, another, more compelling magical feminist-themed game, Dontnod Entertainment's 2015 *Life is Strange,* was built in Unreal 3, though with far less interactive agency afforded to the player than was present in *Infinite.* There have also been games built in the Unreal Engine that play with player's perceptions of Euclidian space, such as Alexander Bruce's *Antichamber* and Valve's *Portal.* Rather, the case of Elizabeth is intended to serve as a call to feminist and postcolonial media scholars to more deeply study the material affordances and political agencies embedded in the governing code of game systems themselves, as well as for critical and activist game designers to explicitly engage in the design and coding of feminist and postcolonial game *architectures* in addition to game narratives.

# Bibliography

Alter, Robert. 1975. *Partial Magic: The Novel as a Self-conscious Genre.* Berkeley: University of California Press.

Barad, Karen. 2007. *Meeting the Universe Halfway: Quantum Physics and the Entanglement of Matter and Meaning.* Durham, NC: Duke University Press.

Bogost, Ian. 2013. How the Video-Game Industry Already Lost Out in the Gun-Control Debate. *The Atlantic,* January 11. Accessed February 29, 2016. http://www.theatlantic.com/entertainment/archive/2013/01/how-the-video-game-industry-already-lost-out-in-the-gun-control-debate/267052/.

Bolter, Jay David, and Richard Grusin. 1999. *Remediation: Understanding New Media.* Cambridge: The MIT Press.

Crawford, Kate. 2016. Can an Algorithm Be Agonistic? Ten Scenes from Life in Calculated Publics. *Science, Technology, and Human Values* 41 (1): 77–92.

Davis, Martin. 1995. Influences of Mathematical Logic on Computer Science. In *The Universal Turing Machine a Half-Century Survey*, 289–299. Vienna: Springer.

Ellison, Cara, and Brendan Keogh. 2015. The Joy of Virtual Violence. In *The State of Play*, ed. Daniel Goldberg and Linus Larsson, 141–156. New York/Oakland: Seven Stories Press.

Flanagan, Mary. 2009. *Critical Play: Radical Game Design*. Cambridge: The MIT Press.

Gallagher, James. 2011. Ken Levine Interview: Taking *BioShock* from Rapture to Columbia. *Playstation.blog*, November 10. Accessed February 26, 2016. http://blog.us.playstation.com/2011/11/10/ken-levine-interview-taking-BioShock-from-rapture-to-columbia/.

Gee, James Paul. 2007. *What Video Games Have to Teach Us About Learning and Literacy*. New York: St. Martin's Griffin.

Goldfarb, Andrew. 2013. How Playing as Elizabeth Changes *BioShock Infinite*. *IGN*, August 7. Accessed February 18, 2016. http://www.ign.com/articles/2013/08/07/how-playing-as-elizabeth-changes-BioShock-infinite.

Hart, Patricia. 1989. *Narrative Magic in the Fiction of Isabel Allende*. Rutherford: Fairleigh Dickinson University Press.

Irrational Games. 2014. *BioShock Infinite: Burial at Sea Episode 2*. USA: 2K Games.
———. 2013. *BioShock infinite*. USA: 2K Games.

Lizardi, Ryan. 2014. BioShock: Complex and Alternate Histories. *Games Studies* 14, No. 1.

Manovich, Lev. 2001. *The Language of New Media*. Cambridge: The MIT Press.

McDonald, Liam T. 1998. *Maximum PC 3*, No. 10, p. 43. November.

Mouffe, Chantal. 1993. *The Return of the Political*. New York: Verso Books.

Nardi, Bonnie. 2010. *My Life as a Night Elf Priest: An Anthropological Account of the World of Warcraft*. Ann Arbor, MI: University of Michigan Press.

Romero, John. 2009. The Tidiness Theory. http://rome.ro/2009/11/tidiness-theory.

Rushdie, Salman. 1991. *Imaginary Homelands: Essays and Criticism 1981–1991*, 209–234. London: Granta Books. Cited in Wilson, Rawdon. 2005. The Metamorphoses of Fictional Space: Magical Realism. In *Magical Realism: Theory, History, Community*, ed. L. Zamora and W. Faris. Durham, NC: Duke University Press.

Sample, Mark. 2013. Criminal Code: Procedural Logic and Rhetorical Excess in Videogames. *Digital Humanities Quarterly* 7 (1). http://www.digitalhumanities.org/dhq/vol/7/1/000153/000153.html.

Sarkeesian, Anita. 2013. Ms. Male Character – Tropes Vs. Women. *FeministFrequency*. Accessed September 28, 2016. https://feministfrequency.com/video/ms-male-character-tropes-vs-women/.

Slemon, Stephen. 1995. Magical Realism as Postcolonial Discourse. In *Magical Realism: Theory, History, Community*, ed. L. Zamora and Wendy B. Faris, 407–426. Durham, NC: Duke University Press. Cited in Bowers, Maggie Ann. 2004. *Magic(al) Realism*. New York: Routledge.

Turing, Alan. 1937. On Computable Numbers, with an Application to the Entscheidungsproblem. *Proceedings from the London Mathematical Society*.

von Uexküll, Jakob. 2010. *A Foray into the Worlds of Animals and Humans: With a Theory of Meaning*. Minneapolis, MN: University of Minnesota Press.

VanOrd, Kevin. 2013. The Break Room: We Can Kill the Industry with Cynicism – Ken Levine – BioShock. *Gamespot*, published on *Youtube*, March 20. Accessed March 3, 2014. http://www.youtube.com/watch?v=JwsjALh2vYA.

Wells, Kimberly Ann. 2007. *Screaming, Flying, and Laughing: Magical Feminism's Witches in Contemporary Film, Television, and Novels*. Ph.D. Dissertation, Texas A&M University.

Wikipedia. List of Unreal Engine Games. Aggregated List on *Wikipedia*. Accessed March 1, 2016. https://en.wikipedia.org/wiki/List_of_Unreal_Engine_games.

Wilson, Rawdon. 1995. The Metamorphoses of Fictional Space: Magical Realism. In *Magical Realism: Theory, History, Community*, ed. L. Zamora and Wendy B. Faris. Durham, NC: Duke University Press.

Winner, Langdon. 1986. *The Whale and the Reactor: A Search for Limits in an Age of High Technology*. Chicago: University of Chicago Press.

# 4

# From Sirens to Cyborgs: The Media Politics of the Female Voice in Games and Game Cultures

Milena Droumeva

*'Voice' is one of those apparently simple everyday words that have astonishingly prismatic qualities. It is a term that at once encapsulates ideas of the body, identity, expressiveness and subjectivity as well as ideas of agency, opinion, power, and political participation*
*(Lacey 2013, 123)*

Over the past decade, scholarly interest and cultural discourses surrounding gender and gaming have grown significantly. The popularization of gaming, changing definitions of the gamer identity, and the expansion of gaming practices across media platforms have been accompanied by a growing public conversation about the gender politics of games as systems of representation (Consalvo 2012). These conversations directly challenge normative understandings of game cultures and industries as exclusive spaces for men and boys, therefore disrupting the patriarchal order (Penny 2014). Consequently, women's sonic participation in these spheres—whether as critics, voice-over actors, or players—has made them targets of everything from ridicule, to harassment, to doxxing (Gray 2012; Jenson and de Castell 2013). But this is nothing new. Since antiquity, men have positioned women's voices as lacking *sophrosyne* (balance and harmony)—using their supposed physical deficiencies to explain why they are threatening to men and sound so bad (Carson 1995; James 2015). In classic forms of performance such as opera, singers undergo

M. Droumeva (✉)
Simon Fraser University, Burnaby, BC, Canada

© The Author(s) 2018
K. L. Gray et al. (eds.), *Feminism in Play*, Palgrave Games in Context,
https://doi.org/10.1007/978-3-319-90539-6_4

rigorous training in order to occupy heavily gendered roles (Clément 2000). The gendered sonic positioning of women's voices in popular media suggests that little has changed. In film, radio, and television, men have been cast as the voice of authority and confidence, while women are often coded as hysterical, nurturing, or seductive (Doane 1985; Loviglio 2007; Williams 1985). Although there have been notable exceptions (Loviglio 2007; Butkus 2012; Ehrick 2015), it is important to acknowledge these as transgressing the dominant gender order.

A marked absence in this emergent conversation has been the gender coding of sonic representation in games. Which tropes and conventions from traditional media have been imported? What novel developments have occurred? What role does interactivity play in the production, mediation, and reception of gendered sound? This chapter examines these questions by considering how women's voices have been historically positioned, translated, and policed across different media spaces. Beginning with the stages of the opera house, it considers gendered voice in terms of its physicality, regulation, and opportunities for transgression. Next, it examines the gendered voice broadcast across the screens and through the speakers of film, radio, and television—with specific attention paid to the role of the announcer and function of the voice-over.

Considering the history and ongoing nature of women's exclusion and underrepresentation, the gendered nature of authority, and (dis)embodiment, it also examines how the integration and separation of voice and image have cultivated new modes of subjectivity that challenge the status quo. These histories provide a rich context for us to examine the gendered voice of gaming and play, where reconfigured forms of corporeality, regimes of control, and dialogic possibilities co-exist and unfold within the rubrics of interactivity and player identities. Here, I consider how role-playing games (RPGs) exist within an ambivalent space of constraint and opportunity that are instructive in informing new ways of undoing and unpolicing gendered identities in the media (see Bonenfant 2014). As such, this chapter provides a unique methodological paradigm and model for drawing connections between women's sonic representation and participation across different media, and how dominant ideologies of gender are both re-articulated and transgressed. The gendered disciplining and social construction of voice begins in antiquity (Beard 2014; Carson 1995) in tandem with the political framing of women's role in society and the corresponding policing of their bodies and voices. It also begins by acknowledging the profound physicality and materiality of sound. This chapter is thus organized around several guiding themes that set up the gendering of sound and voice across media and lead us into the staging of women's voices in video games: (1) embodiment and physicality; (2) gender coding and voice typologies; and (3) transformation and transgression.

# Embodiment/Physicality

## Vocal (cis)-cipline

Voice is literally the body resounding itself. It is uniquely modulated through the physical size, shape, and consistency of bodies and further honed by biology, race, socialization, and environmental factors. The voice always hearkens to a body—a gendered, political, racialized, social body. It is no surprise then that the physical characteristics of women's voices have been subject to scrutiny, discipline, and regulation respective to their social position. Feminist film scholar Kaja Silverman argues that similarly to impossible standards for female beauty, 'the female voice is as relentlessly held to normative representations and functions'. (Silverman 1988, viii). Nowhere is vocal training as rigorous and gendered as throughout the history of opera, the precursor to modern entertainment including both musical theatre and genre media. As opera theorist Christine Clément emphasizes, operatic and pre-operatic traditions are important to this discussion because they set the cultural stage not only for types of narratives but also more importantly for the presentation and vocal training of character typologies—a kind of 'dominant and institutionalized cultural heritage [that includes] the realities of gender politics' alongside vocal aesthetics (Clément 2000, 24–25).

In the operatic tradition, singers spend years disciplining their voices and bodies to fit into a certain category of voice, established by the lower and upper limits of human capacity and continuously re-inscribed by a rigid musical canon (e.g. you are *either* a soprano or mezzo-soprano). Engendering a kind of vocal perfection (*sophrosyne*) that requires years of rigorous physical training and self-regulation, this high-pitched *siren-like* (Carson 1995) female voice is culturally coded as an ideal performance synonymous with physical beauty. Technology shifts these relationships significantly: while in musical performance it is the physical body that produces sound, the history of sound recording and reproduction is marked by a continual separation between the body on screen and the vocal performance of gender; between the symbolic body and the gendered voice. Thus, looking into the way technologies for audio reproduction and early aural media (e.g. radio) evolved to accommodate the female voice is a core aspect of the story of voice in games: a screen medium where the voice actress is necessarily an 'othered' embodiment than that of the avatar.

One of the subtle, yet insidious ways in which female voices are policed and excluded within the very *technologies* of sound reproduction has to do with their configuration to specifically fit the male voice and other normative forms of soundmaking: a practice Frances Dyson (1996) calls encoding the body in technology. The aural presence of women on radio is a story that most starkly reflects how the physicality of voice is used to justify difference and exclusion in an increasingly mediated public sphere (Douglas 1999; Lacey 2013). Throughout the 1920s to the 1940s, the physical qualities of women's voices were deemed unsuitable for the airwaves of radio. Too high pitched and thus unable to be 'modulated' properly for radio, women's voices seemed at odds with a broadcast spectrum implicitly suited for the lower-register male voice (Zakharine 2013). In that, the mediated female voice (and by extension, the female body) was framed as lacking, non-normative, distorted (Thompson 2016). Similarly, the advent of the microphone instantiated a kind of intimate voice of authority, the lower tones of male speech overly emphasized into booming baritones—a quality Roland Barthes (1991) praises as rich and (intrinsically) pleasant in his essay *The Grain of the Voice*. Female radio announcers' voices were trapped in a double bind: too shrill and noisy for the airwaves while also too emotionally unbridled, 'cackling', and informal to be 'taken seriously'. In her historic account of listening publics, Kate Lacey (2013) observes how women were accused of dramatizing factual news with their 'emotive' speech while simultaneously criticized for speaking 'too public/ not private' enough in tone (129). In other words, female voices failed to achieve the right kind of *sophrosyne* of microphone intimacy.

This cultural construction of women's media voices as shrill, creaky, and noisy is mapped in the contemporary media space to one of two categories of vocal performance considered to be 'inappropriate', a sign of insecurity, and unprofessional on air: *the vocal 'fry'* and the (Valley girl) *upspeak*. Both are particular embodied performances that push the limits of gendered tonality by either lowering the voice to the point of 'creaking' and growling (vocal fry) or modulating pitch inflection in a sentence, elevating the last word to a pronounced higher tone (upspeak). While these qualities are demonized and coded as feminine failings in informational media (Thompson 2016; Loviglio 2007), they are considered positively desirable in women's voices in genre media. For example, vocal fry—specifically in the form of creaking and breaking—is central to the hyper-sexualized sonic presence of the seductress in film, popular music, and games (Thompson 2016). Similarly, the upspeak can be aligned with the high-pitched exhalations that often mark the female battle cry in fighting RPG and arcade games.

## Technologizing the Voice

When it comes to encoding the body into audio technology, particularly one that is pertinent to the realm of sound design for gaming, the history of the vocal synthesizer (vocoder) brings another example of policing and exclusion. Roberts (2015) observes that robotic voice synthesis polices gender down to actual wavelength coming at around 100–150 HZ for male, and 200–250 Hz for female speech. Arguing that such tools reinforce normative definitions of sexed and gendered personhood, she states that simulated speech articulates a series of assumptions about what neutral inflection is, what a female voice is, and whose voice technology can ventriloquize. This approach is not dissimilar to operatic categorizations of exclusive voice registers (e.g. soprano, alto) as tropes that have influenced subsequent performance domains. Technologically speaking, synthesized sound opens potentials for transgression and fluidity. This is why it is notable that in practice the synthesizer reifies and encodes already gendered sonic tropes. From electronic music to early video game 8bit sound, the strict vocal ranges of femininity and masculinity are artificially recreated and emphasized.

A case in point, many classic RPGs such as Final Fantasy or Zelda have their humble roots in electronic music (Droumeva 2011) which itself could be considered not particularly gendered and even transgressive. Yet the very limitations of game processing and synthesizer technologies—coupled with an increasing appetite for character-driven 'realistic' narratives—led to the rather binary representation of gendered sound: low synth=male; high synth=female, with trans-diegetic (Jørgensen 2011) characters such as magical or robotic creatures represented through vocal distortion and ambiguous pitch. With the advent of Foley for film and the increased processing power of gaming consoles, RPGs have evolved to incorporate a mixture of tonal audio cues and representational or 'realistic' sound effects. In terms of player-driven narrative, this includes both sounds that the avatar makes and sounds that she or he produce by interacting with the environment as a gendered body. This sonic embodiment of playable character brings with it a number of inherited media tropes that I discuss in the next section.

## Disembodiment

As Mary Ann Doane (1985) points out, screen voices open remarkably different ways of gendering vocal expression, with the tropes of 'disembodiment' and aural 'gaze' as key audiovisual features. However, we must begin by casting away the moniker of disembodiment. As Christine Ehrick (2015) puts it, 'to refer to voices from unseen sources as "disembodied" is to suggest that the voice is somehow separate from the body, a problematic formulation'. In film, women's voices *are* their bodies. The voice-over in the flashback of film noir often separates the voice from the body—creating an unseen voice that is staged as separate from the character's body, yet is still remarkably gendered. In examining the hierarchies and the radical otherness of the narrator in film, Mary Ann Doane (1985) notes that this has always been a male voice, 'with its power residing in the possession of knowledge and privileged unquestioned activity of interpretation' (168; Silverman 1984, 31). From a psychoanalytic lens, the *disembodied* female voice is subordinated to subjective and affective elements such as voice-over commentary, interior monologue, and flashbacks (Doane 1985, 169). Kaja Silverman builds off the work of film scholar Laura Mulvey in arguing that just as the male gaze is central in film, so too is the voice, through an implicit *aural gaze*. She argues that in comparison to the disembodied male speaker, women's voices are excessively embodied to signify their symbolic gendered characteristics (1984, 46–47).

In entertainment media, when there is an active interest in hearing women's voices, it often comes in the form of a *scream*. Sounds of pleasure and torture are often associated with women in film in a gendered divide that resides in the embodiment of what is shown and what is heard (Sullivan 2015). The scream queen/damsel in distress is shrill or sexy, a seductive falling victim to male voices and one whose feminized embodiment is aurally hyper-emphasized as a narrative device and an emotive centerpiece of genre media (Zakharine 2013, 207). As Gordon Sullivan (2015) argues, there is a long history of women's vocalizations serving as aural fetishes for the pleasure of male listeners (Fig. 4.1). Sullivan cites the work of John Corbett and Terri Kapsalis (1996), who observe that the sounds of female pleasure are 'more viable, less prohibited, and therefore a more publically available form of representation than, for instance, the less ambiguous, more easily recognized "money shot" that characterizes hard core pornography' (104).

Picking up on the construction of 'realism' through sound effects and vocalizations in RPG games, the female body (when a playable character) is sounded out in specifically gendered ways. While male grunts and battle cries caricature overflowing masculinity connoting power and energy, female vocalizations often express their limits in navigating the game world—through sounds of pain, frustration, annoyance, and hysteria. Following established female leads in adventure games such as *Tomb Raider, Uncharted, Bayonetta, Mirror's Edge, Assassin's Creed* (more recently), as well as classic RPG series such as *Final Fantasy* and *Dragon Age*, women as playable characters are aurally represented (while performing action sequences) through higher pitched

**Fig. 4.1** Voice actress sounding out Elizabeth: 'Putting the body into it': source 1 (https://goo.gl/6dzbaj); Lara Croft in Tomb Raider 2013 navigates the environment with breathy moans and pants at the forefront of gameplay: source 2 (https://goo.gl/gTqqcM)

vocalizations, a variety of breathy exhalations, grunts, and moans. In challenging feminist game scholars' reading of Lara Croft's aural presence as pornographic, Liana Kerzner (2015) points out that these vocalizations were recorded as part of the motion capture sequence and were thus the natural sounds made by the actress and not a 'misogynist conspiracy'. In her words, 'sometimes women grunt and gasp for reasons that don't involve a penis'. Similarly, the female talent playing Elizabeth in *Bioshock Infinite* says this about using voice to portray her character in the narrative: 'you have to put your entire body into it. There are times when I'm literally drenched in sweat because my body is working so hard' (Fig. 4.1). Yet this is precisely the point that Mary Ann Doane (1985) and others make about women's aural presence on screen—that it is unforgivingly embodied, with the voice anchoring the *fantasmic* body to a real feminized body in space. We are never allowed to forget that the character is female, in contrast to the normativity established for male playable characters who get to be simply 'heroes' of the story.

# Gender Coding and Voice Typologies

This brings us to the semiotics of voice and gender. In opera—the birthplace of (Western) vocal performance—Clément (2000) breaks down common gendered narrative typologies by vocal register: the high female soprano voice is the persecuted victim (tragic, humiliated, haunted, driven mad, bodily victimized). Men who perform the role of the soprano become 'less than' other men—the 'castratos' who are similarly diva-like and full of 'hubris' are coded with tragedy and despair. Their pathos reaches spiritual levels, and yet they are never the heroic victors of the story. The female mezzo-soprano, on the other hand, encodes notions of resistance, witchcraft, and treason. In these roles, women start out with an agency and heroism of their own, which paradoxically often focuses on a 'masculine' way of life and freedom. Tenors are typified by courage and rebellion. Although they are often tragic like sopranos, they are allowed heroism in their sacrifice—and are agents of that sacrifice, not victims. But no role is more celebrated, more regal, than that of the bass. Connoting spirituality, gravitas, and power, the bass is a king or a priest. He occupies the position of supreme symbolic power, a quality that can be traced to the deep male tones of the 'announcer' voice-over, the disembodied voice of authority that is central to radio, television, film, and advertising (Doane 1985, 168; Zakharine 2013, 208). In informational mass media, the relegation of women's voices and talk to the unimportant, trivial, or gossipy has been a dominant trope since antiquity (Carson 1995). In the realm of early mass media, Dmitri Zakharine notes that there was a strong and enduring resistance to the high pitch of women's voices when it came to news categories in broadcasting journalism (2013, 208). Women's voices were confined to 'soft' news connected to the domestic, while men announced the 'serious' news with the authority of 'truth'. In mass media, as with opera, we see the typifying of vocal registers to represent and embody specific narratives (227):

> The genre of the news broadcast demands a certain iconic similarity between the tonality of voice and the type of event to which the voice refers. The voices of hosts, in turn, have an indexical function of reference: they refer the speakers to the listeners and vice versa. (Zakharine 2013, 208)

Extending media tropes to video games reveals a similar narrative coding of gendered vocal performances. In some ways game sound is already a binary synthesis of digital audio, so choices around the soundmaking of gendered characters are necessarily encoded in technological constraints. However, as we saw in the previous section, a drive toward greater realism has resulted in the adoption of more cinematic vocal tropes. An emphasis on the physicality of gendered speech and vocalization is coupled with inherited semiotic coding. For instance, taking stock of the character set in *Dragon Age* reveals some familiar archetypes from genre media that carry through similar RPG titles. Alongside the cultural coding of male battle cries as exaggeratedly low, grunty, and aggressive, female voices are coded in terms of character typologies: the 'witch' voice is almost a growl, animalistic, with heavy vocal fry; the supporting racialized voice is often coded as seductress, featuring breathiness, urgency, and emotional affect; the mythical fey figure (e.g. Spirit of the Forest) is typically vocally coded as white and British, breathy, whisper-like, erotic, but in a way that is pure. The fey figure evokes the myth of idealized femininity and acceptable otherness, in contrast to the non-conforming sexuality of the witch (e.g. Desire Demon). In the next sections, I expand on these tropes under three broad and malleable categories of vocal performance: female masculinity, the service voice, and the scream queen.

## Female Masculinity/Joan of Arc

Picking up on the gendered broadcast voice in film, Mary Ann Doane (1985) notes that while the male voice is endowed with 'the possession of knowledge and privileged, unquestioned activity of interpretation' (168), the female voice when used as voice-over is subjective, autobiographical, 'evoking in a reminiscent fashion the diegesis which constitutes the film's present' (Silverman 1988, 136). Sonically, narrative female voices are distinctly recorded close to the microphone in an imposed position of intimacy that is lower in register, almost whisper-like, and with emotionality encoded in the form of 'creaking' and vocal 'breaking' (Thompson 2016). As Butkus (2012) observes, strong female voices of authority remained sparse in televised and filmic narratives well into the 2000s, a notable exception being the voice of Kate Mulgrew (Captain Janeway in the *Star Trek* franchise). Mulgrew's commanding, anchoring, deep Bacal-like voice introduced a novel tonality for the mediated female voice that resisted both the categories of 'seductress' and 'damsel' (186) in favor of what Loviglio (2007) refers to in American public radio as 'female masculinity' (cf. Halberstam 1998). In games, the vocal performance of female masculinity is relegated to the few playable female action heroes and leads, in order to audibly inscribe their legitimacy as warrior-types. Yet even in those cases, re-embodying markers of traditional femininity seems inevitable. In this excerpt, a player complains about *Mass Effect's* FemShep's overt emotionality in comparison to the consistent male action voice of her counterpart:

Jennifer Hale [FemShep] only really does two voices: strong, gruff female warrior, with a penchant for talking really low when shit gets real, and happy, flirtatious sweetheart. That, and she ... sighs with each and every word, especially when she's trying to sound gruff. MaleShep is more consistent, able to be gruff and tough, while still being able to tackle the more sombre moments well, all with the same voice direction.

The sonic depictions of the female action heroine of titles such as *Tomb Raider, Bayonetta, Mirror's Edge*, as well as playable female leads in *Uncharted, Assassin's Creed*, and *Final Fantasy* (among many others) invoke a similar timbre of female masculinity. Here, the confident female voice is of medium register and timbre akin to the mezzo-soprano in opera or the 'masculine' female voice in radio. It is coded as middle-class and white, often featuring a British or (non-regional) American accent, clearly marking this sonic archetype as the normative narrative lead voice. Yet, in comparison with the gamut of male character voices featured in typical RPGs, both secondary non-playable female characters and to some degree female action leads read as overly close-miked and breathy, unable to contain the overflowing femininity of the character. The cross-over between the vocal performance of female masculinity and the seductive voice is perhaps best expressed in a fan comment about *Assassin's Creed Liberation*'s playable lead Avelyne, whom he describes as a 'gorgeous sexy black woman with a killer French accent who seduces everybody and frees slaves' (Thawne 2016). Enough said.

## The Service Voice/Sexy Female Robot

The voice-over or narrator trope from film and radio also directly informs another important space for female vocalization: the artificial intelligence (AI) service voice and, more generally, the companion voice. The female service voice is a particularly relevant case for game sound because it not only espouses and transgresses traditional gendered semiotics inherited from other media genres, but it also encodes them in a specifically technological paradigm. AO Roberts (2015) notes how AI is already gendered and tied up with stereotypical ideas of femininity down to the bandwidth and frequency ranges allocated to speech. Thinking back to the backlash against women on radio, it is interesting how context changes everything. When it comes to having a handy personal assistant who is even-tempered, sanitized from the emotional excesses of stereotypical femininity, everyone seems to prefer female AIs (Giggs 2011). Rebecca Zorach from the University of Chicago is quoted in Brian Giggs' article as saying: 'yes, probably these compliant female robot voices reinforce gender stereotypes, not just because they serve the user but because the technology itself is about communication and relationships (areas that women are presumed to be good at)'. Of course with the personal assistant role comes the cultural imaginary of human-robot romance with the implied male user. Cortana, one of the longest standing game AIs in the series *Halo*, presents a strong trope of both female service voice and AI-human romance transgressing the game screen to become Android's voice-operated mobile personal assistant. Notably, in 'real life' the designers of Android's *Cortana* have already had to develop her defenses against the onslaught of sexual harassment 'she' receives from mobile users. Similar characters include computer system aides in *Star Wars Republic*, *Gears of War*, and many other tactical FPS games. However, the promise of a robotic, unemotional female companion is anything but reality in terms of sonic conventions. Similarly to female AIs in cinema, ranging from *Blade Runner* to *I, Robot* and *Ex Machina*, the female service voice is still prominently grounded in a gendered vocal performance marked with seduction, cunning, heightened emotionality, and affect.

A related trope of the service voice is the female companion in games. The companion is essentially AI (a non-playable character) but not necessarily a robot. In games, her voice occupies the traditional cinematic female voice-over trope, expressing inner thoughts and self-doubt, narrating her actions in real time, and providing helpful tips and emotional reactions to the actions of the male lead. Some of the more notable female 'service' companions include Quiet from *Metal Gear Solid*, which a fan reviewer calls 'useful if distracting companion' in reference to her nearly nude attire; Elizabeth (*Bioshock*) who starts out as a typical damsel in distress and becomes Booker's aide; Elena in *Uncharted*; and Alyx Vance (*Half Life 2*) who, as the same reviewer points out, is 'so good she might as well have been the main character' (WitchMojo 2016). Yes, why isn't she the main character?

## The Scream Queen/Damsel in Distress

In the history of entertainment and genre media, gendered voices have been coded and stratified in ways that both subvert and reinforce the dominant gendered order. We can again trace this tradition back to opera, where, a precursor to the *female scream* trope in film, the piercing falsetto of the (tragic) heroine has long been 'central to the *jouissance vocale* of the male opera lover' (Bosma 2003, 12; Poizat 1992). Cathérine Clément (1988) discusses the tendency for female arias to become higher and higher as a kind of gradual de-voicing, occupying registers where speech becomes unintelligible, which Heather Bosma describes as a type of 'melismatic singing and coloratura fragmenting the word into sound' (2003, 12). The female character is then pure voice, a siren-like *objéct sonore*. In pop music and genre media the female scream is a contradiction—described both as feminized noise, a *screeching* (Brophy 2013; Thompson 2016), and at the same time as the aural evidence of female pleasure, a sonic reward for an implied male player (Corbett and Kapsalis 1996; Carson 1995). In that, the *scream queen* trope of (horror) cinema manifests in games as the pornographic voice of female exertion.

This trope is most remarkably evident in the vocalizations of female characters as they inflict or receive damage: their 'battle cries'. In similar ways to the hyper-real and animalistic masculinity espoused in respective male characters, female battle cries and accompanying vocalizations of exertion (such as running, climbing, falling, and picking up objects) are undeniably feminized. Breathy, gaspy, at once guttural and high pitched, creaking and breaking with overflowing emotionality, female characters often connote what Anita Sarkeesian and others refer to as the 'fighting fuck toy'. They are sometimes animalistic, bordering on hysterical, and conveying a lack of control and urgency. In what is clearly a wink-wink comment to a male fan base, a video blogger has this to say on the voicing of *Street Fighter*'s iconic character Chun-Li: 'she is known for her epic cry and of course we are referring to the sound she makes every time she gets knocked down' (list25 2014).

## Transgressions/Transformations

And yet voice has always been a site of possibility and transformation. In opera, the castrati and travesti have always been part of the operatic tradition as cross-dressing voices (Hadlock 2000), as have decades of gender bending vocal performance in popular music (Brophy 2013). In the realm of media, as narratives have progressed in complexity from the days of early radio and silent cinema, so has the range of acceptable media voices. This has created more space for typological differences and transgression. One of the most interesting examples in terms of both cinematic and game-based narratives manifests in fantasy and science fiction narratives as the representation of AI. Keeping in mind that the AI voice in games is itself a creative reconstruction of the technological constraints of real-world voice synthesizers, it both inherits and plays with technological norms of gender encoding.

Looking closely at some notable examples of AI voices reveals a fascinating overlap between traditions of game sound and the wider field of assistive technology. The iconic AI of the *Halo* series, Cortana—incidentally to become the signature Android voice-based assistant—displays a wide range of vocal performances depending on the context and narrative event. Her natural speaking voice is relatively sultry and pleasant—a 'neutral' friendly service tone. However, in emotional settings her voice is heavily transformed. When interacting with the Chief in a romantic context, her voice becomes breathy, high with emotive breaks, and comes across as almost hyper-human—the same way the OS Samantha in the movie *Her* is sonified as raw and sultry, fragile. When Cortana displays anger (coded as hysteria) her voice transforms almost comically through vocoder processing. It is heavily reverberated with an added 'chorus effect', evoking multiplicity—an unstable, non-normative femininity, an almost non-conforming multiple gender. Her overall character is sassy and playful while her vocal character matches her role in the context: from very vulnerable and human to quite robotic, cold, and detached.

A quick scan through other cyborgian or hybrid female characters reveals similar patterns: for example the character of Liara T'soni in *Mass Effect* speaks with a sultry British accent in a lyrical way, thickened with light reverberation. Sarah Kerrigan in *Starcraft* (a Zerg hybrid creature) is an even more extreme case of a transgressive vocal treatment. Her voice changes to signal her Zerg transformation: from an even medium-timbre 'Joan of Arc' officer, to a base of sultry, heavily processed, almost slowed-down voice marked with a lot of breathiness, augmented with reverberation and chorus effects. The use of reverberation on 'disembodied' female voices (e.g. the inner voice, memory flashback or guide) as well as nonconformist types of femininity such as witches and mythical creatures is a well-documented trope in cinematic narratives (Creed 1993; Caputi 2004; Doane 1985). Dating back to antiquity, Anne Carson (1995) traces the metaphorical associations of the echo effect with femininity; with unbridled subjectivity and lack of vocal agency (after the nymph Echo, destined to repeat the speech of others but not speak herself). In cinema and games, 'multiplicity' effects such as chorus or a pitch randomizer are interesting devices that signal, I would suggest, the inherent gender ambiguity of the hybrid, artificial (proto female) character— semiotically coded as transgressive and non-binary. Often AIs in games are explicitly androgynous, such as the computer voice in the *Portal* series, or the child-like pitched-up voice of the guide Midna in *Zelda*. Sonic transgression then hides in the nuance of already 'othered' characters.

## The Public Voice of Women

Technical changes in media production and dissemination continuously usher in new types of audiences, new forms of democratization of voices, and transgressions of canon. Although the rise of interactive media can support new modes of audience participation, it can also make criticism and backlash more participatory (Loviglio 2007). Feminist mobilizations have often been about gaining a voice and using it for political change and as Kate Lacey (2013) notes, political and technical changes coincided with women's entrance into the public sphere. But who exactly is allowed to vocally transgress, and when? As Jason Loviglio (2007) notes in his study of NPR, while public radio is a space where women's voices tend to narrate and report a majority of the content, the disparities in professionally acceptable vocal range for women and men call into question the 'progressiveness' of the current era. Loviglio notes that while male hosts and announcers seem to have long been afforded to opportunity to vary their speaking style and engage in upspeak or vocal fry, women have learned the language of a more sober 'masculine' feminism, a vocal performance of 'male drag'. When speaking freely on the air, women are still relentlessly criticized for perceived incompetence, sounding 'unprofessional', or possessing annoying voice qualities. For Lacey (2013), speaking is a political act corresponding to the act of *listening in* to the 'electrified voices' that form the contemporary public sphere. She notes that we have a responsibility to listen differently: listen to the voices that jar or grate and not only to those that are familiar, easy, or reassuring (131).

Like many traditionally male technocratic domains, game culture is excessively policed and guarded against transgressive voices—particularly those that have recently come from women who make, study, critique, and play games. Without re-appropriating the metaphor of voice-as-agency, a striking pattern is evident in the transmedia histories of women's exclusion from broadcasting, as well as the typologizing of female voices in media, and the vitriolic harassment that female game critics receive on the social web: the re-inscribing of women (back) into their bodies. Even when male commentators may be 'trash talked at' online, it is with women specifically that threats and insults take on a visceral gendered character, literally reducing women to their respective body parts and implying unmistakably sexualized violence. In Anne Carson's words (1995), we are right back to antiquity where the female mouth and the vagina are called the same, where both women's sexuality and their public participation need to be vehemently guarded, disciplined, and policed.

As *interactive* narratives, games are uniquely positioned to evoke the player's identification with a character, and one of the injustices of the last decades of game design that is geared almost exclusively to young (white) men is the entrenched paradigm of players necessarily identifying with a male action hero. With small exceptions, female characters have been after-thoughts of the industry, and alongside their hyper-sexualized visual presentation, their sonic presence and vocalizations undeniably embody stereotypical media tropes of femininity. I do not mean to suggest that women should not sound like women when exerting themselves on the adventure terrains of game worlds. Rather, I am suggesting that the aim of inclusive design in gaming when it comes to visual and sonic presentation of characters should be to make them relatable to any player—not as an othered or exotic object, but as a full-bodied, nuanced protagonist that players of any gender can identify with. If anything, I advocate for more and greater vocal transgressions, while we as gamers should be prepared to *listen in* to difference, to unexpected sonic presence, and agency.

**Acknowledgments** I'd like to acknowledge the generous support of the ReFiG SSHRC partnership grant, as well as Maggie MacAuley's vital contribution to the theoretical background review.

# Bibliography

Barthes, Roland. 1991. *The Grain of the Voice: Interviews 1962–1980*. Translated by L. Coverdale. Berkeley: University of California Press.

Beard, Mary. 2014. The Public Voice of Women. *London Review of Books* 36 (6): 11–14.

Bonenfant, Yvon. 2014. On Sound and Pleasure: Mediations on the Human Voice. *Sounding Out!* Accessed June 1, 2016. https://soundstudiesblog.com/2014/06/30/on-sound-and-pleasure-meditations-on-the-human-voice/.

Bosma, Hannah. 2003. Bodies of Evidence, Singing Cyborgs and Other Gender Issues in Electrovocal Music. *Organised Sound* 8 (1): 5–17.

Brophy, Philip. 2013. Evaporate Music 1: Revoicing and Gendered Vocalization. In *Electrified Voices: Medial, Socio-historical and Cultural Aspects of Voice Transfer*, ed. Dmitri Zakharine and Nils Meise, 93–105. Göttingen: V&R Unipress.

Butkus, Clarice. 2012. Sound Warrior: Voice, Music and Power in Dark Angel. *Science Fiction Film & Television* 5 (2): 179–199.

Caputi, J. 2004. *Goddesses and Monsters: Women, Myth, Power, and Popular Culture*. Madison: University of Wisconsin Press.

Carson, Anne. 1995. *Glass, Irony, and God*. London: New Directions.

Clément, Constance. 1988. *Opera or the Undoing of Women*. Translated by B. Wing. Minnesota: University of Minneapolis Press.

———. 2000. Through Voices, History. In *Siren Songs: Representations of Gender and Sexuality in Opera*, ed. Mary Ann Smart, 17–28. Princeton, NJ: Princeton University Press.

Consalvo, Mia. 2012. Confronting Toxic Gamer Culture: A Challenge for Feminist Game Studies Scholars. *Ada: A Journal of Gender, New Media, and Technology* 1. Accessed May 12, 2014. http://adanewmedia.org/2012/11/issue1-consalvo/.

Corbett, John, and Terri Kapsalis. 1996. Aural Sex: The Female Orgasm in Popular Sound. *TDR* 40 (3): 102–111.

Creed, Barbara. 1993. *The Monstrous-Feminine: Film, Feminism, Psychoanalysis*. New York: Routledge.

Doane, Mary Anne. 1985. The Voice in the Cinema: The Articulation of Body and Space. In *Film Sound: Theory and Practice*, ed. Elizabeth Weis and John Belton, 162–176. New York: Columbia University Press.

Douglas, Susan. 1999. *Listening In: Radio and the American Imaginatio*. New York: Times Books.

Droumeva, Milena. 2011. An Acoustic Communication Framework for Game Sound: Fidelty, Verisimilitude, Ecology. In *Game Sound Technology and Player Interaction: Concepts and Developments*, ed. Mark Grimshaw, 131–152. Hershey, PA: IGI Global.

Dyson, Frances. 1996. When Is the Ear Pierced? The Clashes of Sound, Technology, and Cyberculture. In *Immersed in Technology: Art and Virtual Environments*, ed. Mary Ann Moser, 73–101. Cambridge: MIT Press.

Ehrick, Catherine. 2015. Vocal Gender and the Gendered Soundscape. *Sounding Out!* Accessed June 14, 2016. https://soundstudiesblog.com/2015/02/02/vocal-gender-and-the-gendered-soundscape-at-the-intersection-of-gender-studies-and-sound-studies/.

Gray, Kishonna L. 2012. Intersecting Oppressions and Online Communities: Examining the Experiences of Women of Color in Xbox Live. *Information, Communication & Society* 15 (3): 411–428.

Griggs, Brian. 2011. Why Computer Voices Are Mostly Female. *CNN*. Accessed May 20, 2015. www.cnn.com/2011/10/21/tech/innovation/female-computer-voices/.

Hadlock, Heather. 2000. The Career of Cherubino, or the Trouser Role Grows Up. In *Siren Songs: Representations of Gender and Sexuality in Opera*, ed. Mary Ann Smart, 67–92. Princeton, NJ: Princeton University Press.

Halberstam, Jack. 1998. *Female Masculinity*. Durham, NC: Duke University Press.

James, Robin. 2015. Vocal Gender and the Gendered Soundscape: At the Intersection of Gender Studies and Sound Studies. *Sounding Out!* Accessed January 11, 2016. https://soundstudiesblog.com/2015/02/02/vocal-gender-and-the-gendered-soundscape-at-the-intersection-of-gender-studies-and-sound-studies/.

Jenson, Jennifer, and Suzanne De Castell. 2013. Tipping Points: Marginality, Misogyny and Videogames. *JCT (Online)* 29 (2): 72.

Jørgensen, Kristine. 2011. Time for New Terminology? Diegetic and Non-diegetic Sounds in Computer Games Revisited. In *Game Sound Technology and Player Interaction: Concepts and Developments*, ed. Mark Grimshaw, 78–97. Hershey, PA: IGI Global.

Kerzner, Liana. 2015. Fighting Back Against the Fighting F\*\*ktoy Trope. *Metaleater*. Accessed June 1, 2015. http://metaleater.com/video-games/feature/why-feminist-frequency-almost-made-me-quit-writing-about-video-games-part-4.

Lacey, Kate. 2013. Speaking Up and Listening Out: Media Technologies and the Re-sounding of the Public Sphere. In *Electrified Voices: Medial, Socio-Historical and Cultural Aspects of Voice Transfer*, ed. Dimitri Zakharine and Nils Meise, 123–136. Göttingen: V&R Unipress.

Loviglio, Jason. 2007. Sound Effects: Gender, Voice and the Cultural Work of NPR. *Radio Journal: International Studies in Broadcast & Audio Media* 5 (2–3): 67–81.

Penny, Laurie. 2014. Why We're Winning: Social Justice Warriors and the New Culture War. *Laurie Penny* [Blog]. Accessed July 2, 2016. http://laurie-penny.com/why-were-winning-social-justice-warriors-and-the-new-culture-war/.

Poizat, Michael. 1992. *The Angel's Cry: Beyond the Pleasure Principle in Opera*. Ithaca, NY: Cornell University Press.

Roberts, A.O. 2015. Echo and the Chorus of Female Machines. *Sounding Out!* Accessed June 20, 2016. https://soundstudiesblog.com/2015/03/02/echo-and-the-chorus-of-female-machines/.

Silverman, Kaja. 1984. Dis-embodying the Female Voice. In *Re-vision: Essays in Feminist Film Criticism*, ed. Mary Anne Doane, Patricia Mellencamp, and Linda Williams, 131–149. Frederick, MD: University Publications of America.

———. 1988. *The Acoustic Mirror: The Female Voice in Psychoanalysis and Cinema*. Bloomington: Indiana University Press.

Sullivan, Gordon. 2015. A Conversation with Themselves: On Clayton Cubitt's Hysterical Literature. *Sounding Out!* Accessed June 20, 2015. https://soundstudiesblog.com/2015/10/22/a-conversation-with-themselves-on-clayton-cubitts-hysterical-literature/.

Thawne, K. 2016. Top 10 Kickass Female Video Game Characters. *Unpause Asia*. Accessed June 20, 2016. http://unpauseasia.com/?p=3232.

Thompson, Marie. 2016. Creaking, Growling: Feminine Noisiness and Vocal Fry in the Music of Joan La Barbara and Runhild Gammelsæter. *Paradoxa: International Feminist Art Journal* 37: 5–11.

WhitchMojo.com. 2016. Top 10 Most Helpful A.I Companions In Video Games. Accessed September 15, 2016. https://www.youtube.com/watch?v=gxfOSb6_y6s.

Williams, Linda. 1985. *Hardcore: Power, Pleasure and the 'Frenzy of the Visible'*. Berkeley, CA: University of California Press.

Zakharine, Dimitri. 2013. Voice-e-voice-design-e-voice-community: Early Public Debates about the Emotional Quality of Radio and TV Announcers' Voices in Germany, the Soviet Union and the USA. In *Electrified Voices: Medial, Socio-historical and Cultural Aspects of Voice Transfer*, ed. Dimitri Zakharine and Nils Meise, 201–231. Göttingen: V&R Unipress.

# 5

# The Magnificent Memory Machine:
# The Nancy Drew Series and Female History

## Robyn Hope

In Herinteractive's long-running *Nancy Drew* series, the player takes on the role of the iconic teenage detective, commanding her actions, choosing her dialogue, and solving mysteries in her shoes. In the course of their investigation, the player and Nancy frequently encounter a particular kind of historical mystery: they find themselves searching for the lost truths left behind by a historical-fictional woman. These women hail from eras across time, and locations across the world. The player unlocks their secret passageways, unearths their buried treasures, and discovers their true stories. Each *Nancy Drew* adventure is, in its essence, an assemblage of interactive parts that, when manipulated by a capable player, will reveal a mysterious, forgotten past. In this way, the series expresses the complex relationship present-day women have with female history through narrative and gameplay. Records and primary sources of women's history have been largely erased over time, and it is from this absence that the challenge of the *Nancy Drew* games emerges (Sayer 2003; Spender 1982). Re-discovering women's history, the gameplay suggests, requires an *investigation*.

While the recovery of female history is presented as a worthwhile goal (Nancy always comes away victorious), it does not come without its challenges and pitfalls, and many female side characters in the series have far more troubled relationships with history than Nancy. In particular, the villainesses of the series—female thieves and con artists—repurpose harmful feminine stereotypes to obfuscate their criminal activity. As this chapter progresses, it will demonstrate how positive and negative relationships with female history,

R. Hope (✉)
Concordia University, Montreal, QC, Canada

© The Author(s) 2018
K. L. Gray et al. (eds.), *Feminism in Play*, Palgrave Games in Context,
https://doi.org/10.1007/978-3-319-90539-6_5

and the process of its reconstruction, manifest through the gameplay and storylines of different *Nancy Drew* titles. First, we must take a closer look at Nancy's digital incarnation, before progressing to the relationship between games and history more generally. Following this groundwork, we will undertake close readings of three games from across the 32-installment series: *Curse of Blackmoor Manor, Danger By Design,* and *Labyrinth of Lies.*

## Heroine of Her Time(s)

Nancy Drew makes a fitting avatar for an exploration of women's history, because she is already a historical icon herself. The first *Nancy Drew* novel was published in 1930, and Nancy-related media has been produced and consumed ever since. Scholars frequently observe that Nancy changes slightly to fit contemporary cultural and market demands (Siegel 1997; Pecora 1999). Some of her characteristics stay the same: she is proactive, independent, and mobile; she is both physically and mentally fit; she is logical and level-headed; and she solves mysteries to sate her own curiosity, without the desire for compensation (Perry 1997). She has been affectionately and accurately described as a "feminist superheroine," a hyper-competent, unfettered young woman who can change a tire or break a code better than any man she encounters (Siegel 1997, 162). The general consensus is that Nancy's best evolutions bring her heroism in line with the technology of the times; if her independence is ever hamstrung, the critical tone becomes delightfully bitter. Any reincarnation of the girl detective of the 1930s must, above all else, retain Nancy's ability to reject societal conventions and transcend the restrictions of her gender; Nancy will never be prevented from doing something just because she is a girl.

In 1998, this "feminist superheroine" stepped into the male-dominated world of the computer game. Computer gaming culture, especially in the 1990s, has always been an aggressively gendered space. Games were for boys and young men, and if girls were encouraged to play, they were encouraged to play games *for girls.* So the influx of Barbie games, and so the subsequent tide of critical scholarship deriding them for reinforcing misogynist stereotypes (Millar 1998; Cassell and Jenkins 1998). With this in mind, Nancy's transition into the digital put her in a difficult position: rather than acting as an unfettered heroine in her own world, she became a transgressor in a masculine one. Herinteractive seemed aware of their impertinence; one of the earliest series taglines advertised the games as "For girls who aren't afraid of a mouse." The suggestion that a mouse—a pun on computer mouse—could induce fear in girls implied that there was, in fact, some kind of gendered threat against women who wanted to access the digital world. However, any girl brave enough to challenge this patriarchal structure was welcome to join Nancy on her adventure.

Still, the ripple effect of this transgression is felt within the diegesis of Nancy's adventure games: one of the most significant changes to Nancy's character is the restriction of her legendary mobility (Perry 1997). Nancy is still a globetrotter—across 32 games, she has visited numerous European countries, Japan, New Zealand, Canada, and many different American states—but her freedom within these spaces is frequently challenged. Nancy makes it very clear that during a case, *she cannot leave*; clicking on the most obvious exit will cause Nancy to chastise herself for thinking that she can depart before the case is solved. Many games take place in forcibly isolated settings: a snowed-in chateau, a moving train, or a prison cell. Nancy's iconic blue roadster is altogether absent (but for its homage in *Secret of the Old Clock*, a game set in the 1930s), and whenever Nancy uses other vehicles, she has to *earn* them first. She must fix the boat in *Ghost Dogs of Moon Lake* before she can start it; she must demonstrate a knowledge of horses before she can ride one in *Secret of Shadow Ranch*. If the player tries to explore, their options may be artificially limited: the secret caves in *Danger on Deception Island* cannot be accessed before Nancy discovers their GPS coordinates, despite the fact that the caverns are visible from the water.

All of these obstacles actually serve a particular purpose; the primary goal of the *Nancy Drew* games is to overcome these restrictions and explore new spaces. Some strands of digital game theory characterize games as spaces that can be colonized by a dominant class (Fuller and Jenkins 1995). Chapman observes that historical games in particular are prone to "linking space and power," and points out that space—whether it be ground gained against an enemy in a shooter, or freshly conquered territory in *Civilization V*—is a reward for player victories (2016, 107). However, the acquisition of space can be much more difficult depending on the gender of the adventurer. Women also seek spaces of play, but a number of factors—including the masculine colonization of digital territory and the feminized tasks of girls' toys and games—can limit their success (Cassell and Jenkins 1998, 268). Conversely, T.L. Taylor identifies the freedom of exploration in certain games as one of the most appealing features for their female players. Her context is MMOGs, particularly *Everquest;* she explains that while exploring certain areas may be dangerous due to high-level monsters, "the threat is not based on gender," and that earning the right to explore by triumphing over non-gendered challenges affords women an experience that they would not necessarily have in the real world (Taylor 2006, 98).

This type of achievement—overcoming non-gendered threats to explore new space—is a major principle in the *Nancy Drew* series. The trials standing Nancy's way are never gendered, but they do provide a challenge and a sense of triumph when the player overcomes them. Moreover, in Taylor's example, exploration is challenging due to higher-level monsters (who could kill the avatar) acting as deterrents (Taylor 2006). In Nancy's case, she investigates places that have been *actively* rather than *implicitly* prohibited. Not only will the door not open when the player clicks on it, but it will be adorned with a "Keep Out" sign, or another character will say the room is forbidden, or Nancy will despairingly comment "it's locked." As *Nancy Drew* games generally limit the objects the player can interact with to objects that are important to Nancy's case, these cues don't mean the player should abandon the locked room; on the contrary, they confirm that progressing in the game will *require* breaking into it. Many of the "clues" Nancy collects are either keys, or miscellaneous objects functioning as keys, and progressing in the game involves deducing what to unlock next and how. Nancy is also frequently captured by her enemies (she quips in *Alibi in Ashes*, "I get knocked out and thrown into a dungeon every other week"). If Nancy has been tied up in a burning shed or a flooding room, breaking her out is simply the player's next challenge. Even fatal errors do not deter the player/Nancy team, as the player can rewind to the moment immediately before their deadly decision simply by clicking the "Second Chance" button. For women who naturally suffer restrictions on their mobility due to their gender, playing as Nancy offers the cathartic experience of shattering such restrictions.

Because of this pattern of prohibitions and transgressions, Nancy's mysteries are centered on her explorations of spaces. Each mystery is more accurately a *narrative garden*, to borrow Chapman's term, in which a historical narrative is embedded in the rich sensory details of a location, waiting to be discovered. He even explains that "in these games, the player is invited to function as a detective trying to piece together the sequence from environmental clues" (Chapman 2016, 102). The *Nancy Drew* series makes the *avatar* a detective alongside the player, and centers its gameplay around this investigation of space. What secrets lie in this mansion, in this city, in this museum, and *who put them there?* By combining the idea of narratives of place and female transgressors, the series developed a fascinating investment in the exploration of female histories. It is in the exploration of these forbidden places that Nancy finds her lost foremothers.

# Discovering the Historical Woman

Before we dive more deeply into Nancy's exploits, however, it will be useful to understand the typical relationship historical games create with the past. Kapell and Elliot, in their introduction to *Playing with the Past*, consider player agency to be the defining factor in how games interact with history. They explain that granting a player agency within a certain event "allows for an in-depth understanding not just of facts, dates, people, or events, but also of the complex discourse of contingency, conditions and circumstances, which underpins a genuine understanding of history" (Kapell and Elliott 2013). Additionally, the process of writing history involves assembling facts into a narrative, and historical games grant the player the ability to partially construct this historical narrative themselves (Kapell and Elliott 2013). Chapman, in *Digital Games as History*, also observes this phenomenon, stating "the historical narrative produced in these games is always produced by the actions of the developer-historian *and* the player" (2016, 34). In this way, players learn how to think like historians by examining the cause-and-effect relationships of historical contingency, conditions, and circumstances, and they learn this by creating their own historical narratives through play. The *Nancy Drew* series creates an interesting intervention into this established discourse of historical games through its gameplay and narrative. With but one exception (*Secret of the Old Clock*), these games are not set in a historical time period, as with many historical games. Instead, Nancy is herself a historian investigating previous eras. This brings the creation of a historical narrative from the background into the foreground: now "making history" is no longer a side consequence of the player's play process, but rather its *goal*. Recalling Chapman's description of how players move through a narrative garden—assembling environmental clues like a detective—Nancy gradually exposes historical data through investigation, puzzle-solving, and interrogation, and she pieces together historical narratives (often the stories of misremembered women) through this process. In order for this process to be a challenge, the historical women Nancy investigates are shrouded in mystery.

Here, we will benefit from a specific example. The main historical figure of the fourteenth game in the series, *Danger by Design*, is Noisette Tornade, a Parisian woman who was allegedly a German spy during World War Two. Years later, it was revealed that the accusations were baseless: she was not a German spy, but a double agent for the French Resistance. During the war, she also removed a number of stained-glass windows from Parisian churches, and hid them to keep them safe from German bombings. Noisette never revealed what she had stolen, even after the war ended, fearing the public would turn on her again. Her confessions remain hidden until Nancy unearths them and recovers the stolen stained glass. Due to this fear of persecution, Noisette hides her treasures behind layers of obfuscation. Her instructions must be literally decoded using an M-380 codebreaking machine (a fictional version of the German Enigma), and the instructions on how to use the machine are hidden in riddles throughout Paris. Noisette's situation is not unique in the *Nancy Drew* series, but rather typical of the historical women in it. Other examples include Marie Antoinette, who hides a diamond in *Treasure in the Royal Tower*; Charlotte Thorton, who locks away her family's controversial will in *Ghost of Thorton Hall*; and Elinor Penvellyn, who protects a 100-year-old family heirloom in *Curse of Blackmoor Manor*. The first is a slightly fictionalized version of her historical counterpart, the latter two are entirely fictional: all three, just like Noisette, hide their secrets behind layers of puzzles, codes, and passageways.

Here, we begin to see why the idea of players creating historical narratives through gameplay is so vital to the discussion of this particular series. Players not only learn to "think like historians" by assembling historical evidence but they also act *counter to* established patriarchal histories by highlighting women whose stories were erased. The gameplay process recovering the testimonies of silenced women is strikingly similar to the *actual* process of writing women's history. For example, in her volume on the history of women and technology, Melanie Stewart Millar describes her project thusly: "Telling the story of women's historical relationship to technology involves piecing together fragments of archaeological data ... and extrapolating from existing evidence" (Millar 1998, 15–16).

Millar is using the language of puzzle-solving and crime-solving almost unintentionally: she is "piecing together" disparate puzzle pieces, and drawing conclusions from "evidence," as a detective would. A fundamental difficulty of *all* women's history is the absence of women from primary sources (Sayer 2003; Spender 1982). Women have always produced information and text, but the *flow* of information is controlled by patriarchal forces; as a result, the artifacts of women's history tend to vanish en masse (Spender 1982). As a result, historiographers must seek sources of historical information outside conventional primary records. Sayer includes the examination of "diaries, letters, newspapers ... literary texts, poetic [and] prose-based ... cartoons, oil paintings, architectural plans ... photographs; [and] material culture" as "fundamental" to the practice of researching women's history (2003, 12). In her games, Nancy finds many clues in paintings, poems, or private letters. Noisette's codes are hidden in pieces of public art: she has built a passageway under a sculpture in a park, and embedded a cipher in Parisian metro stops. The ultimate historical trophies of *Danger By Design* (the stained-glass windows and a letter written in Noisette's own hand) also belong on this list of alternative texts.

In order to understand these unconventional sources, Nancy uses a number of unconventional tools. As aforementioned, one of Nancy's major strengths is that she is largely unrestricted by the expectations of her gender. Therefore, she can *combine* the masculine crime-solving tools of technology with feminized skills and objects. She collects keys, books, papers, jewelry, tools, art supplies, miscellaneous household objects, gadgetry, and even food. Melanie Stewart Millar mentions that technologies associated with home-making tasks, such as cooking technologies, are often rejected *as* technology because they are developed and utilized primarily by women; Nancy and the women of the past both ingeniously use these technologies to encode and decode information (Millar 1998). Nancy uses butter to grease a lock, or an artist's paintbrush to sweep for fingerprints. At the same time, Nancy retains her technological and athletic competence. She uses a spectroscope to detect art forgeries in *Labyrinth of Lies*, and dons a wetsuit to swim through catacombs in *Danger By Design*. Nancy can use feminine technologies in order to solve her mysteries, but she is not *restricted to* those technologies; rather, she must simultaneously understand technologies that, because feminine, have been devalued, *and* make transgressive use of technologies that are "not for girls." This may resonate with the experiences of the female-identified player, who is using a masculinized technology (the computer game) to save the day as a female hero.

In parallel to Nancy's androgynous ingenuity, the games also blend gendered conventions of setting (Fiske 1989). Soap operas and melodramas—traditionally "female" genres—are set in the home, while masculine crime dramas are set in public arenas of politics or power. Nancy's games are set in places where the boundaries between the home and the public sphere begin to weaken: where wartime double agents hide art in their cellars, or where political prisoners write in their diaries while Revolutions rage on outside. Chapman laments that historical games do not investigate the private sphere as frequently as they model massive, violent conflicts; the *Nancy Drew* series is an excellent demonstration of how games *can* examine private spaces and domestic history (2016).

In light of this resourcefulness, Nancy in her digital incarnation is as much a "superheroine" as her literary predecessor—but what of women who are not quite so superheroic? A great number of female characters in this series do not have Nancy's advantages: some are beholden to men, some are impaired by debt or legal constraints, and many of them have difficult, even traumatic relationships with history. In the worst cases, these women react violently against societal pressures and historical injustices, and commit crimes. While the series presents solving the case—and thereby recovering female history—as a worthwhile goal, it also does not shy away from the painful experience of belonging to a historical gender minority. Many games with female culprits express these frustrations: three of the most relevant are *Danger by Design*, *Labyrinth of Lies*, and *The Curse of Blackmoor Manor*.

## I've Always Been the Queen: Nancy's Female Foils

In *The Curse of Blackmoor Manor*, Nancy is invited to Blackmoor to investigate the strange behavior of a family friend, Linda. Linda is convinced that she is transforming into a beast, and refuses to show her face, spending the game hidden behind a white curtain. She has recently married into the Penvellyn family, the owners of Blackmoor; her husband, Hugh, is not present when Nancy arrives. Aside from Linda, there are three other women at the manor: Jane, Hugh's daughter from a previous marriage; her tutor, Ethel; and her great-aunt, Leticia Drake. Alongside them is an unaffiliated scholar, Nigel Mookerjee, who is researching the Penvellyn family. The key historical Penvellyn figure is Elinor. Allegedly, she was a witch who transformed her husband into a beast, and Linda believes Elinor's spirit has cursed her with the same fate.

Gothic tropes are hard at work in this particular mystery, including the grim setting in an English manor; the monstrous woman undergoing a hysteric breakdown and magical transformation; and the ghosts, witches, and secrets (Gilbert and Gubar 1984). Elinor is the traditional Gothic "monster in the house," that villainous, partly bestial, magical female creature, a cousin to Medusa and Lilith, as described in *The Madwoman in the Attic* (Gilbert and Gubar 1984). The women of Blackmoor appear to be either Elinor's victims or her handmaidens: Linda believes herself to be transforming into a beast, and the player catches a glimpse of her hairy hand; Jane and Ethel conduct a midnight ritual involving chanting, candles, and pouring oil down a drain. However, these mysterious occurrences have rational explanations. Linda is growing hair on her hands because her moisturizer was mixed with balding cream; the ritual Jane and Ethel conduct provides fuel for a forge in the basement. Elinor was not a witch, but rather rebel working against Oliver Cromwell, and she—along with every Penvellyn "heir" for the last 600 years—has left behind a puzzle within Blackmoor, not to bestow curses, but to protect a family heirloom (a meteorite, hidden in a basement vault).

As it turns out, the lair of the "monstrous woman" is simply the manor's masquerade, and much can be gleaned by examining the people who fall for that disguise. Firstly, there is Nigel Mookerjee. Throughout the game, Nigel stands for the presence of institutionalized, masculine academia. He is attempting to write an "unauthorized tell-all," as Nancy dubs it, by conducting conventional, book-based research in Blackmoor's library. He answers many of Nancy's questions with dates and facts, and dismisses curses and ghosts as nonsense. Near the end of the game, Nancy discovers one of Elinor's gadgets in a secret passageway, which will cause a statue in the library to move of its own accord. If Nigel is in the library when Nancy moves the statue, he will panic, throw a sheet over the statue, and insist that Blackmoor Manor is "genuinely haunted." The player is the cause of this haunting, and yet they do not have the option of informing Nigel of their deception, painting him more as a subject of ridicule than pity. Unlike the women bound up with the history of the castle, Nigel does not have the capacity to comprehend Blackmoor. Knowledge in Blackmoor is passed down through puzzles, pictures, icons, stories, games, and codes—through the unconventional artifacts of women's history—and it cannot be retrieved from standard historical texts.

More importantly, the culprit herself—the 12-year-old Jane—has also been taken in by the mystery of Blackmoor. She was the one who tampered with her mother's moisturizer and left the curse on her nightstand. Nancy even associates her behavior with the "monstrous woman" in the epilogue; she narrates, "Well, there *is* a Beast of Blackmoor—Jane." As in traditional Gothic tales, Nancy and Jane share thematic parallels (Chess 2015). Jane is also an intrepid puzzle-solver, who forces Nancy to play games with her before she will reveal the location of a secret passage. She is also the rightful heir to Blackmoor's secrets: as her ancestors explain in a diary hidden in the Blackmoor vaults, creating puzzles to hide the meteorite is a Penvellyn tradition, which every other generation has upheld since the fifteenth century. In a better world, Jane would have been another Nancy, an intrepid female detective uncovering the secrets of her lineage. So why, then, does Jane end up as the "Beast of Blackmoor" instead of the heroine?

The answer is, quite simply, that Jane is not in the same liberated position as Nancy. She is frustrated by expectations for her behavior, and her powerlessness due to her age. To return to *The Madwoman in the Attic*, Gilbert and Gubar retell the story of Snow White, arguing that it represents the conflict between the two literary manifestations of the woman: the angel and the monster. Importantly, the innocent, angelic Snow White and the monstrous witch Queen are "in some sense one—while the Queen struggles to free herself from the passive Snow White in herself, Snow White must struggle to repress the assertive Queen" (Gilbert and Gubar 1984, 41). Jane is this tension incarnate. Throughout the game, Jane has been manipulating, deceiving, and drugging her stepmother, but she behaves innocently all the while, and her machinations stem from the sincere yet impossible desire to leave Blackmoor and be reunited with her biological mother. Pulled in these two directions, Jane's villainy emerges from her inability to fully inhabit either role. She can no more resist the desire for the love of her true mother than she can quell her cunning. Because Jane is imprisoned, isolated, largely ignored, and misunderstood, her energies are misdirected. She models herself after the powerful, mysterious Elinor—not the *real* Elinor, but the monstrous Elinor constructed by the patriarchy, and she attempts to drag her mother into that Gothic narrative through a faked lycanthropic curse.

In another case of the "Queen and Snow White" becoming one, Linda and Jane actually suffer a nearly identical neglect. Gilbert and Gubar identify the voice of the patriarchy in the form of the King in Snow White, while in *Curse of Blackmoor Manor* the masculine authority emerges from an equally absent figure: Hugh Penvellyn, Jane's father and Linda's spouse, who can only be contacted over the phone. It is Hugh's abject ignorance of the social dynamics at work between Linda and Jane that causes their conflict. He is too easily fooled by Jane playing the innocent and addressing Linda as "mummy"; he too swiftly dismisses Linda's devolution into the Blackmoor Beast as hysteria, calling her rages "temper tantrums … [that] make rational discourse … impossible"; and he turns up his nose at the history of the Penvellyns, claiming to be disinterested. Both Jane and Linda are functionally imprisoned in Blackmoor: Jane by her age, and Linda by a legal clause that states she must remain there for six months after marrying a Penvellyn. Hugh, meanwhile, is both able to ignore the history of Blackmoor—the title of the official Penvellyn "heir" skips a generation—*and*, as he is called away for work before the game even begins, he is clearly free to leave it. The game reaches its resolution by not only forcing Hugh to return to his family and apologize, but also sparking his curiosity in his own history.

Such a happy ending is unconventional; traditionally, the monstrous Queen is destroyed by her inability to conform to the role of the sweet, inoffensive, domestic woman (Gilbert and Gubar 1984). Yet Jane is one of the few culprits who is *not* punished. This last-minute swerve away from the traditional tropes of the fairytale opens a new reading. Jane does not return to a state of purity and submissiveness, nor is she condemned forever to suffer as a monster. Rather, she finds her place in the matriarchy, and develops her own puzzle to protect the Penvellyn treasure. Nancy Drew then delivers on its promise of matriarchal lineage in a metatextual way, tying its female puzzle-makers, inside the diegesis and out, together: in *Danger By Design*, the struggling, paranoid fashion designer Minette is revealed to be one of the beta-testers of Jane's first computer game.

Minette and Jane share another similarity: they are the villains of their respective games, and both perform female stereotypes to obfuscate their sinister activities. In *Danger By Design*, Minette is both the cause and culprit of her case. Nancy has been sent to Minette's studio to investigate her bizarre behavior, similar to how she was sent to Blackmoor to help "diagnose" Linda. Minette wears a mask, throws violent tantrums, and has fallen behind in her work. Her crime is that she has been spying on a politician by designing a dress with surveillance equipment in it, under promise of payment from a cabal of spies. Nearly all of her behavior can be attributed to how Minette suffers under a crushing weight of societal pressure. She is desperate to be financially independent, and so she takes an illegal job for the pay. Other characters constantly reiterate that reputation can make or break a designer, so when Minette gets a tattoo on her face, which is a mistake that would likely get her laughed out of the fashion world, she begins wearing a mask. The very design of her studio provokes paranoia; it is full of secret passageways, and it is constantly bombarded with threatening letters, cockroaches sent in chocolate boxes, and even a paint bomb created to ruin Minette's designs. Magazines found on tables emphasize how vital a designer's *image* is to the world of fashion, and discuss the enemies Minette has made in her work; e-mails on her computer reveal that her assistants are pressured into high-paying, tell-all interviews. The more the player explores, the more confined and threatened they feel. While many people in the game—Nancy included—deride Minette for being a "nutjob," she has cracked under very real stresses for women in positions of cultural power. She suffers pressure from all sides, while lacking financial freedom of her own. And yet, like Jane, there is some implication that Minette is using the stereotype of the hysterical woman to her own advantage; many of the threats against her are faked, and it is possible that the paranoia is a construction as well, crafted so that Nancy will indeed dismiss her as a "nutjob" instead of realizing she is a criminal.

From these cases, a pattern begins to emerge: women suffering sexist societal pressures may employ sexist stereotypes as tools of deception. Jane performs innocence and stages Linda's monstrosity; Minette performs hysteria to displace scrutiny. The villain who uses such stereotypes more masterfully than any other is Xenia, the self-styled "Queen" of *Labyrinth of Lies*. Through organizing a stage play on location at a museum, Xenia plans to steal a number of priceless Greek artifacts by switching them out for stage props. The play is the Greek myth of Persephone's abduction by Hades, and Xenia, citing her sympathy with the legendary distressed damsel, plays Persephone. At the end of the game, she reveals that she sympathizes with Persephone because she believes the Queen of Hades, like so many other women, is historically *misread*. Persephone was not the Underworld's captive, Xenia insists, but its ruler. When Nancy argues that Xenia is not like the petty criminals she has been commanding, Xenia replies "No. I'm smarter," and flaunts her dominance over her subordinates, declaring that she stands with her "heel on [Nancy's] throat."

In many ways, the brilliant, scheming Xenia parallels the villainesses in melodrama, who manipulate the men around them, acting as power fantasies before their defeat restores the patriarchal status quo (Fiske 1989). However, the most vital difference between Xenia and the characters in melodrama that she, like Nancy, never uses her sexuality to obtain information; she relies entirely on her intellect. The struggle between the heroine and the villainous seductress does not rely on the manipulation of a man. Xenia manipulates people more generally, but also, like Nancy, manipulates historical information to get what she wants—reinforcing the damsel-in-distress reading of Persephone's story, and creating false historical data through forgeries. She is another anti-Nancy, independent and clever, but intent on profiting from history rather than retrieving it. Near the end of the game, Nancy is knocked out, and wakes to the image of Xenia on a hellish throne, surrounded by flames; Nancy then chases Xenia down and thwarts her plan by riding a lift to the stage and forcing Xenia to confess her crimes in the middle of her own play. This final confrontation—including Xenia's claim that she has "always been the Queen," suggesting a matriarchal authority, and the fact that Nancy defeats Xenia by overtaking her onstage space in the middle of her show—takes us back to the idea of historical games demonstrating change and progress by an exchange of space and power. Here, the confrontation is non-violent but very public; Nancy defeats her opponent in a battle of wits and presence, rescues the museum's artifacts and—according to her ending monologue—accidentally creates a smash-hit stage show in the process, praised for its "unconventional ending."

With but a few exceptions, *Nancy Drew* games have two components to their endings. Firstly, in every game, Nancy—with the help of the player, of course—conquers her opposing villain, often by using the environment cleverly or solving a timed puzzle. Secondly, in a majority of titles, Nancy recovers a treasure of some kind, an artifact that redeems a historical woman or, in some cases, a modern one—as when the recovery of the meteorite in Blackmoor Manor both helps to prove Elinor's innocence *and* spurs Jane's repentance. The endings of these games are idyllic, and tellingly, the rediscovery of a lost story is often painted as Nancy's biggest victory. In these endings, Nancy always delivers a concluding monologue. The ending monologue of an early installment, *Treasure in the Royal Tower*, spells out what could be Nancy's creed and the player's: "it's never too late to change history."

## Conclusion

The *Nancy Drew* series models different relationships with women's history. Nancy recovers the secrets of female history by decoding their messages and liberating their stories, while a slew of female villains subvert gender stereotypes—the innocent girl, the hysterical artist, the hapless ingénue—by playing them up to cover their criminal plots. This puts a new spin on the "guilty pleasure" of identifying with a female villain and, most importantly, it enables investigations of female *conflict* as well as female history. Conflict drives every plot, but these conflicts do not revolve around sexual competition over a man. Taken together, I conclude that the *Nancy Drew* series character-izes the recovery of female history as a process of ongoing negotiation between women of the past and present, rather than a singular task of solidifying his-tory into an authoritative Truth. There are always conflicts and tensions, and many of these emerge in the unfortunate yet unavoidable rivalries *between* women fighting for recognition and independence in a patriarchal world. This is why the agency of the player is perhaps the key role in this entire nego-tiation of history; they are the force that characterizes history, and women's history in particular, as open to reconstruction and reinterpretation. The *Nancy Drew* games are relatively loose in their structure, and they demand creative and logical thinking, but more importantly, they require *action*. The player is not just learning history, but actively excavating it—they build what history *is* by solving puzzles and exploring with Nancy, and are even encour-aged to create their *own* puzzles for posterity. History, as this series represents it, is a process; better yet, it is a game.

## Bibliography

Cassell, Justine, and Henry Jenkins. 1998. *From Barbie to Mortal Kombat: Gender and Computer Games*. Cambridge, MA: MIT Press.
Chapman, Adam. 2016. *Digital Games as History: How Videogames Represent the Past and Offer Access to Historical Practice*. New York: Routledge.

Chess, Shira. 2015. Uncanny Gaming. *Feminist Media Studies* 15 (3): 382–396. Accessed March 1, 2016. https://doi.org/10.1080/14680777.2014.930062.

Fiske, John. 1989. *Television Culture*. London: Methuen & Co Ltd.

Fuller, Mary, and Henry Jenkins. 1995. Nintendo and New World Travel Writing: A Dialogue. In *Cybersociety: Computer-Mediated Communication and Community*, ed. Steven G. Jones, 57–72. Thousand Oaks: Sage Publications.

Gilbert, Sandra, and Susan Gubar. 1984. *The Madwoman in the Attic: The Woman Writer and the Nineteenth-Century Literary Imagination*. New Haven: Yale University Press.

Kapell, Matthew Wilhelm, and Andrew B.R. Elliott. 2013. Introduction: To Build a Past That Will "Stand the Test of Time". In *Playing with the Past: Digital Games and the Simulation of History*, ed. Matthew Wilhelm Kapell and Andrew B.R. Elliott, 1–23. London: Bloomsbury.

Millar, Melanie Stewart. 1998. *Cracking the Gender Code: Who Rules the Wired World?* Toronto: Second Story Press.

Pecora, Norma Odom. 1999. Identity by Design: The Corporate Construction of Teen Romance Novels. In *Growing up Girls: Popular Culture and the Construction of Identity*, ed. Sharon R. Mazarella and Norma Odom Pecora, 48–79. New York: Peter Lang Publishing Inc.

Perry, Sally E. 1997. The Secret of the Feminist Heroine: The Search for Values in Nancy Drew and Judy Bolton. In *Nancy Drew and Company: Culture, Gender, and Girls' Series*, ed. Sherrie A. Inness, 145–158. Bowling Green: Bowling Green State University Popular Press.

Sayer, Karen. 2003. Modern Women's History: A Historiography. In *Proceedings of History Week*, ed. T. Curtis. Veritas Press.

Siegel, Deborah L. 1997. Nancy Drew as New Girl Wonder: Solving it All for the 1930s. In *Nancy Drew and Company: Culture, Gender, and Girls' Series*, ed. Sherrie A. Inness, 159–177. Bowling Green: Bowling Green State University Popular Press.

Spender, Dale. 1982. *Women of Ideas and What Men Have Done to Them: From Aphra Behn to Adrienne Rich*. London: Routledge & Kegan Paul.

Taylor, T.L. 2006. *Play Between Worlds: Exploring Online Game Culture*. Cambridge, MA: The MIT Press.

# 6

# The Sexual Politics of Video Game Graphics

Robert Mejia and Barbara LeSavoy

A patriarchal legacy continues to haunt mainstream video game culture even though the industry has expanded well beyond its "the valley of the geeks" stereotype (Lalley 2005). Coded in implicit and (later) explicit gendered terms, the early 1980s to late 1990s stereotype of the geek and subsequent fanboy emerged as a normative framework that effectually wrote women out of gaming history (Williams 2003; Mejia 2012). This erasure of women was visible in the arcade division at Atari, for example, where in 1980, one of its mockumentaries featured "Club Atari" as a brothel, depicting Dona Bailey, co-creator of *Centipede* (1980), as one of the Club Atari women (Kent 2001). Despite the industry's mainstream prominence, sexist narratives like the 1980 Atari example have persevered, signifying patriarchy's enduring hold on video game culture. Hence, we use the field of critical visual studies to examine how graphical trends reproduce gender and sexual disparity in the video game industry.

Contrasted against other major media venues, patriarchal influence in the video game industry is significant. For instance, the New York Film Academy (2014) found that, in the top 500 American films from 2007 to 2012, only 10.7 percent featured equally balanced female and male roles, and women in these films spoke only 30.8 percent, wore sexually revealing clothing 28.8 percent, and got partially naked 26.2 percent of screen time. Dismal as that

R. Mejia (✉)
North Dakota State University, Fargo, ND, USA

B. LeSavoy
The College at Brockport (SUNY), Brockport, NY, USA

© The Author(s) 2018
K. L. Gray et al. (eds.), *Feminism in Play*, Palgrave Games in Context,
https://doi.org/10.1007/978-3-319-90539-6_6

**83**

dataset may seem, Edward Downs and Stacy Smith (2010) examined the top selling video games of 2003 and found that women were featured only 14 percent, wore sexually revealing clothing 41 percent, and were partially or fully nude 43 percent of the time. These findings have remained relatively consistent across time (see Dietz 1998; Williams et al. 2009). Compared to film then, women in video games are roughly 50 percent more likely to wear sexually revealing clothes and appear partially or fully nude and about 50 percent less likely to perform in principal roles let alone appear in a video game at all.

## Understanding the Patriarchal Legacy of Video Game Culture: Developer Demographics, Market Demand, and Platform Design

Social, political and economic inequality between the sexes (see Launius and Hassel 2015) likely contributes to female underrepresentation in video games, but key arguments focused on developer demographics and perceived audience demand are limited. For instance, Williams et al. (2009) note that numbers of primary female characters were nearly identical to developer demographics in 2005–2006 (at 10.45 percent and 11.5 percent, respectively), but the increased numbers of women working in game development (22 percent) have had minimal effect on representations of female characters (Edwards et al. 2014). Major publishers have developed a large number of games that offer players the opportunity to select either male or female protagonists, but those featuring exclusively playable female protagonists (9 percent) are significantly less than those featuring exclusively playable male protagonists (32 percent) (Sarkeesian 2015). Likewise, although significant performative nuances do distinguish player-selected female characters from male characters—especially those using voice actors (Patterson 2015)—game scripts and marketing efforts are often crafted with male-selected characters in mind (Heron et al. 2014). These design choices do not match audience indicators. The Entertainment Software Association, in tracking decades of video game demographics, has long recognized the market as heterogeneous (Baka 1998; Lien 2013). Using industry measures, women have constituted from 31.1 percent (1998) to 44 percent (2015) of video game markets, so one would expect to see a wider range of gendered representations (Baka 1998; Entertainment Software Association 2015). Video game programmers, designers, and team leads recognize diversity as important in the workplace

(75 percent) and industry (79 percent) and critical for industry growth (65 percent) (Edwards et al. 2014), but diversity awareness has not translated into increased female representation.

Gender disparity would be a moot point if audiences were resistant to or not interested in character diversity, but studies suggest that video game players want (or at least are receptive to) more complex representations. For instance, a study of 1400 middle and high school students found that "47% of middle school boys agreed or strongly agreed, and 61% of high school boys agreed or strongly agreed" that "female characters are treated too often as sex objects" (Wiseman 2015). Arguably, some gamers are voting for hypermasculinity and sexist representations with their dollars, but this is not true across the board. For instance, *Doom* (an icon of hypermasculinity) and *Myst* (a puzzle game noted for both its complex story and popularity among women) were both released in 1993, and it was *Myst* that "dominated the charts" (Brenda Romero qtd. in Lien 2013).[1] The same has proven true of *The Sims* franchise (2000–present), which sold over 175 million copies by 2013 (Gaudiosi 2013), a sales outcome on par with the 175 million copies the *Call of Duty* (2003–present) and roughly 185 million copies the *Grand Theft Auto* franchises (1997–present) sold by 2015 (Makuch 2015). Despite success among franchises like *Myst* and *The Sims*, game developers model consoles to accommodate design philosophies common to other franchises.

While women's presence in video games has (slowly) improved across workforce and audience size, audience desire, and character representation, platform design is complicating the positive effects in gender representation that we would expect from these advances. One concern researchers raise is design platforms that code gender using narrowly construed market ideals of female behavior and appearance (Downs and Smith 2010; Martins et al. 2009). For instance, Martins et al. (2009) argue that "highly photorealistic games may be more likely than less photorealistic games to activate body dissatisfaction and a drive for thinness among female gamers, and to support the idealization of a markedly thin female body among male gamers" (831). Martins et al. (2009) optimistically hope that an "uncanny valley" effect may mediate against negative sexual effects of these representations, but they recognize that advances in video game graphics may make it so that "body shapes found in games may have a norming influence akin to manipulated advertising images like magazine […] and television characters" (832). Trends like this further distort female imagery where agency and voice in video game culture are already compromised.

This chapter turns to the field of critical visual studies to inform an understanding of how the photorealistic imperative that dominates graphical trends in the video game industry is affecting the gender and sexual politics of the industry. Our interest in graphical trends means that we are less interested in specific visual representations but rather the broader question of visual regimes: for though all representations are "fundamentally questions about […] the operation of social power," transformations of visuality are "inseparable from [broader reorganizations] of knowledge and social practices that [modify] in a myriad [of] ways the productive, cognitive, and desiring capacities of the human subject" (Crary 1992, 3). To this end, we organize this chapter by first exploring how the sexual politics of visuality evolved across the Atari 2600 and Nintendo Entertainment System (NES) consoles. We then focus on the *Final Fantasy* and *Tomb Raider* franchises to illustrate how the transition from realism of the PlayStation 1 era to the photorealism of the PlayStation 3 era resulted in a convergence in sexual representation. We selected these two franchises because each franchise has been perceived as starting from relatively opposite poles of the sexualization spectrum, with *Final Fantasy* becoming more sexualized and *Tomb Raider* becoming less sexualized (Crawley 2015; Oxford 2016). Leveraging Laura Mulvey's (1975/2006) project, which uses "psychoanalysis to discover where and how the fascination of film is reinforced by pre-existing patterns of fascination already at work" (833), we argue that the sexual politics embedded in the visual structures of contemporary gaming is negatively impacting how games represent women.

## From Action to Object: The Evolution of the Visual Pleasure of Video Game Play

Laura Mulvey (1975/2006) argues that advanced representation systems allow us to understand "the ways the unconsciousness (formed by the dominant order) structure ways of seeing and pleasure in looking" (834). Mulvey's (1975/2006) analysis of how the Hollywood style had established a formal mise-en-scene and cinematic apparatus that facilitated the production of a "skilled and satisfying [patriarchal] manipulation of visual pleasure" can be used as a model for analyzing the sexual politics embedded in the visual structures of the video game industry (835). Just as Mulvey (1975/2006) argues that "cinematic codes and their relationship to formative external structures […] must be broken down before mainstream film and the pleasure it provides can be challenged," so too are we arguing that engagement with the visual structures of video games must be apprehended before its sexual politics can be adequately challenged (843). Hence, this section offers a psychoanalytic analysis of the gender and sexual visual structures that evolved across the Atari 2600 and NES consoles.

Patriarchal desire has been embedded in the video game industry since its earliest days. One of the first video games, *Spacewar!* (1962), emerged from a cultural mindset that idealized "overdeveloped Hardy Boys [going] off through the universe to punch out the latest gang of galactic goons, blow up a few planets, kill all kinds of nasty life forms, and just have a heck of a good time" (Graetz 1981, 56). But these male-centered interests were not inserted into the visual structures of the video game industry until the advent of the Atari 2600 (1977), because prior to the Atari 2600, video games were played on either (1) multipurpose commercial or personal computers or (2) specialized machines developed specifically for a small number of games. As a result, the visual structures for the video game industry had not yet been standardized.

Patriarchal visuality with the launch of Atari 2600, although not the first to introduce interchangeable cartridges, dominated the video game industry during what is widely considered the golden age of gaming (Kent 2001). The reason this dominance matters is twofold: (1) the technical and discursive framework that constitute a platform constitute "real and substantive interventions into the contours of public discourse" (Gillespie 2010); and (2) the politics of these platforms is not just constrained to their technological manifestations (i.e., the console) but also create normative expectations on how other platforms ought to operate (Postman 1985/2005). In essence, the Atari 2600 made a real and substantive intervention into the contour of public discourse precisely because, by offering itself as a platform for other games to be played (as a general purpose gaming machine): (1) it had to define in advance the range of graphical representations it could accommodate; *and* (2) to the extent that game developers wanted to create games that could appear both on the Atari 2600 and elsewhere, those games had to be designed with an eye toward the Atari 2600. This is not to say that the Atari 2600 had a determinant effect on *everything* that could appear on its platform, but rather, that system architectural choices make certain games easier to make than others (Montfort and Bogost 2009). For the Atari 2600, this design choice was engineering its graphical interface with five movable objects in mind: two sprites, two missiles, and one ball. Though developers were able to use these objects creatively—with Warren Robinett designating the ball graphic as the player's avatar in *Adventure* (1979) so as to free up the sprites for other in-game non-playable characters—these design characteristics emphasized action over representation (see Fig. 6.1).

These design choices affect the sexual politics of the games that appeared on the Atari 2600 so that gender and sexuality emerged from character interaction as opposed to representation. For instance, Pitfall Harry of *Pitfall!* (1982) fame expresses his masculinity not necessarily through his physique or attire

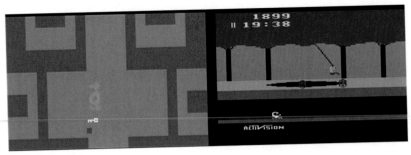

**Fig. 6.1** Screenshots from *Adventure* (*left*) and *Pitfall!* (*right*). Courtesy of the Wikimedia Foundation

but rather through his actions (see Fig. 6.1). The same is true for *Adventure*, with identification emerging from what the interaction represents (a hero on a quest to recover an enchanted chalice) as opposed to what the images represent (a red square moving from screen to screen). This is made more apparent when one looks at games that featured sexually explicit material during this time. If *Adventure* and *Pitfall!* conceived of the avatar as a mere vehicle for player desire—that coincidentally happened to be male-bodied—and hence could afford to neglect the representational qualities of player-avatar character, then one would think this would prove different for pornographic games like *Beat'em and Eat'em* (1982) and *Philly Flasher* (1982). Yet this is not the case. Modeled after the style of *Kaboom!* (1981), players control either two nude women (*Beat'em*) or two male prisoners with exposed penises (*Philly*) attempting to catch semen from a man ejaculating off of the top of a building (*Beat'em*) or a witch expressing breast milk off of the top of a building (*Philly*) (see Fig. 6.2). Although marketed for different audiences, the representational aspect of these two games is of such poor quality, that the head, arms, and legs of the player-controlled character models are interchangeable between the two games. Combined with the motion-blur that occurs as an artifact of the Atari 2600's Television Interface Adapter, this interchangeability matters because it suggests it was not character representation but rather the interaction between the ambiguously represented characters that produced their gender and sexual identities. And these two examples are not unique; nearly every game produced by Mystique and PlayAround (which purchased the rights for Mystique's "Swedish Erotica" line of games) featured "gender" swapped versions of the same game (Rolfe and Matei 2007). These examples illustrate that for the Atari 2600, gender and sexuality were mapped on the interaction and not yet the body.

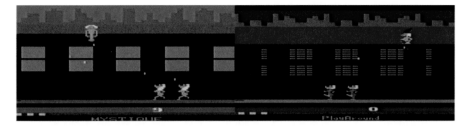

**Fig. 6.2** Screenshots from *Beat'em and Eat'em* (*left*) and *Philly Flasher* (*right*). Courtesy of James Rolfe and Mike Matei of *Angry Video Game Nerd*

The advent of the NES (1983) altered this textual and graphic narrative, resulting in two design decisions: one technical and the other sociocultural. On the technical side, the NES could process a significant number of unique, visually sophisticated sprites simultaneously, thus enabling a wider range of representations than previously allowed for by the Atari 2600. This technical capacity on its own, however, does not guarantee the emergence of an oppressive gender and sexual regime. Thomas Apperley and Jussi Parikka (2015) note, platforms "are not just technologies but techniques that sustain interactions as well as offer an epistemological framework" (5). As it pertains to the NES, the sociocultural techniques that emerged around the possibility of displaying numerous (up to 64) unique sprites at any given time—in contrast to the typical limit of two for the Atari 2600 (outside of creative programming [see Montfort and Bogost 2009])—were to map some sprites as active and others as passive.

While exceptions existed, these sprites were often segregated as active or passive according to gender designation, with "male" sprites active and "female" sprites passive. This effectually transformed passive, typically "female" sprites into trophies for the active, typically "male" sprites. For instance, the plot for the unlicensed *Menace Beach* (1990) centers upon rescuing your kidnapped girlfriend; after completing each level, the player is shown a short clip of her chained to a wall, with each subsequent clip featuring less clothing (which is decaying due to the passing of time) (see Fig. 6.3). James Rolfe and Mike Matei (2009) of Angry Video Game Nerd fame humorously comment, "Seriously, that's the only explanation. I think she would die of starvation before her clothes would rot, [...] but the funny thing is that it's a strangely effective way to get you to play the game, because just for curiosity's sake, it makes you wonder: how much of her clothes are going to come off?" But one need not look to unlicensed video games to understand the sexual politics of the passive female versus active male sprite designations. Indeed, sometimes the same character embodied both attributes, as with Samus Aran at the end

**Fig. 6.3** Screenshot from *Menace Beach* (*left*) showing Bunny's decaying clothes. Courtesy of James Rolfe and Mike Matei of *Angry Video Game Nerd*. Screenshot showing Samus Aran without her Power Suit (*right*). Courtesy of the Wikimedia Foundation

of *Metroid* (1986), whom "becomes" female by stripping off her Power Suit at the very same moment in which she transitions from an active player-controlled character to a passive sprite—in other words, from doing to being seen (see Fig. 6.3).

This trend in mapping gender and sexual desire on the body above and beyond that of the interaction (as with the Atari 2600) continued relatively unabated for the next decade, as the next two major consoles, the Sega Genesis and Super Nintendo Entertainment System (SNES), operated as extensions of the general representational logic established by the NES. That is, whereas the Atari 2600's visual structures were built around interaction—two character sprites, two missiles, and a ball—the NES' technical and sociocultural design philosophy established a new, dominant visual regime for the home video game ecology premised upon active male sprites and passive female sprites. This visual regime had the effect of extending the gender and sexual logics of the Atari 2600, with masculinity emerging as a manifestation of doing, but also added a new representational layer that defined femininity as a matter of being. This resulted in introducing into video games what Laura Mulvey (1975/2006) identifies in film as the *to-be-looked-at-ness* of women: "the presence of woman is an indispensable element of spectacle in normal narrative film, yet her visual presence tends to work against the development of a story line, to freeze the flow of action in moments of erotic contemplation" (837). The famous refrain of "Thank you Mario! But our Princess is in another Castle!," from the original Super Mario Bros (1983), is at once both a freeze in the flow of action and a deferral of the erotic contemplation of having obtained one's "trophy." This visual regime of freeze and erotic deferral would not change until the advent of the three-dimensional visual regime that the Sony PlayStation established in the mid-1990s.

# The Sexual Obsession with Polygons

As we have been arguing, visual regimes emerge as a product of *both* technical and sociocultural design philosophies. The relationship between the two is complicated in that technology is affected by sociocultural norms and designed toward specific ends, but these ends are not absolute and those with technical skill and sociocultural desire can circumvent these mechanisms (to an extent) to offer alternative cultural logics (Benkler 2006; de Certeau 1980/1988; Montfort and Bogost 2009). Nonetheless, it is precisely because technology operates as a form of politics by other means that we ought to understand how sociocultural design philosophies are embedded in technical infrastructure so that certain cultural logics are considered more legitimate than others (Starr 2004; Williams 1974/2005). This is no less true when it comes to the video game industry in that its visual regime is governed by the cultural logics of its AAA titles as opposed to its indie titles, precisely because systems are designed around their AAA offerings as opposed to their indie offerings. Since the advent of the Sony PlayStation (1994), this visual regime has been obsessed with polygons.

This transition from sprite- to polygon-based visual environments introduced a sort of crude cubism to the aesthetics of video games. Just as the cubists broke down the visual image into geometric components so as to create new understandings of the human body (MOMA 2006), so too did the polygon challenge graphic artists to conceive of new means for mapping gender and sexual desire. This transition, however, presented a unique challenge for video game artists; unlike the cubists, who freely chose to leverage geometry to challenge our understanding of the subject, video game artists had to work within a limited geometric domain to reproduce our understanding of the subject. In other words, the technical limits of 180,000 textured polygons per second, combined with the sociocultural limits of realism, meant that video game artists had to decide which physical attributes mattered most for the existing gender and sexual regime. To be clear, there was nothing technically inherent in making this choice. The video game industry could have slid back toward an abstract interaction-orientated sexual and gender regime, but the sociocultural logics that mobilized the transition to three-dimensional graphics were driven by a sense of realism: the belief that three-dimensional graphics could better show what was really there. In other words, the transition to three-dimensional graphics did not overturn the freeze and erotic deferral that was a part of the prior visual regime so much as it made the freeze the erotic itself: pausing to admire a game's graphical fidelity was no longer conceived as an interruption to narrative pleasure but rather an essential pleasure in its own

**Fig. 6.4** Screenshot from *Final Fantasy VII* featuring a long shot of Aerith Gainsborough's home in the sector 5 slums. The grandeur of this shot—combined with the relative insignificance of the game character (bottom left corner) due to the disparate character-to-screen ratio—encourages the player to pause and become consumed by the exceptional beauty of the game world. Such moments have become a part of modern gaming since the advent of the PlayStation, and cannot be thought of as "pauses" or "deferrals" but rather an essential feature of world building. Screenshot by first author

right (see Fig. 6.4). This fetishizing of graphical fidelity—as evidence of the game world's realism—would quickly be applied to the body of women: female characters bear the burden of realism.

By transforming the freeze in the flow of action into the erotic itself, the transition to three-dimensional graphics introduced a pleasure that had hitherto been absent: that of fetishistic scopophilia. Fetishistic scopophilia, Mulvey (1975/2006) argues, emerges as a particular response to the idea that the sexual desire for women might result in the symbolic castration of men. The typical response is either to evaluate a particular woman and accept or reject her presence as a castration threat (voyeurism) or disavow the possibility for this symbolic castration by delimiting her presence (fetishistic scopophilia) (Mulvey 1975/2006). This fetish is created by reducing the complexity of the feminine into a beautiful object: something that exists solely for the viewer and whose beauty obscures and displaces the threat she might otherwise represent (Mulvey 1975/2006). This fetish manifested in three-dimensional video games for two reasons: (1) to the extent that polygons were offered as an aesthetic capable of expressing realism, graphic artists had to make choices as to which attributes captured the essence of gender and sexuality; (2) these selected attributes had to overcompensate for an unbridgeable distance that existed between the sexual object and the sexual act desired. In other words, graphic artists overcome the second by overcompensating on the first. But again, to be clear, this argument is not a crude form of technological determinism; rather, the argument is that because sexual desire served as a sociocultural motive, graphic artists embraced the polygon as an aesthetic model capable of manifesting this sexual desire, and the consequence of this embracement was the production of a new type of sexual fetish: the polygon.

The particular configuration of this polygonal sexual fetish and the relationship between technology and sociocultural desire is best understood by briefly discussing the aesthetics of two divergent franchises: *Final Fantasy* (1987–present) and *Tomb Raider* (1996–present). Though different in terms of genre, with the first being a role-playing game and the second an action adventure, both franchises are powerful exemplars for considering the relationship between technology and sociocultural desire because each have made important contributions to our popular understanding of graphical realism: *Final Fantasy VII* (1997) is widely regarded for having offered gamers one of the first convincing, immersive three-dimensional worlds for players to explore; and the original *Tomb Raider* (1996) produced one of the most iconic three-dimensional representations of a woman. It is their evolving treatment of gender and sexual representation that is of interest, because each series' initial three-dimensional foray began and continues in a similar and often overlapping manner, even if there are important distinctions.

In spite of their differences, the introductory sequences for both *Final Fantasy VII* and *Tomb Raider* began in a similar fashion. Both start with magnificent long shots that establish the scope and scale of the game, and then, notably, the first focused full-, mid-, or close-up shot the player sees is that of a woman's face: Aerith Gainsborough for *Final Fantasy VII* and Lara Croft for *Tomb Raider* (see Fig. 6.5). Notably, as it pertains to our argument, in *Final Fantasy VII*, Aerith's face serves as the focal point for her gender and sexual identity; in contrast, for *Tomb Raider*, Lara's face deflects attention and indeed relies on a standard film convention of shot/reverse shot in order to create a sense of identification—not with Lara—but with the man reflected in her glasses. This latter point is further reinforced by the fact that the man reflected in her glasses is stating at this exact same moment: "What's a man gotta do to get that kind of attention from you." The differences become even more apparent once we see their full bodies, with Aerith's face continuing to serve as the fetish object in contrast to Lara Croft's iconic body, with her large rectangular breasts, pencil waist, and short shorts. What these differences illustrate is that, although the technical requirements of the PlayStation platform

**Fig. 6.5** Aerith Gainsborough from *Final Fantasy VII* (*left*) and Lara Croft from *Tomb Raider* (*right*). Regarding the image of Lara Croft, as we are introduced to her in this sequence, the man in her reflection states: "what's a *man* gotta do to get that kind of attention from you." Screenshots by first author

encouraged the production of a sexual fetish capable of capturing and over-compensating for the (im)possibility of gender and sexual presence, the socio-cultural politics of this sexual fetish had not yet crystalized, hence allowing for the existence of two divergent claims to graphical realism. This would change after the next major graphical intervention nearly a decade later, the advent of the PlayStation 3.

We have skipped console generations (e.g., NES to PlayStation, skipped the SNES) because transformations in visual regimes only seem to happen every other generation. This was roughly true of the transition from the NES to the SNES—in spite of important innovations such as the introduction of mode 7 graphics—and seems to be roughly true of the transition from the PlayStation to the PlayStation 2, with the latter operating as more of a visual extension of the prior regime. For instance, the evolutionary trend of Lara Croft's character model remained relatively consistent from the advent of her first appearance in *Tomb Raider* (1996) to *Tomb Raider: Underworld* (2008) (see Fig. 6.6). Though we do register a substantive change in Lara's character model in *Tomb Raider: The Angel of Darkness* (2003), which was the first *Tomb Raider* built for the PlayStation 2, the difference is primarily one of resolution and detail. This evolution of degree as opposed to kind holds true for Lara up until *Tomb Raider* (2013), which is notable for this was the first *Tomb Raider* developed exclusively for PlayStation 3 equivalent platforms. Likewise, though the *Final Fantasy* series was known for its artistic experimentation on the PlayStation 1, with *Final Fantasy VIII* (1999) attempting a hyper-realistic visual style and *Final Fantasy IX* (2000) offering a cute, nostalgic "chibi" aesthetic, the general trend holds true as well in that the transition from the NES/SNES (1987–1994) to the PS1/PS2 (1997–2006) resulted in a similar sexual fetishizing of the polygon—though for the *Final Fantasy* franchise, this fetishizing often centered on the face.[2]

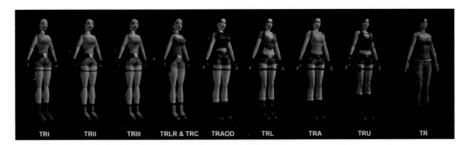

**Fig. 6.6** The Evolution of Lara Croft's character models from 1996 to 2013. *Tomb Raider Chronicles* (TRC [2000]) was the last *Tomb Raider* developed solely for PlayStation 1 equivalent platforms; and it is important to note that while *Tomb Raider: Anniversary* (TRA [2007]) and *Tomb Raider: Underworld* (TRU [2008]) were developed for PlayStation 3 equivalent platforms, their visual design was held back by the need to operate on "last generation" equivalent platforms. Courtesy of Ron from Cloud Gaming (2014)

With the advent of the PlayStation 3 (and Xbox 360), however, we witness not just a mere extension but a particular crystallization of the visual regime that the original PlayStation had established: from realism to photorealism. The difference between these two regimes is that while the first (realism) enabled a range of sexual and gender representations as evidenced by the cubist iconography present in *Final Fantasy* (1997–2006) and *Tomb Raider* (1996–2008), photorealism encourages a narrower range of gender and sexual legitimacy. The reason is because while artists for the PlayStation 1 and 2 had to grapple with limitations in the console graphic engines' ability to process polygons—and thus had to make choices about what constituted the essence of sexual and gender representation—this limitation has been relatively removed from the last and current generation models (or rather there is a diminishing return on graphical realism). And yet, though advances in contemporary graphic engines have enabled artists to bypass the threshold of graphical fidelity (from the realm of realism to photorealism), patriarchal desire is unable to bypass the fear of castration. Hence, the transition from realism to photorealism meant that prior sexual fetishes had to be replaced with new sexual fetishes.

The consequence of this new visual regime is that on the one hand, the polygon has been tamed, in that the absurd body measurements of the original *Tomb Raider* are likely a thing of the past (Crawley 2015); on the other hand, the new photorealistic normal seems to have agreed on a particular body type, facial structure, and even messy hairstyle (see Fig. 6.7). The problem with this second development is that, although this new photorealistic visual regime has moved away from the implausible body expectations of the prior regime, these new sexual and gender representations that are being

**Fig. 6.7** Lightning from *Final Fantasy XIII* (*left*) and Lara Croft from *Tomb Raider* (*right*). Screenshots by author

crystalized are no more plausible—nor desirable—for a significant portion of the population. This last point is of particular concern for as Nicole Martins et al. (2009) argue, photorealistic video game characters may result in more powerful normative effects than less realistic characters. Indeed, as Kimberly Bissell (2006) notes, these types of images are persuasive even among women with higher levels of visual literacy (see also Martins et al. 2009). This may be because, in spite of the artificiality of photorealistic video game characters by definition, their plausibility communicates a sense of attainability: we know this body type is not universal, but we know it could exist and that it should exist.

## Conclusion: A Crisis of Technical Imagination

This chapter has sought to illustrate how the technical and sociocultural design of home video game consoles makes some gender and sexual representations more legitimate than others. To make this claim, we have traced the video game evolution of gender and sexual representation from action (Atari 2600) to object (NES) to sexual fetish (PlayStation and beyond). In doing this, our interest has been to illustrate how concern regarding gender and sexual representations must take into account the sexual and gender politics of the platform itself: how it makes some representations not only easier but also more desirable than others. To this end, three themes made throughout this chapter are worth reiterating in the conclusion.

First, as important as it is, there are limiting returns on the gender and sexual politics of improving developer demographics *without also taking into account platform politics*. We want to be clear on this last point: developer demographics matter, but the positive contributions one would expect from this improvement in diversity are complicated by the prevailing technical and sociocultural expectations surrounding game development. As it currently stands, there have been significant strides made in the increased presence of female characters, and yet the majority of this growth has been for games that allow players to select either male or female protagonists. Though this notion of choice is better than the alternative of not having access to playable female characters, the male characters still typically operate as the default as game scripts are often designed around the presumed male protagonist (Heron et al. 2014). So even when there are some meaningful gameplay differences, it is not surprising that most players see the female character as the alternative and never explore this option (see Patterson 2015).

Second, exploring the gender and sexual politics of a given platform requires taking into account not only the technical specifications of the hardware but also the sociocultural norms surrounding it. For instance, there is no reason why gender had to be transformed into a hybrid action–object configuration (with active "male" sprites and "passive" female sprites) for the NES as there was plenty of processing power, sprites, and controllers to spare; however, a sociocultural choice was made to designate one as active and the other as passive, and it just so "happened" to coincide with the prevailing cultural norm of the (male) hero saving the (female) damsel in distress. The same trend continues today with Ubisoft, for instance, claiming that they lacked the resources to create "active" animations for their female characters (Corriea 2014; Farokhmanesh 2014), but apparently had enough resources to create plenty of animations for its (sometimes naked) non-playable female characters. From this perspective, the technical operates as an alibi for patriarchal politics.

And yet, to conclude, the technical matters, and hence should not be thought of as subservient to the sociocultural any more than the sociocultural should be thought of as subservient to the technical. They are two sides of the same coin (Williams 1974/2005). Indeed, as Paul Starr (2004) reminds us, "architectural choices are often politics by other means, under the cover of technical necessity" (6). So yes: sociocultural interests are at play when a platform is designed to accommodate two unique sprites, two missiles, and a ball; sociocultural interests are at play when a platform is designed to accommodate up to 64 unique sprites; and, sociocultural interests are at play when a platform is designed to accommodate an ever increasing number of polygons in the drive toward photorealism. And yet, these sociocultural design choices become codified in the technical specifications of the hardware so that it is seen as wasteful or unsatisfying to operate within the old visual regime; players buy new consoles precisely so as to move to the next visual regime—though not necessarily aware of what that means. In this regard, technical specifications encourage developers to live up to a particular sexual and gender visual regime, for to do otherwise would be seen as not taking advantage of the hardware. Hence, as this chapter has argued, if we wish to create an environment hospitable for a more progressive range of gender and sexual representations, hardware has to be a part of the conversation.

## Notes

1. The comparison between Myst (1993) and Doom (1993) warrants clarification. Some will argue that Doom had a larger install base because it was available as shareware. While true, perhaps a better comparison would be Myst against Doom II (1994), which sold roughly 2 million copies in contrast to Myst's 5.5 million. See: Giantbomb. "Doom." Giantbomb, http://www.giantbomb.com/doom/3025-156/; NPD Intelect. "Npd Intelect: Myst Franchise Continues Success with Myst III: Exile". https://www.npd.com/press/releases/press_010619.htm.

2. It is important to note that this sexual fetishizing does not extend to male characters for the simple fact that the design of male characters does not often rely upon reductive gender markers. Whereas a range of aesthetic types exist for male characters, female options are often limited. This disparity in options between male and female character designs is the video game equivalent of Simone De Beauvoir's (1949/2010) famous observation that "one is not born, but rather, becomes woman" (330). In essence, gender manifests in three-dimensional video games precisely through the presence of women: female characters bear the burden of gender.

## Bibliography

Apperley, Thomas, and Jussi Parikka. 2015. 'Platform Studies' Epistemic Threshold. *Games and Culture*. https://doi.org/10.1177/1555412015616509.

Baka, Jeremy. 1998. *Video and PC Games Are the Most Fun Home Entertainment Activity, Reveals New National IDSA Survey*. Interactive Digital Software Association.

de Beauvoir, Simone. 1949/2010. *The Second Sex*. Translated by C. Borde and Sheila Malovany-Chevallier. New York: Vintage.

Benkler, Yochai. 2006. *The Wealth of Networks: How Social Production Transforms Markets and Freedom*. New Haven, CT: Yale University Press.

Bissell, Kimberly L. 2006. Skinny Like You: Visual Literacy, Digital Manipulation and Young Women's Drive to Be Thin. *Simile: Studies in Media & Information Literacy Education* 6 (1): 1–14.

de Certeau, Michel. 1980/1988. *The Practice of Everyday Life*. Berkeley: University of California.

Cloud Gaming. 2014. Lara Croft, Archaeologist, Explorer, Sex Symbol. https://cloudvidgaming.wordpress.com/2014/02/01/lara-croft-archaeologist-explorer-sex-symbol/.

Corriea, Alexa Ray. 2014. *Far Cry 4 Devs Were 'Inches Away' from Women as Playable Characters*. Polygon. http://www.polygon.com/2014/6/11/5801330/far-cry-4-women-ubisoft.

Crary, Jonathan. 1992. *Techniques of the Observer: On Vision and Modernity in the Nineteenth Century*. Cambridge, MA: MIT Press.

Crawley, Dan. 2015. The Sexualization of Lara Croft Is a Thing of the Past, Says Rise of the Tomb Raider Writer. *Venturebeat*. http://venturebeat.com/2015/11/09/the-sexualization-of-lara-croft-is-a-thing-of-the-past-says-rise-of-the-tomb-raider-writer/.

Dietz, Tracy L. 1998. An Examination of Violence and Gender Role Portrayals in Video Games: Implications for Gender Socialization and Aggressive Behavior. *Sex Roles* 38 (5/6): 425–442.

Downs, Edward, and Stacy Smith. 2010. Keeping Abreast Hypersexuality: A Video Game Character Content Analysis. *Sex Roles* 62 (11/12): 721–733.

Edwards, Kate, Johanna Weststar, Wanda Meloni, Celia Pearce, and Marie-Josée Legault. 2014. *Developer Satisfaction Survey 2014*. International Game Developers Association.

Entertainment Software Association. 2015. 2015 Sales, Demographic and Usage Data: Essential Facts about the Computer and Video Game Industry. http://www.theesa.com/wp-content/uploads/2015/04/ESA-Essential-Facts-2015.pdf

Farokhmanesh, Megan. 2014. Ubisoft Abandoned Women Assassins in Co-Op Because of the Additional Work. *Polygon*. http://www.polygon.com/e3-2014/2014/6/10/5798592/assassins-creed-unity-female-assassins.

Gaudiosi, John. 2013. 'The Sims 4' and Other Upcoming Games to Watch. *CNN*. http://www.cnn.com/2013/09/02/tech/gaming-gadgets/games-watch-gamescom/.

Gillespie, Tarleton. 2010. The Politics of 'Platforms'. *New Media & Society* 12 (3): 347–364.

Graetz, J. Martin. 1981. The Origin of Spacewar. *Creative Computing* 18 http://www.wheels.org/spacewar/creative/SpacewarOrigin.html.

Heron, Michael J., Pauline Belford, and Ayse Goker. 2014. Sexism in the Circuitry: Female Participation in Male-Dominated Popular Computer Culture. *Computers & Society* 44 (4): 18–29.

Kent, Steven L. 2001. *The Ultimate History of Video Games: From Pong to Pokemon and Beyond—The Story Behind the Crazy that Touched Our Lives and Changed the World*. New York: Three Rivers Press.

Lalley, Jacqueline. 2005. Beyond the Valley of the Geeks: Notes on Gender and Gaming. *Bitch*. August 31, 42–47.

Launius, Christie, and Holly Hassel. 2015. *Threshold Concepts in Women and Gender Studies: Ways of Seeing, Thinking, and Knowing*. New York, NY: Routledge.

Lien, Tracey. 2013. No Girls Allowed. *Polygon*. http://www.polygon.com/features/2013/12/2/5143856/no-girls-allowed.

Makuch, Eddie. 2015. 175 Million Call of Duty Games Sold to Date, Still Fewer Than GTA. *Gamespot*. http://www.gamespot.com/articles/175-million-call-of-duty-games-sold-to-date-still-/1100-6426188/.

Martins, Nicole, Dmitri Williams, Kristen Harrison, and Rabindra A. Ratan. 2009. A Content Analysis of Female Body Image. *Sex Roles* 61 (11–12): 824–836.

Mejia, Robert. 2012. *Playing the Crisis: Video Games and the Mobilization of Anxiety and Desire*. Dissertation, Institute of Communications Research, University of Illinois at Urbana-Champaign.

MOMA. 2006. Modern Art and Ideas 3: 1907–1914. *The Museum of Modern Art*.

Montfort, Nick, and Ian Bogost. 2009. *Racing the Beam: The Atari Video Computer System*. Cambridge, MA: MIT.

Mulvey, Laura. 1975/2006. Visual Pleasure and Narrative Cinema. In *Media and Cultural Studies: KeyWorks*, ed. Meenakshi Gigi Durham and Douglas M. Kellner, 342–352. Malden, MA: Blackwell Publishing.

New York Film Academy. 2014. Gender Inequality in Film. *New York Film Academy Blog*. https://www.nyfa.edu/film-school-blog/gender-inequality-in-film/.

Oxford, Nadia. 2016. Final Fantasy XV's Lack of Core Female Characters Goes Against Tradition. *US Gamer*. http://www.usgamer.net/articles/final-fantasy-xvs-lack-of-core-female-characters-goes-against-tradition.

Patterson, Christopher B. 2015. Role-Playing the Multiculturalist Umpire: Loyalty and War in BioWare's Mass Effect Series. *Games and Culture* 10 (3): 207–228.

Postman, Neil. 1985/2005. *Amusing Ourselves to Death: Public Discourse in the Age of Show Business*. New York: Penguin Books.

Rolfe, James, and Mike Matei. 2007. AVGN: Atari Porn. *Cinemassacre*. http://cinemassacre.com/2007/08/22/atari-porn/.

———. 2009. Bible Games 2. *Cinemassacre*. https://www.youtube.com/watch?v=_dUVZozf-i0.

Sarkeesian, Anita. 2015. Gender Breakdown of Games Showcased at E3 2015. *Feminist Frequency*. http://feministfrequency.com/2015/06/22/gender-breakdown-of-games-showcased-at-e3-2015/.

Starr, Paul. 2004. *The Creation of the Media: Political Origins of Modern Communications*. New York: Basic Books.

Williams, Raymond. 1974/2005. *Television: Technology and Cultural Form*. New York: Routledge.

Williams, Dmitri. 2003. The Video Game Lightning Rod: Constructions of a New Media Technology, 1970–2000. *Information, Communication & Society* 6 (4): 523–550.

Williams, Dmitri, Nicole Martins, Mia Consalvo, and James D. Ivory. 2009. The Virtual Census: Representations of Gender, Race and Age in Video Games. *New Media & Society* 11 (5): 815–834.

Wiseman, Rosalind. 2015. Everything You Know About Boys and Video Games is Wrong. *Time*. http://time.com/3948744/video-games-kate-upton-game-of-war-comic-con/.

# Part II

## All Made Up: Gendering Assemblages

# 7

# Women's Experiences on the Path to a Career in Game Development

Johanna Weststar and Marie-Josée Legault

Considerable research has been conducted about career pipelines, specifically regarding the underrepresentation of women in male-dominated fields such as science, technology, engineering, and mathematics. The underrepresentation of women in the video game industry is well known, but has received limited attention. This chapter seeks to examine and critique women's experiences with the career pipeline of game development.

Initially it was posited that if more women were put into the developmental 'pipeline' for a career, more women would come out the other end (Schweitzer et al. 2011). This occurs through the normative general career trajectory process depicted in Fig. 7.1, where initial exposure leads to further reinforcement through formal schooling, which leads to successful early job experiences and a sustained career in a field. However, the lack of success in interventions geared to increase the number of women entering the pipe demonstrated a more complicated process and sparked research into what can be conceptualized as 'blocked pipes' and 'leaky pipes' (Bennett 2011; Lucena 2000; Vitores and Gil-Juárez 2016). A blocked pipeline conceptualizes the barriers to initial entry into the career path. It also captures the 'sticky floor' and 'glass ceiling' effects of vertical segregation within a workplace (Yap and Konrad 2009). The sticky floor effect suggests that women are more likely to stay at lower levels of an occupational ladder and/or pay grade (i.e., they are stuck) and the glass

J. Weststar (✉)
Western University, London, ON, Canada

M.-J. Legault
TÉLUQ-Université du Québec, Montréal, QC, Canada

© The Author(s) 2018
K. L. Gray et al. (eds.), *Feminism in Play*, Palgrave Games in Context,
https://doi.org/10.1007/978-3-319-90539-6_7

**Fig. 7.1**  General model of a traditional career pipeline

ceiling effect refers to the struggle women have faced in achieving the highest levels of an occupational hierarchy. A blocked pipeline also includes occupational/horizontal segregation within a larger field where jobs are male- or female-dominated and garner differential occupational and societal status (i.e., female nurse and male surgeon in the health care field). The leaky pipeline conceptualizes reasons, some related to the blockages, why a person would leave a career path once they have begun. This can include not pursuing higher education in the field, not beginning a career in the field after achieving a credential, or leaving the field.

The pipeline metaphor has received sustained critique, due to its influence on how we view the 'problem' of, and articulate 'solutions' to, women's under-representation (Vitores and Gil-Juárez 2016). For some, the pipeline metaphor is insufficient as it assumes a neutral pipe and disregards that the career pipelines into male-dominated fields are systemically gendered (Mariani 2008). This implies that the methods used to conceptualize and measure people flowing through the pipeline and into careers may be inherently narrow or biased (Metcalf 2010, 2014). Also, a focus on getting women into a specific pipe and making sure they do not leave may miss the point that these pipes and the resultant careers are inhospitable or problematic—to women, but also to others who do not fit the norms or expectations of that pipe (Hammonds and Subramaniam 2003; Subramaniam 2009).

This chapter seeks to explore these topics with respect to the video game industry. Specifically, it seeks to identify whether there is a dominant, presupposed pathway to a career in game development and then to look for women and women's experiences at each stage of that pipeline. It concludes such a dominant pathway does exist and this pathway both disadvantages women who attempt it and marginalizes other pathways. In most fields in the game industry, only a minority of women follow the assumed pathway, enroll in good proportions in appropriate training programs, obtain and remain with jobs in the industry. Along the way, they deal with obstacles that can delegitimize their choices and experiences and/or make the assumed pathway inhospitable.

This chapter relies on published literature as well as exclusive data from the 2014 and 2015 Developer Satisfaction Surveys (DSS) ($n$ = 2198 and 2928, respectively) conducted by the International Game Developers Association (IGDA) in partnership with the authors. The DSS is the most comprehensive international survey of people who study or work in any capacity in relation to the game industry. It therefore primarily captures people working in core development or support roles in game studios, but also includes students, academics, journalists, and those working in game-related event planning. It is the culmination of the IGDA's earlier survey work on demographics, diversity, and quality of life issues and also includes detailed questions about employment status and type, working conditions, compensation, education and training, developer perceptions of the industry and industry trends (for more detail about the survey, the questions it asks, and additional reports using its data see http://www.igda.org/?page=surveys and http://gameqol. org). It is particularly useful for research about diversity and gender in the game industry as it contains an extensive set of questions about demographics in the industry and in educational programs, organizational policies, and programs about diversity, as well as developers' experiences of discrimination and inequity and their perceptions of diversity in the industry. When survey data is presented it is from only those respondents who were working in non-managerial development roles, unless otherwise stated. Included in development roles are: programming, visual and audio art and production, game and level design, writing, user-experience and user-interface research and design, and localization.

## The Career Pipeline of Game Development

There is a dominant and accepted starting point for a career in game development: a love of games, passion for gaming, and a devoted history of playing games. This is made strikingly clear through studio job advertisements that literally state as specific requirements, 'must love games' or 'be an avid gamer' (Weststar 2015). The shared experience and language of games bonds people together and begins to develop a community of belonging even before official entry into the field (Weststar 2015).

From that point, the dominant practical path to the industry is through formal schooling in a relevant discipline. The 2014 and 2015 DSS asked developers their highest level of schooling and the type and relevance of their obtained degrees/diplomas. Student respondents were also asked about their educational programs. Data from the 2015 DSS show that 88% of developers have a college degree/diploma or higher. For many, this schooling is a generic degree in art, design, computer science or computer engineering where skills are then applied to game-making, but colleges and universities increasingly offer specific degree and diploma programs in game development, game/computer art, and game design.

This credentialization and the rise of specific game development designations is a recent shift. Similar to the history of IT and computer programming, when the game industry was emerging in the 1970s, entry into the field was more porous; people came from diverse educational and professional backgrounds because they were drawn to this new exciting medium. As an immature field, many were also self-taught (Adams and Demaiter 2008; Ensmenger 2001, 2003). Shades of this ethos remain in the industry as evidenced by the advice given to people looking to enter the field; veterans indicate that the most important requirement is to be able to show, in any way, the ability to make great games and they advise hopefuls to fully devote themselves to this task (Weststar 2015). As well, the rise of independent publishing due to the affordances of digital distribution, the emergence of the mobile game market, the ubiquity of game-making tools, and growth of the maker and hobbyist movements may maintain some non-formalized routes for entry. However, for most new entrants, the pathway is through formal schooling. This paints the picture of a rather typical career pipeline for game developers and encourages us to look for and then examine the experiences of girls and women at each stage: exposure/access, education and training, and job experiences.

## Exposure and Access

Research over the past decade has consistently argued against a gendered view of gameplay and game preferences (Carr 2005; Jenson and de Castell 2008; Jenson et al. 2011) and emphasized that it is not a dislike or disaffinity for video games that keeps girls and women from playing. Specifically, the work of Jenson and colleagues shows that distinctions in video game interest among girls and boys that have been previously attributed to gendered preferences should be more accurately attributed to differential skill levels. When girls were given the opportunity to develop expertise and mastery in a girls-only video game club, they behaved in ways previously ascribed to males. In subsequent co-ed environments, observed differences in gameplay and corresponding social interactions were based on skill differentials and not gender.

Understanding the gameplay of girls and women from this socially deterministic standpoint acknowledges that the simple act of playing is 'embedded in existing social dynamics and hierarchies' and that mixed gender households are not environments of equal access to gameplay (Schott and Horrell 2000, 42). This means that girls and women are not given the same opportunities to develop the requisite level of interest and mastery to sustain investment in the video game medium. As Schott and Horrell (2000) discuss, females usually have secondary access to game devices and they must continually negotiate that access because they often engage in play in the presence or under the sanction of males. In most instances, this stunts the ability of female players to acquire mastery in a game. In this context, Schott and Horrell (2000) suggest that games with easily learned mechanics, reduced risk of dying or losing, and free exploration to acquire goods or powers might be appealing not because of a gendered preference, but because of a learned response to acquiring and maintaining control. These games do not require a large time commitment to achieve desired mastery and the game experience is not cut short by dying or failing in the objective. The player can thus maintain control of the game rather than lose the controller to a more 'expert' (male) player who will disenfranchise the female player in 'showing them how to do it' or doing the hard parts for them.

These barriers to access have implications for the accepted career pipeline to game development because they reduce the opportunity for girls and women to develop the investment and expertise of an avid gamer that is publicly and normatively required by the industry. Winn and Heeter (2009) reported that a gaming orientation develops at an early age; early game play predicted later game play, and non-gamers were less likely than gamers to anticipate an increase in their gaming even if 'better' games were available. Due to the immense investment of time that gamers have made to hone their skills, simply knowing where to place one's hands on the keyboard for a PC game or casual familiarity with complex modern controllers immediately signals belonging in the game community (Schmalz 2016). This belonging is denied or made harder for those without the required investment and experience.

Issues of access and expertise also exist in terms of the games played. As Consalvo and Paul (2013) articulated, the game community cultivates a system of insiders and outsiders by privileging 'real' games and positioning those who play them as 'real gamers.' Consalvo and Paul (2013) identified the importance of developer pedigree, particular game mechanics, the depth of interactive meaning, and the price/pay structure of games as tacit signals of which games matter and which do not. This is largely an approach to occupational closure that is common to many professional and professionalizing occupations as it effectively denigrates new entrants and forces them to comply with the standard in which natives are heavily invested (Witz 1990). However, this protectionist attitude and the reification of real games and gamers further disenfranchise women who have invested time in the wrong games. It also may prevent girls and women from leveraging innovations in technology to gain access to the game space rather than evening the playing field if these innovations are devalued (Jenson and de Castell 2008). Research suggests that women have taken up the social and casual games populating Facebook and mobile devices and that casual games and innovation in game controllers such as the Wii may have removed some barriers to entry (ESA 2016; Fron et al. 2007; Juul 2009). Industry statistics suggest that women represent 45–49% of gamers and are the fastest growing consumer group (ESA 2013; ESAC 2013). However, statistics about the rise of casual games and gamers may overstate as they often include traditional games such as cards that have migrated to computer interfaces (Jenson and de Castell 2005). These are not considered real video games. As well, figures about the number of people who play games belie the existence of a stratum of gamers that is based on factors like the type of games purchased and the time devoted to play; again, the manufactured sense of 'real' games and gamers (Fron et al. 2007).

This suggests that even if gamer/non-gamer distinctions decrease, a gendered dichotomy or hierarchy of hard-core/casual may remain (Harvey 2011). Hard-core gamers may play casual games like everyone else (Bouça 2012), but casual gamers do not engage in the hard-core universe from which most future game makers are drawn. The gravitation of women to particular forms of play can ghettoize and delegitimize that experience and expertise in the face of dominant, masculine interpretations of technical competence and the industry maintained hegemony of 'real' games. It has been noted that much of the play by women is not considered true gaming by themselves or others (Fron et al. 2007; Harvey 2011; Jenson and de Castell 2005). Therefore, even girls and women who gain some access to games and achieve some mastery of gameplay may not see themselves or be seen as future game makers under the dominant screening and signaling norms and mechanisms. They are a square that does not fit in the round pipe and therefore have the potential to be disregarded.

# Education and Training

Accepting the argument above—that collectively girls and women have less investment in the game industry due to limited opportunities to gain valued expertise—leads to the assumption that fewer girls and women pursue additional training in this field. The DSS data we use for this chapter included a number of respondents who were students studying to enter the game industry or studying games. They were asked questions about their domain of study as well as the gender representation of their classes. In the DSS 2015, 20% of the survey respondents identified as students. Their data show a lack of women in formal game-related education as only 25% of the student respondents to the survey identified as female compared to 73% as male. Self-selection response bias is a concern with this data; however, students were also asked what percentage of their class was women and this provides supportive evidence. The majority responded that women made up less than half of the class; 22% indicated that their class was less than 10% women (Fig. 7.2).

The DSS 2015 data also show a gendered bifurcation in the type of education game developers have obtained. Men were found to outnumber women in obtained computer science and software engineering degrees by more than 2:1 while the opposite was true for degrees in animation, art, art and design, and graphic design. The distribution was more balanced for degrees specifically in game design and game development. This gendered segregation by degree type is also present among the student respondents to the DSS 2015 survey. Students were asked, 'What kind of game industry job are you most interested in?' 'Programmer/software engineer' was selected by 32% of males and 20% of females, while 'visual art' was selected by 9% of males and 20%

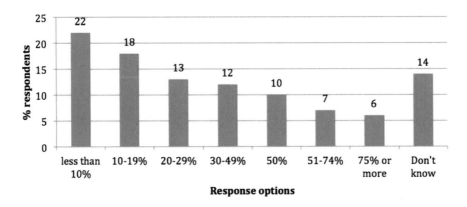

**Fig. 7.2**   Percentage of class that is women. Source: IGDA DSS 2015

of females. 'Writer' also displayed a gender split; it was selected by 6% of males and 14% of females. The distributions for key roles such as 'producer/project manager' and 'game designer' were roughly similar.

Despite these differences in degree and occupation, among the student respondents, there was no gendered difference regarding a love for the industry and the importance of early experiences. Males and females responded similarly to questions about being passionate about games and wanting to share this by being in the industry, about playing games as a hobby and turning that into a career, and about making games as a hobby and turning that into a career. Both groups were also similarly confident about their ability to get a job in the industry after graduation. That said, females were significantly less likely than males to agree that there was 'equal treatment and opportunity for all in game-related educational programs'; 40% of females versus 17% of males said there was not equal treatment for all.

## Sustained Career in the Field

Not surprisingly under a dominant pipeline model, the representation gap and occupational segregation between males and females persist from formal schooling to game developer jobs. Among the respondents to the DSS 2015 survey who work in non-managerial core development jobs, 19% identified as female while 78% identified as male. Males were heavily represented in programming roles and females were more likely to be found in artist, writer, user experience/user interface (UX/UI), and localization roles (Fig. 7.3). When we examine the 2015 DSS data for managerial roles in the industry, females are slightly more represented across the board at 22%. Specifically, they are underrepresented in senior management roles compared to males (47% vs. 61%), but overrepresented in producer/project manager roles (40% vs. 21%). There was equal gender representation in the managerial sub-sample for middle managers and team leads.

Given the critiques about narrow career definitions often leveled at pipeline research (Metcalf 2014), it is informative to look for women in game industry roles off the dominant path of commercialized development. When we include the whole sample of the DSS 2015, the representation of females rises to 23%. This is due to a slightly higher tendency for females to work in game-related journalism, academia, and event planning and a much higher tendency for women to work in roles that support game development. Across all the occupations classified as support roles in the DSS 2015, there was an equal gender split; however, there was still strong occupational segregation

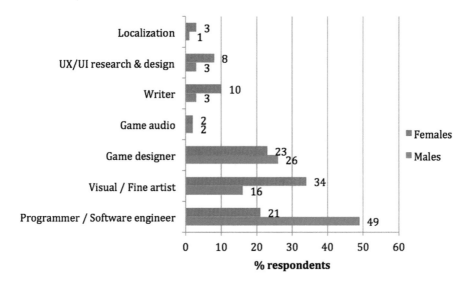

**Fig. 7.3** Occupational segregation of non-managerial core developer roles by gender. Source: IGDA DSS 2015

within those roles. Females were much more likely to work in community management and administration (e.g., human resources, accounting, legal, and office manager), while males were more likely to work as consultants and in technical and customer support. Public relations and marketing had more equal balance.

Despite the differences in representation and occupational sub-group, male and female game developers held similar sentiments toward their jobs. Most felt that their job making games was their career and reported that it was a large part of their life (53% males, 57% females). Some reported that making games was their life and a smaller number acknowledged that it was just one part of their life, but the pattern of response showed no gender difference. However, data from the 2014 DSS suggest some gender differences in the intention to stay in the industry. When asked how long they planned to remain in the industry, the dominant response for both males and females was to stay indefinitely (80% and 71%, respectively), but almost twice as many females as males selected options of six years or less. The data also suggest that the path to a game development career may not be as direct for some women. In both the 2014 and 2015 DSS data, females were more likely than males to report that their career path into the game industry was unintentional, though the majority response for both groups was an intentional career path. This data should be considered carefully, however, due to the conflation of gender and occupational role. Respondents who identified as programmers (mostly men) were much more likely to report an intentional career path into games than an unintentional path. Conversely, roles comprised of more women (UX/UI research and design, writing, localization) were associated with an unintentional career path into games. Visual artists and game designers were as likely to report an intentional career path as unintentional.

In addition to differences in representation and occupational role, women experience a different lived experience as game developers. The past two years have seen intense interest in the topics of sexism, discrimination, and harassment in video games, video game workplaces, and the broader gamer community. The challenges women face as developers came to the fore through the Twitter hashtags #1reasonwhy and #1reasontobe that went viral in 2013. #1reasonwhy was flooded with personal accounts of struggle in answer to the question, 'Why are there not more women game developers?' And #1reasontobe arose in solidarity, but also in challenge, to document reasons why women *should* be in the industry and to share stories of success and perseverance.

The DSS surveys contained numerous questions about diversity and equity and the data echo many of the challenges surfaced in the Twitter movement and expressed publicly by female game developers at industry conferences and in the press. In both the 2014 and 2015 data, a high percentage of respondents across genders reported that sexism in games, among gamers, and in the workforce contributed negatively to the industry (Weststar and Andrei-Gedja 2015, 2016) and 49% of the DSS 2015 respondents felt that there was not equal treatment and opportunity for all in the industry (12% were not sure). Similar to this question as posed to students, when analyzed by gender, these sentiments were reported more by females than males in all cases. For instance, compared to males, twice as many females reported experiencing inequity in recruitment and hiring processes, four times as many females reported experiencing inequity in the promotion process, five times as many females reported inequity on monetary grounds, six times as many females reported microaggressions in the workplace (verbal, behavioral, and environmental indignities), and seven times as many females reported experiencing inequity in both discipline and social/interpersonal interactions. The absolute incidence of these inequities for all genders ranged from 8 to 16% of respondents, but the relative incidence for women is striking.

As well, the work environment of the video game industry poses challenges that are not unique to women, but may present greater barriers. The long hours culture has been well documented (Peticca-Harris et al. 2015; Legault and Weststar 2015; Weststar and Legault 2012, 2015), and it has been concluded that long hours and/or crunch time and the project-based organization of work are a significant challenge to women in the game industry (Chasserio and Legault 2010; Consalvo 2008; Legault and Chasserio 2012; Legault and Ouellet 2012). For these reasons, it has been argued that game work tends to favor young and unattached males who better conform to the dominant professional identity of long hours and the required national and international mobility (Deuze et al. 2007). It is notable that the mean industry age is 32 and the number of game developers answering the DSS surveys who have children is very low (Weststar et al. 2017). Additional studies have also found a particular lack of women with children among game developers (Deuze et al. 2007; Consalvo 2008; Prescott and Bogg 2010) as opposed to men (Prescott and Bogg 2011a, b). Interruption in career path is a long-enduring burden in women's professional lives (Simpson 1998). Women also tend to experience more work-family conflict than men, and this can lead to reduced opportunities for promotion and advancement as women may be more likely to refuse overtime, refuse extra work, or turn down high-profile, yet high demand projects (Chasserio and Legault 2010; Weststar 2011). Recalling the 'real' games argument of Consalvo and Paul (2013), game studios or lower-profile projects within studios that do tend to support flexible working time policies or resist crunch time are not often those that are esteemed as prestigious in terms of the games that they make (i.e., casual games, children's games, educational games, and serious games) (Legault and Ouellet 2012). Therefore, they do not build the kind of reputation that can leverage a developer's career.

This said, the industry may slowly be changing. Regarding working time, Legault and Weststar (2015) used the IGDA data as well as interviews with developers to review trends over a ten-year period. They found that the duration, frequency, and intensity of crunch time are decreasing. However, crunch remained a challenge for a significant population of game developers. For instance, in the 2015 DSS, respondents reported that crunch time or long hours had negatively affected their family relationships (50%), their emotional health (58%), and their physical health (55%). There were no significant differences found across gender with respect to these experiences. Importantly, this indicates that the structural features of the industry such as long hours may increasingly be a barrier to both men and women.

## Discussion

There is a dominant pathway into a career in game development that begins with exposure and investment in the medium through play. According to data from the IGDA surveys over the past ten years and from anecdotal experience with the industry, a majority of people who work in video games counted playing video games as a major hobby (IGDA 2004; Legault and Weststar 2012; Weststar and Legault 2015) and immersion in the medium is part of the occupational community of game developers (Weststar 2015). As these are conditions of entry to the dominant pathway toward a career in game development, it is therefore a problem if girls and women are underrepresented among gamers, or if they are segregated into playing certain games that are themselves stereotyped. It is also a problem if girls and women play games, but face negative and marginalizing experiences both within the game and from the gaming community.

Following the dominant pipeline through formal schooling shows that some women are pursuing game development as a career choice and they are no less interested or passionate than their male peers. However, these women remain greatly outnumbered and may exist in occupational ghettos within academic programs. As expected this pattern translates into the industry at large where women remain underrepresented, occupationally segregated, and in many instances marginalized through systemic and overt sexism.

There are some alternative pathways for women into the game industry, though they are not without challenges. First, the important roles of game designer and producer/project manager seem to be of equal interest to male and female students and show more balanced gender distribution in the workforce. Particularly coupled with an increase in specialized game design/development programs, these jobs could be alternative pathways of a sort, where women can gain access to and influence the field, but sidestep the need to break into programming or software engineering as a domain. However, these roles present opportunities for change only insofar as they are imbued with meaningful power and influence that is leveraged to enact change rather than to reproduce the gendered status quo of so-called womens' skills, game intellectual property, and/or working conditions (Powell and Sang 2015). Work that is done primarily by women, even if once dominated by men, faces a legacy of devaluation (Levanon et al. 2009; Miller 2016). Recent attacks against female game designers under the Gamergate mantle could be considered an example of outright attempts at this delegitimization.

There is little known research on the internal hierarchy and power dynamic among the sub-disciplines that contribute to the making of a game; therefore, some occupational roles will be more influential than others. We would suggest that the male-dominated field of programming is dominant due to the hegemony of hard science and technical skill, the centrality of computer coding to the game-making process, and the sheer relative number of programmers. Certainly, the DSS survey data indicates that programmers are among the highest paid occupational groups, while artists and disciplines with higher numbers of women receive lower compensation; within occupations women also make less than their male counterparts (see also Gamasutra 2014). The roles of writer or UX or localization specialist allow for alternative educational pathways and roles in journalism and event planning provide game-related careers, but these jobs do not sit at the core of game development in terms of compensation or influence on the medium.

Trends toward improved hours of work will benefit all developers and in particular ease additional burdens that may be faced by women. As well, the rise of independent studios, self-employment, and the increased democratization of game development through the new technological affordances of self-publishing, digital distribution systems, sophisticated open-source development tools, and mobile platforms may also present opportunities for both women and men to create new pipelines toward revisioned career endpoints that are more representative and sustainable. In the DSS 2014, 48% of the respondents said they worked as independent developers and in 2015 39% identified as indies. As well, the percentage of respondents who identified as self-employed was 15% in 2014 and 19% in 2015. Self-employed respondents reported choosing that path to gain greater intellectual control over their work, but the most common reason was that self-employment gives more control over their working conditions. In the 2015 DSS, males and females were equally likely to report working in an indie environment and the representation of women in independent studios was higher than the general developer sample which included all studio types (23% vs. 19%). Females were as likely to be self-employed as males (14% vs. 18%).

It would be an overstatement to claim that indie development presents a nirvana of ideal game development practices or that it is a safe haven for female developers in particular. This form of employment comes with its own challenges in terms of work-life balance, the downloading of employment risks and uncertainties onto the individual and the lack of access to many legal protections or social security programs. As well, the market is increasingly crowded with games and indies must work very hard to achieve and sustain success. However, there are exemplars. For instance, Dames Making Games is a feminist non-profit organization in Toronto, Canada, dedicated to 'supporting dames interested in making, playing and changing games' (https://dmg. to/about). Part of their mission statement reads, 'We believe that creating *space and time* to make and talk about games in an explicitly feminist context elevates the craft, amplifies alternative and diverse narratives, and supports the socio-cultural changes that are necessary to make game design accessible to all' (https://dmg.to/about; emphasis theirs). Here, women may claim a segment of the industry by creating it themselves.

# Conclusion

This chapter argued that, like many other industries, the dominant pipeline to a career in game development is one of early experience → additional training → first job → sustained career (see Fig. 7.1) and it is not working for women. Though men and women are equally predisposed to love playing and making games, girls and women face more barriers than boys and men in gaining access to and legitimacy in early gaming experiences and they are underrepresented, occupationally segregated, and perceive negative differential treatment in game-related degree and diploma programs. These patterns persist into employment where women remain in the minority, may occupy roles that are lower in the occupational hierarchy or more tangential to what is considered the 'core' work of developing games, may be confined to low-scaled or less prestigious projects, and may be disadvantaged under a project-management regime that emphasizes extreme commitment, long hours, and high employment insecurity. These findings are not surprising as similar stories have been told about somewhat cognate fields in the domains of science, technology, engineering, and mathematics as well as entertainment fields such as film and television (Chasserio and Legault 2010; Cicmil et al. 2009; Henderson and Stackman 2010; Lindgren and Packendorff 2006; Turner et al. 2009; Watts 2009). Research has documented how project-management theory and training is also deeply gendered. Masculine assumptions about time allocation, professionalism, and masculine cognitive styles are embedded into the Project Management Body of Knowledge (PMBoK) (Buckle and Thomas 2003; Thomas and Buckle-Henning 2007).

The evidence presented above demonstrates that women do experience blocks and leakages when trying to navigate the dominant career pathway into game development. They are sorely underrepresented as a whole and generally experience the glass ceiling and sticky floor effects of vertical segregation, as well as occupational segregation in core domains and genres. However, there is also some evidence that women are finding alternative pathways/pipelines to work in the industry. They are better represented in industry roles outside of core development occupations, some enter the industry through non-game-related educational programs, and some are creating new spaces for the making and distribution of video games that challenge industry norms. As well, the challenges faced by women in the game industry are receiving growing attention as women game developers speak out at industry events, through the attention of the women developers' associations and grassroots movements and through social media movements. As such, the inhospitality of the traditional pipes is increasingly revealed and is being rejected by both men and women. As Subramaniam (2009, 964) succinctly put it, 'Imagining the regimented travels in pipes that give the travelers no agency in their journey, we might start rooting for the leaks and for those who escape the drudgery of pipe travel.'

It remains to be seen whether imagined new pathways will lead to a sustained and influential presence for women and whether they will also promote a reimagining of the game industry as a whole, or whether they will be devalued like the old 'mommy track' (Lewin 1989). Thus, it remains important to analyze the experiences of girls and women both along the dominant pipeline and in areas that may provide refreshing alternatives for all game workers. As knowledge work is more important, so are project-based organizations. We should also pursue the study of project-based organizations as a whole, as they pose many common challenges to their workforce and often share a common gendered workplace culture.

**Acknowledgments** This work was supported by the Social Sciences and Humanities Research Council of Canada under Grant 435-2013-0187.

# Bibliography

Adams, Tracey L., and Erin I. Demaiter. 2008. Skill, Education and Credentials in the New Economy: The Case of Information Technology Workers. *Work, Employment and Society* 22 (2): 351–362.

Bennett, Cinnamon. 2011. Beyond the Leaky Pipeline: Consolidating Understanding and Incorporating New Research: About Women's Science Careers in the UK. *Brussels Economic Review* 54 (2–3): 149–176.

Blickenstaff, Jacob Clark. 2003. Women and Science Careers: Leaky Pipeline or Gender Filter? *Gender and Education* 17 (4): 369–386.

Bouça, Maura. 2012. Angry Birds, Uncommitted Players. In *Proceedings of DiGRA Nordic 2012 Conference: Local and Global – Games in Culture and Society*, vol. 10.

Buckle, Pamela, and Janice Thomas. 2003. Deconstructing Project Management: A Gender Analysis of Project Management Guidelines. *International Journal of Project Management* 21 (6): 433–441.

Carr, Diane. 2005. Contexts, Gaming Pleasures, and Gendered Preferences. *Simulation & Gaming* 36 (4): 464–482.

Chasserio, Stéphanie, and Marie-Josée Legault. 2010. Discretionary Power of Project Managers in Knowledge-Intensive Firms and Gender Issues. *Canadian Journal of Administrative Sciences* 27 (3): 236–248.

Cicmil, Svetlana, Damian Hodgson, Monica Lindgren, and Johann Packendorff. 2009. Project Management Behind the Façade. *Ephemera: Theory and Politics in Organization* 9 (2): 78–92.

Consalvo, Mia. 2008. Crunched by Passion: Women Game Developers and Workplace Challenges. In *Beyond Barbie and Mortal Kombat: New Perspectives on Gender and Gaming*, ed. Y.B. Kafai, C. Heeter, J. Denner, and J.Y. Sun, 177–192. Cambridge, MA: MIT Press.

Consalvo, Mia, and Christopher A. Paul. 2013. Welcome to the Discourse of the Real: Constituting the Boundaries of Games and Players. In *Proceedings of the 8th International Conference on the Foundations of Digital Games (FDG 2013)*, 55–62.

Deuze, Mark, Chase Bowen Martin, and Christian Allen. 2007. The Professional Identity of Gameworkers. *Convergence* 13 (4): 335–353.

Ensmenger, Nathan L. 2001. The 'Question of Professionalism' in the Computer Fields. *IEEE Annals of the History of Computing* 23 (4): 56–74.

———. 2003. Letting the "Computer Boys" Take Over: Technology and the Politics of Organizational Transformation. *International Review of Social History* 48 (S11): 153–180.

Entertainment Software Association (ESA). 2013. *Essential Facts about the Computer and Video Game Industry*. http://www.theesa.com/facts/pdfs/esa_ef_2013.pdf.

———. 2016. *Essential Facts about the computer and Video Game Industry: 2016 Sales, Demographic and Usage Data*. http://essentialfacts.theesa.com/Essential-Facts-2016.pdf.

Entertainment Software Association of Canada (ESAC). 2013. *Essential Facts About the Canadian Computer and Video Game Industry*. Report, Canada.

Fron, Janine, Tracy Fullerton, Jacquelyn Ford Morie, and Celia Pearce. 2007. The Hegemony of Play. In *DiGRA Conference. Situated Play*, Tokyo, September 24–27.

Gamasutra. 2014. Gamasutra Salary Survey. http://www.gamesetwatch.com/2014/09/05/GAMA14_ACG_SalarySurvey_F.pdf.

Hammonds, Evelynn, and Banu Subramaniam. 2003. A Conversation on Feminist Science Studies. *Signs: Journal of Women in Culture and Society* 28 (3): 923–944.

Harvey, Alison. 2011. Constituting the Player: Feminist Technoscience, Gender, and Digitalplay. *International Journal of Gender, Science and Technology* 3 (1).

Henderson, Linda S., and Richard W. Stackman. 2010. An Exploratory Study of Gender in Project Management: Interrelationships with Role, Location, Technology, and Project Cost. *Project Management Journal* 41 (5): 37–55.

International Game Developers Association (IGDA). 2004. *Quality of Life in the Game Industry. Challenges and Best Practices*. White Paper. http://www.igda.org.

Jenson, Jennifer, and Suzanne de Castell. 2005. Her Own Boss: Gender and the Pursuit of Incompetent Play. In *Proceedings of DiGRA 2005 Conference: Changing Views—Worlds in Play*. Vancouver, Canada.

———. 2008. Theorizing Gender and Digital Gameplay: Oversights, Accidents and Surprises. *Eludamos. Journal for Computer Game Culture* 2 (1): 15–25.

Jenson, Jennifer, Stephanie Fisher, and Suzanne de Castell. 2011. Disrupting the Gender Order: Leveling up and Claiming Space in an After-School Video Game Club. *International Journal of Gender, Science and Technology* 3 (1).

Juul, Jesper. 2009. *A Casual Revolution: Reinventing Video Games and Their Players.* Cambridge, MA: MIT Press.

Legault, Marie-Josée, and Stéphanie Chasserio. 2012. Professionalization, Risk Transfer, and the Effect on Gender Gap in Project Management. *International Journal of Project Management* 30 (6): 697–707.

Legault, Marie-Josée, and Kathleen Ouellet. 2012. So Into It They Forget What Time It Is? Video Game Designers and Unpaid Overtime. In *Managing Dynamic Technology-Oriented Business: High-Tech Organizations and Workplaces*, ed. D. Jemielniak and A. Marks, 82–102. Hershey: IGI Global.

Legault, Marie-Josée, and Weststar, Johanna. 2012. More than the Numbers: Independent Analysis of the IGDA 2009 Quality of Life Survey. http://gameqol.org.

———. 2015. *Working Time among Video Game Developers, 2004–14.* Accessed February 9, 2016. http://www.gameqol.org/igda-qol-survey/.

Levanon, Asaf, Paula England, and Paul Allison. 2009. Occupational Feminization and Pay: Assessing Causal Dynamics Using 1950–2000 US Census Data. *Social Forces* 88 (2): 865–891.

Lewin, Tamar. 1989. Mommy Career Track Sets Off a Furor. *The New York Times*, March 8. Accessed August 5, 2016. http://www.nytimes.com/1989/03/08/us/mommy-career-track-sets-off-a-furor.html.

Lindgren, Monica, and Johann Packendorff. 2006. What's New in New Forms of Organizing? On the Construction of Gender in Project-Based Work. *Journal of Management Studies* 43 (4): 841–866.

Lucena, Juan C. 2000. Making Women and Minorities in Science and Engineering for National Purposes in the United States. *Journal of Women and Minorities in Science and Engineering* 6 (1): 10.

Mariani, Mack D. 2008. A Gendered Pipeline? The Advancement of State Legislators to Congress in Five States. *Politics & Gender* 4 (2): 285–308.

Metcalf, Heather. 2010. Stuck in the Pipeline: A Critical Review of STEM Workforce Literature. *InterActions: UCLA Journal of Education and Information Studies* 6.

Metcalf, Heather E. 2014. Disrupting the Pipeline: Critical Analyses of Student Pathways through Postsecondary STEM Education. *New Directions for Institutional Research* (158): 77–93.

Miller, Claire Cain. 2016. As Women Take Over a Male-Dominated Field, the Pay Drops. *New York Times.* Accessed August 5, 2016. http://www.nytimes.com/2016/03/20/upshot/as-women-take-over-a-male-dominated-field-the-pay-drops.html?_r=1.

Peticca-Harris, Amanda, Johanna Weststar, and Steve McKenna. 2015. The Perils of Project-Based Work: Attempting Resistance to Extreme Work Practices in Video Game Development. *Organization* 22 (4): 570–587.

Powell, Abigail, and Katherine J.C. Sang. 2015. Everyday Experiences of Sexism in Male-Dominated Professions: A Bourdieusian Perspective. *Sociology* 49 (5): 919–936.

Prescott, Julie, and Jan Bogg. 2010. The Computer Games Industry: Women's Experiences of Work Role. In *Women in Engineering, Science and Technology: Education and Career Challenges: Education and Career Challenges*, ed. J. Prescott and J. Bogg, 138–158. IGI Global.

———. 2011a. Career Attitudes of Men and Women Working in the Computer Games Industry. *Eludamos. Journal for Computer Game Culture* 5 (1): 7–28.

———. 2011b. Segregation in a Male-Dominated Industry: Women Working in the Computer Games Industry. *International Journal of Gender, Science and Technology* 3 (1).

Schmalz, Michael. 2016. *Limitation to Innovation in the North American Console Video Game Industry 2001–2013: A Critical Analysis*. PhD Dissertation. Scholarship@Western Electronic Thesis and Dissertation Repository. http://ir.lib.uwo.ca/etd/3393.

Schott, Gareth R., and Kirsty R. Horrell. 2000. Girl Gamers and Their Relationship with the Gaming Culture. *Convergence* 6 (4): 36–53.

Schweitzer, Linda, Eddy Ng, Sean Lyons, and Lisa Kuron. 2011. Exploring the Career Pipeline: Gender Differences in Pre-career Expectations. *Industrial Relations* 66 (3): 422–444.

Simpson, Ruth. 1998. Presenteeism, Power and Organizational Change: Long Hours as a Career Barrier and the Impact on the Working Lives of Women Managers. *British Journal of Management* 9 (1): 37–50.

Subramaniam, Banu. 2009. Moored Metamorphoses: A Retrospective Essay on Feminist Science Studies. *Signs* 34 (4): 951–980.

Thomas, Janice Lynne, and Pamela Buckle-Henning. 2007. Dancing in the White Spaces: Exploring Gendered Assumptions in Successful Project Managers' Discourse about Their Work. *International Journal of Project Management* 25 (6): 552–559.

Turner, Michelle, Helen Lingard, and Valerie Francis. 2009. Work-Life Balance: An Exploratory Study of Supports and Barriers in a Construction Project. *International Journal of Managing Projects in Business* 2 (1): 94–111.

Vitores, Anna, and Adriana Gil-Juárez. 2016. The Trouble with 'Women in Computing': A Critical Examination of the Deployment of Research on the Gender Gap in Computer Science. *Journal of Gender Studies* 25 (6): 666–680.

Watts, Jacqueline H. 2009. 'Allowed into a Man's World' Meanings of Work–Life Balance: Perspectives of Women Civil Engineers as 'Minority' Workers in Construction. *Gender, Work & Organization* 16 (1): 37–57.

Weststar, Johanna. 2011. A Review of Women's Experiences of Three Dimensions of Underemployment. In *Underemployment: Psychological, Economic, and Social Challenges*, ed. D.C. Maynard and D.C. Feldman, 105–125. New York: Springer.

———. 2015. Understanding Video Game Developers as an Occupational Community. *Information, Communication & Society* 18 (10): 1238–1252.

Weststar, Johanna, and Marie-Josée Legault. 2012. Facts and Discussion about Hours of Work in the Video Game Industry. In *Cultural Perspectives of Video Games: From Designer to Player*, ed. A. Bracken and N. Guyot, 187–197. Oxford: Interdisciplinary Press.

Weststar, Johanna, and Marie-Josée Legault. 2015. *2014 Developer Satisfaction Survey: Employment Report*. International Game Developers Association. http://www.igda.org/?page=dss2014

Weststar, Johanna, and Maria Andrei-Gedja. 2015. *2014 Developer Satisfaction Survey Report: Industry Trends and Future Outlook Report*. International Game Developers Association. http://www.igda.org/?page=dss2014

———. 2016. *2015 Developer Satisfaction Survey: Industry Trends and Future Outlook Report*. International Game Developers Association. http://www.igda.org/?page=dss2015

Weststar, Johanna, Victoria O'Meara, Chandell Gosse, and Marie-Josée Legault. 2017. Diversity among Videogame Developers: 2004–2015. August. http://www.gameqol.org/igda-qol-survey/

Winn, Jillian, and Carrie Heeter. 2009. Gaming, Gender, and Time: Who Makes Time to Play? *Sex Roles* 61 (1–2): 1–13.

Witz, Anne. 1990. Patriarchy and Professions: The Gendered Politics of Occupational Closure. *Sociology* 24 (4): 675–690.

Yap, Margaret, and Alison M. Konrad. 2009. Gender and Racial Differentials in Promotions: Is There a Sticky Floor, a Mid-level Bottleneck, or a Glass Ceiling? *Industrial Relations* 64 (4): 593–619.

# 8

# Rule Makers vs. Rule Breakers: The Impact of Legislative Policies on Women Game Developers in the Japanese Game Industry

Tsugumi Okabe

Is there a need to recruit and retain more women developers in the Japanese game industry? This question frames this chapter and serves as a springboard to explore the social and legal dimensions of Japanese women in the workforce. This chapter reports from semi-structured interviews with four Japanese women game developers who revealed that education, work ethic, and skill ultimately play a far greater role in the economy of the game industry than gender, but that these aspects are hampered by cultural perceptions of women in relation to technology, working overtime, and child rearing. To understand the current climate of women in the game industry, or the lack thereof, I situate this study within the broader context of women and work in Japan, examining the scholarship on the country's labor laws and its impact on gendered work practices in Japan.

A number of studies have suggested several factors that impact a woman's career path in game development. Issues of work-life balance (Prescott and Bogg 2010, 2013b), gender stereotyping (Prescott and Bogg 2013a, 113), and the glass ceiling effect (Prescott and Bogg 2013a, 113) have been identified as some of the reasons why women leave the industry in North America, but how do these concepts apply within a Japanese cultural context? On September 4, 2014, a small group of women game developers held a panel discussion about women in the Japanese video game industry at the Computer Entertainment Developers Conference (CEDEC)[1] in Yokohama, Japan. According to their findings from the 2011 Japan Ministry of Health, Labour, and Welfare Report,

T. Okabe (✉)
University of Alberta, Edmonton, AL, Canada

© The Author(s) 2018
K. L. Gray et al. (eds.), *Feminism in Play*, Palgrave Games in Context,
https://doi.org/10.1007/978-3-319-90539-6_8

**125**

"women in game development consist of 12 percent of the industry and only five percent continue to work in the field after five years" (CEDEC 2014). In his study, Masahito Fujihara (2014) has found that "the proportion of female developers stands at 12.8% in Japan (Fujihara 2010), 11.2% in the USA (Gourdin 2005), and 4% in the UK (Prescott and Bogg 2010; Skillset 2009). The percentage has been similarly low in Canada, at 10%–15% (Dyer-Whitheford and Sharman 2005), and less than 10% in Australia (Geneve et al. 2008)" (Fujihara 111). In Japan, as well as in other developed nations, then, women are marginalized within the game industry. Fujihara's study describes various career paths taken by Japanese women in game design, but he does not address the underlying social and political conditions that impact them. In her study on the impact of legislative policies on the lives of women, Aya Elise Ezawa (2011) argues: "social policies and institutions, as well as workplace practices create structural conditions and institutional frameworks, which shape women's opportunities and lifestyles, and can influence trends in marriage, family formation and women's lives" (108). It is from this sociocultural and legal perspective that this study investigates why there are so few women in Japan's game industry.

# Method

Several interview-based studies have been conducted that investigate workplace challenges for women game developers. Tracy Fullerton et al. (2008) reveal the importance of creating a space wherein women feel encouraged and safe to explore their potential as game designers. Mia Consalvo (2008) critiques an industry and its exploitive practices that limit and discourage women's professional development. Prescott and Bogg (2011) observe how gender segregation poses career barriers for women within the game industry and Sonja Ganguin and Anna Hoblitz (2014) explore the trials and tribulations of German game developers, offering a cultural perspective of workplace challenges that women encounter in the German game industry.

At the outset of this project, I inquired if one of the contributing factors for the absence of women within the game industry could be traced to the discursive formation of motherhood. To interrogate the validity of this inquiry, while simultaneously being open-minded to an investigation of new themes and concepts to expand the scope of this research topic, I went abroad to Japan to interview Japanese game developers from May 17, 2015 to June 6, 2015. There, I conducted a series of five semi-structured interviews of which four were retained. This study obtained approval from the Research Ethics Office

(REO) at the University of Alberta on April 13, 2015. Research participants were contacted by intermediaries through e-mail to whom I distributed a brief summary explaining the study in Japanese and of the voluntary nature of their participation. Intermediaries included colleagues and professors who had access to industry personnel. Interested participants were asked to contact me via e-mail. Then, they received a translated copy of the "confidentiality agreement form," which I asked participants to sign and return should they agree to participate. In addition, participants received the "participation letter information," which outlined the following: study objectives and procedures; the voluntary nature of participation and their right to withdraw; the collection, use, and storage of data; and procedures to ensure confidentiality and anonymity. Both the names of participants and their current company of employment as well as the games that they have created have been anonymized, using the default Japanese format: A-san, B-san, C-san (meaning, person A, B, and C) and/or company A, B, C and/or Game A, B, C. Finally, participants were provided with a questionnaire, which consisted of a combination of closed and open-ended questions to guide us through the interview process. In addition to the questionnaire, I allowed for comments and inquiries to emerge from the context of participants' responses. The time and location of the interviews were decided by each of the participants. Three were conducted face to face and one via Skype due to distance. Two participants, who were acquaintances, requested to be interviewed together. In this case, the participants agreed to take turns answering questions during the interview process. Individual interviews took approximately an hour and the combined interview took approximately and hour and 30 minutes. After I transcribed the digital recordings of the interviews, the data transcripts were sent to participants for clarification, where needed, and to verify its accuracy, which resulted in some minor changes (such as making corrections to the Romanization of Japanese game titles and the spelling of some words). The revised transcripts were sent to participants, then, I translated them into English.

Several limitations were identified in the study. Ethical questions regarding the interviewer's self-disclosure (Gubrium and Holstein 2002), neutrality, and status as outsider/insider (Dwyer and Buckle 2009) are well documented in literature.[2] Being a Japanese woman but having been raised in Canada, I identify myself as occupying neither outsider nor insider status because I occupy an ambiguous space, or a "third space," as Homi Bhabha might say. For critics such as Ted Aoki (1996), the third space marks "an ambivalent space of both this and that, of both East and West, wherein the traditions of Western modernist epistemology can meet the Eastern traditions of wisdom" (8). Certainly, being equipped with the cultural knowledge of Japanese customs, verbal and non-verbal cues, values and etiquettes may have influenced the study in productive ways. Being a woman and a fluent Japanese speaker may also may have facilitated deeper conversations than, say, if I was a man. However, working from this space of simultaneous inclusivity/exclusivity also has certain limitations. A shared sense of gender does not ensure positive relations between the interviewees and me. "Ramazanoglu (1989) points out that women are divided by other variables and this can affect the research process" (Cotterill 1992, 595). In this particular study, for instance, two of the interviewees were ten years my senior and the other two women were six years my junior. Discrepancies between my age and the interviewees' may have had an impact on what was said and what was not. Also, whereas I identify myself as a feminist, the interviewees may not share the same political view. Bearing this in mind, neutrality was maintained through a conscious effort to use "interpersonal skills merely to encourage the expression of, but not help construct, the attitudes, sentiments, and information in question" (Gubrium and Holstein 2002, 14).

Another challenge of this research involved finding participants and conducting interviews within a limited time frame and on a limited budget. Women in game development make up 12.8% (Fujihara 2010, 111) of the Japanese industry, representing a niche population that is hard to access. The number of research participants to make an adequate sample size for a qualitative study is critically debated. The question of "how many" (Adler and Adler 2012, 8) depends on a number factors, including but not limited to the type of research, the breadth and scope of research questions, costs, resources, and "accessibility of potential interviewees" (Flick 1998, 27). Moreover, as Nancy L. Leech (2005) notes, different research techniques call for different sample sizes: "Specifically, Creswell (2002) has recommended that 3-5 participants be used for case study research" (3). That qualitative studies rely on a smaller sample size than quantitative studies is a widely accepted view and it is well supported. In particular, Adler and Adler (2012) posit that "qualitative researchers, working in the context of discovery, are more open-ended, and often follow emergent empirical and conceptual findings in unexpected ways" (9). This small study takes on strategies of open-ended and discovery-based research techniques. In a close reading of the interview transcripts, I first observed recurring concepts and themes that emerged in each of the interviews. This was followed by a comparative analysis of all four interviews from which I identified points of tension and similarity between participant responses. By working closely with the interview transcripts, individual narratives were analyzed and situated within broader discourses of the social and legal dynamics of Japanese work culture and its impact on women game developers. Detailed analyses of the interviews are followed by the literature review.

# Issues with Women's Employment in the Japanese Game Industry

## Legislative Policies and Education Reforms

This section explores, in brief, the development of Japan's legal and educational system to contextualize current issues with women's employment in the Japanese game industry. I begin by outlining two laws that according to Rawstron (2011) "specifically address the intersection of labour and gender in Japan" (59): the Labor Standards Law (1947) and the Equal Employment Opportunity Law (1986) followed by a discussion on cultural norms around technology.

Prior to postwar reformations of the Japanese Constitution, following Japan's defeat in the Second World War, women in Japan had few legal rights and had limited access to education and employment opportunities. In the Meiji Period (1868–1912) and "under the prevailing *ie*, or family, system, which was the foundation of prewar Japanese society, the proper place for women was considered to be within the home, under the authority of the male family head" (Kaneko 2011, 3). According to the *ie* system, "the patriarchal head of the family (usually the eldest son) held unquestioned authority over the rest of the family. Together with the privilege of primogeniture, he had an obligation to support the family financially" (Kaneko 2011, 4). Informed by the "Confucian conception of the role of women, which confined them to childbearing, and child rearing and which held that learning was not only unnecessary, but, indeed, harmful for women" (Hara and Fujimura-Fanselow 2011, 73), this hierarchical formation of the family unit prevailed throughout the Taisho (1912–1926) and early Showa Periods (1926–1989). Cultural idioms such as "*mitsugo no tamashii hyakumade*," meaning that "the soul of a three-year-old remains the same until the age of 100" (Takahashi 2014, 85), reflects the cultural realities of a time when the ideology of *ryōsai kenbo* (good wife, wise mother) was used to educate women.

While the reformation of the Civil Code in 1947 helped to emancipate women from the patriarchal *ie* system by granting them the right to work and participate within the public domain, it strategically reinforced the implementation of the *josei hogo kitei* (Women's Protection Provisions) and the *bosei hogo* ("protection of motherhood"), which regulated working conditions for women on the basis of sex difference. For example, women under the age of 18 were not allowed to work between 10:00 pm and 5:00 am and they were restricted from working in certain occupations, which were deemed unsuitable for a woman such as underground work, which has now been banned under Article 64-2 (Labor Standards Act 24). While these protectionist provisions provided women with greater access to employment, they limited women from attaining equal employment. Conflicted opinions regarding the necessity of protection in order to achieve equality sparked a national debate in the 1960s and 1970s.[3] Although amendments were made to the Labor Standards, which lifted provisions for night work and "dangerous" occupations for women, as Yamada (2009) points out "provisions related to maternal protection were reinforced" under Article 64-3 (Labor Standards Act 24–25) "by the restriction of dangerous and injurious work, holiday work, overtime work and late-night work for pregnant women and the expansion of maternity leave programs before and after delivery" (201).

It was not until 1980 that Japan ratified the Convention on Elimination of Discrimination Against Women (CEDAW), which helped enact the Equal Employment Opportunity Law (EEOL), implemented in 1986 followed by amendments made in 1997 and in 2006 (Assmann 2014, 1). In short, the EEOL, at its various stages, set out to promote equal employment opportunities for women such as by enforcing policies against all forms of discrimination and sexual harassment and the termination of pregnant or child-rearing women (Starich 2007; Assmann 2014). Jennifer S. Fan (1999) discusses at length one of the unintended results of the EEOL such as the two-track hiring system that privileged men to be hired in managerial positions and pushed women into clerical positions. By 2006, formative steps were taken to strengthen the EEOL, resulting in the recognition against various forms of indirect discrimination. However, scholars have identified the limitations of the EEOL primarily because it serves as a mere guideline (Fan 1999; Starich 2007; Yamada 2009; Assmann 2012). The shortfalls of the EEOL may be reflected in the statistics presented in the December 2015 CEDAW report, in which "The Survey on Maternity Harassment (by the Trade Union 'Rengo', 2014), revealed that … 61.2% of female workers gave up their jobs after pregnancy" (1). In the following year, the 2016 alternative report on CEDAW indicated that "Japan ranks 101st out of the 145 countries under the Global Gender Gap Index 2015, remaining at the bottom of the developed nations" (2).

My argument is that protectionist discourses continue to influence the construction of gendered roles that impact a woman's career choice. The myth of protection is still made manifest in the form of the damsel in distress, which is often dealt with thematically in literature and in Japanese popular culture such as in *shōjo* manga narratives, video games, and *moba-ge* (mobile games) targeted to women. Ideas of "femininity" are also embedded in language[4] and in aspects of everyday culture. Phrases such as *josei muke na mono* (things for women) or *josei ni yasashī* (female-friendly) are commonly used to describe the female experience in relation to things from work (*josei ni yasashī shigoto*),[5] to cigarettes, to cars, to choice of physicians, and so on. This type of discourse assumes that women are inherently different from men. It also reveals how notions of female propriety, etiquette, and tastes are governed through market principles that subscribe to patriarchal constructs of femininity. The use of *josei senryōsha* (women-only trains), which are offered during rush hour, to protect women from being groped by men, and themed restaurants exclusively for women function to make natural the "special" treatment of women. The ways in which Japanese society brands femininity and disseminates (patriarchal) ideas of how it *means* to be a "woman" ultimately impacts how a woman sees herself in relation to gendered notions of occupational choice and policies regarding public labor in Japan.

Under a patriarchal belief system that primarily defines women by their reproductive role, they become simultaneously included and excluded from the country's legal and educational reforms. This is particularly evident in how the former ideology of "good wife, wise mother" was gradually replaced in the 1960s with "values of the middle-class family, consisting of a full-time 'professional' housewife, a hardworking salaried husband and two children, [which] became central to the popular image of the postwar Japanese family" (Ezawa 2011, 108). Although by this time, women had greater opportunities to pursue individual careers than ever before, the pressure to uphold social and cultural norms posed a challenge for the privileged few who had access to higher education. It is not surprising, then, that there is a lack of female role models today in fields traditionally characterized as "masculine," which, according to Prescott and Bogg (2010), include Science Engineering and Technology (SET), Information Communication and Technology (ICT), and game development. In Japan, Atsuko Kameda (2011) asserts that "most people cannot name a Japanese woman scientist. Both historically and today, the link between women and science and technology is extremely weak" (90). Kameda (2011) reports on a number of striking statistics: "the percentage of Japanese women researchers in science and engineering fields reached 12.4% in 2008" in comparison to "19.2 percent for Germany, 26 percent for the U.K., 27.8 percent for France, 34.3 percent for the US, 37.1 percent for Greece, 46.2 percent for Portugal, and 51.5 percent for Latvia (Naikakufu 2008, 115, fig 1-6-6)" (91). It was not until 2000 that a number of government-funded programs began to work closely with women's organizations, secondary and postsecondary institutions in the promotion of science and technology for women. Kameda (2011) attributes "the lack of role models" (93) as one of the contributing factors for the lack of women in science and technical fields. This correlates to

Fujihara's findings (2014): "Japanese female game developers do not have role models to guide them in their career at their studios. Therefore, they may have the feeling that their career perspectives in the present or in the future are unclear. However, they try to be leading role models for young women in the Japanese gaming industry, and find meaning in their lives" (124).

## Cultural Norms, Women, and Technology

Since *Angelique* (1994),[6] ideas about women's disinterest in games have changed as game companies capitalized on the genre of *josei-muke gēmu* (women's games), facilitating women's interests in gameplay—but why do so few women pursue a career in game development? The interview data revealed several assumptions about women as players and creators of games. The word and/or concept of *ime-ji* (image) was used in different contexts to describe several aspects of the game industry: the type of job, its demographic, its environment, and the role of women in technological fields. Japanese women game developers describe themselves as exceptions to the norm because they challenge one or more of the following *ime-ji*: women don't play, make, or buy games, women don't like games, and that women can't program or do technically challenging work.

Although statistically speaking, women are outnumbered by men in the industry, at small studios such as A-san's, where the ratio of male to female workers is 5:9, women make up half of the programming team. D-san was also recently hired as the first woman at her company, which has been established for over a decade. Women in the industry are gradually being incorporated into an "*otokoshakai*—a traditional Japanese organizational culture [which] was defined by and for men" (Renshaw 1999, 91)—or an "all-boys" industry mentality. However, a system that places women on the periphery has led to several consequences. Nonetheless, there is an increasing number of college programs that offer courses on game studies and organizations such as WomenWhoCode Tokyo that are redefining cultural perceptions about the relationship between women and digital technologies. There are also online *dōjin*[7] communities that provide "how to" tools, chat venues, and Q&A forums tailored to help women and enthusiasts to create games. Women's involvement in technical fields is important because as Wendy Faulkner (2001) argues, "we cannot transform gender relations without engaging in technology" (90) since technology is often defined in relation to masculinity, authority, and therefore power.

At the same time, a culture of ambivalence and fear about women in technical careers still seems to prevail. In a job fair event that B-san co-hosted with nine other companies, she recalled that "quarter of the job applications were submitted by women." This was a striking contrast to the number of women who attended B-san's technical seminars where she found that "for every female attendee there were approximately 30 to 20 males." B-san explains that "when it comes to technical things like programming, and how to use software and engines ... the percentage [of women] drops drastically." Faulkner (2001) and Judy Wajcman (2006) have examined the ways in which technology is deeply connected to the social construction of gendered identities, whereby it predominantly fosters a masculine image. The lack of female role models in science and digital technologies as pointed out by Kameda (2011) and Fujihara (2014) impacts a woman's perception of her own technical (in)competence. Moreover, the fact that "women were unable to enroll in the science and agriculture faculties of public universities until the 1920s and 1930s" (Kameda 2011, 91) puts into perspective why there are so few role models today. As Kameda further explains (2011), "the advancement of women in science in Japan has finally begun" (91) in 2006. In other words, for over half a century, in Japan, "Technology was seen as socially shaped, but shaped by men to the exclusion of women" (Wajcman 2006, 10). This history of exclusion has created both an internal and external barrier for women pursuing a career in game design.

Organizational prejudice stems from certain stereotypes and myths about Japanese women that influence the lives of female developers. Interview data revealed two prevailing discourses that are believed to have an impact on the professionalization of women in game development—protectionism and motherhood. The issues that emerge from these discourses and the ways in which they are dealt with at the individual and corporate level matter in establishing long-term career goals and career paths for women.

In this study, the interview data revealed that some women felt challenged by corporate expectations of a female worker that conflicted with their work ethic. This is because at some companies, women are told to go home earlier than their male colleagues in consideration of their safety, as C-san reports: "Because I am a woman, I've been told to go home earlier. When it gets around 9 o'clock at night it can be dangerous." D-san also relates that because of her long commute to and from work, she is told to go home earlier than her male coworkers. These two cases highlight how certain "stereotypes can lead to prejudice attitudes of 'them' and 'us' mentality" (Prescott and Bogg 2013a, 113), contributing to "gender segregated occupations and the glass ceiling." C-san debunks the patriarchal logic that underpins discourses of protectionism, as she asserts: "Personally, just because I'm a woman and because I'm told to go home, I'm not going to say 'because I'm a woman, I'm going home now' (laughs). I also work and I'm able to manage my own time so the thought is more than enough." D-san, on the other hand, who is the only woman out of 16 male employees at her company, draws attention to how feelings of guilt are associated with being told to go home describing how she "feels bad" and that "it would nice if everyone went home" not only her. D-san's story illustrates her internal struggle to "fit in" an industry that includes her while simultaneously excludes her on the premise of her "feminine" identity.

This is not to undermine the serious dangers of commuting alone at night. During B-san's employment at her former graphic designing firm, she recalled a time when she was stalked by a man on her way home. When she returned to work the following day, she made a request to leave earlier than the night before, but her boss rejected the idea. B-san's incident, though it did not occur within the context of the game industry, is related to broader concerns of the disadvantageous treatment of women. The integrity behind companies that provide women employees with the option to go home earlier than male employees may seem genuine. However, the extent to which these protective measures serve advantageous to women in occupations where long work hours are the norm depends on individual preferences and career goals. Article 32 of the Labor Standards Act prohibits "working for more than eight hours per week" (9). However, Fujihara's (2014) study on Japanese women game developers reveals that "the average number of work hours per week is 54 (63 during crunch time) in management jobs and 45 (59 during crunch time) in developmental jobs" (115). He further reports that "single females work 48 hour week (62 hours during crunch time); married females with no children work 50 hours (62 hours during crunch time); and married females with children work 42 hours (54 hours during crunch time)" (115). A woman who seeks stability and is family oriented, then, may not find a life-long career in game development appealing (?).

The impact that motherhood has on the professional development of women game designers seems universal—studies ranging from the impact of presenteeism on work-life balance in the UK (Simpson 1998), to the formation of identities in relation to work-life conflict in the US (Raskin 2006), and to the implication of a long work hour culture within an Australian context (Diamond and Whitehouse 2007)—these case studies emphasize a greater need for policies that better harmonize work and family life. Prescott and Bogg (2013a) point out the irony of how "women's identities have been increasingly shifting however, the role of motherhood has remained unchanged" (120). In this study, only one interviewee was married and none of the interviewed women were mothers. The women game developers expressed different opinions regarding the importance of becoming a wife, or mother and how it might affect their individual career paths. However, they all identified marriage, motherhood, and/or child rearing as reasons why they think so few women continue in game development. Those unmarried reported that they feel the pressure to get married and have children. Some expressed that they would like to continue in game development after marriage and even after they have children, while others expressed that they may seek other career opportunities in the future. Some do not want children or say that it is too late to have children. Three women were raised in a typical nuclear household family, and one was raised in household with a single-working mother. This comparison draws attention to how women negotiate and internalize their subjectivity in relation to their role as wives and/or as mothers in highly individualistic ways that is often reflective of the values they grow up with.

Japanese cultural norms regarding motherhood remain a factor that directly contribute to the slow rate at which women are incorporated into the Japanese game industry. However, women who are in positions of authority are transforming the work environment in ways that enable other women to sustain a balance between family obligations and her professional goals. Here, I draw on my conversation with A-san:

> Some time ago, a female programmer consulted me about wanting to have a child. At that time, she thought if she had a child, she would be a burden to the company so she thought of quitting. But, in particular, I thought, if we could decrease her workload—her skills as a programmer up to now would have been for nothing—so I thought, if there's anything we could do, even change the way she works; I wanted her to remain in the game industry… It's really thanks to her that I was able to create leaves for married, pregnant, and child-rearing women… I think it's very sad to hear that someone would want to quit this industry, since they worked hard to get here.

The fact that the female employee thought it best to quit the company to avoid being a burden to her colleagues is revealing of how Japanese workers, in general, are deeply conscientious of their belonging to a group, or *nakamaishiki.* "Loyalty," as Renshaw (1999) writes, "can be attributed to organizational culture directly reinforced by national culture" (88). Renshaw describes that one's loyalty to a company is reinforced by the ways in which "Japanese organizations use a variety of methods to acculturate employees. *Shanai gyoma,* company events or rituals are effectively used to support the shared culture" (88). Companies emphasize the importance of a collectivist work ethic because it is a highly efficient and productive model on which businesses thrive. In her study of women game designers in North America, Consalvo (2008) problematizes the concept of passion because it "serve[s] as a unifying ideology from which development companies can draw in order to justify various practices that might be considered exploitative in other industries" (184). Loyalty, in Japan, functions in a similar way because it holds workers accountable for their commitment within a *nakama* (team or group), which is not only limited within the context of the video game industry, but is used by Japanese companies, broadly speaking, to strategically justify overtime and other (exploitive) work practices.

In returning to the passage above, A-san points out that the fear of letting the group down should not be the deciding factor for a woman to have to choose between work and family. She expresses how companies such as hers are willing to adopt new policies in order to accommodate women (and men) who want to start a family by providing flexible work hours that enable work-life balance. This is important as Patricia Raskin (2006) points out, "If organizations want to minimize turnover in working mothers, and if organizations are committed to increasing diversity at the executive level, family-friendly cultures and policies are necessary" (1377). A-san's intervention also conveys the importance of *compassion* in creating a productive work environment where workers feel valued, which in turn produces loyal and hardworking employees, but not in an exploitive way. Compassion is the key to humane work practices and it has positive results to both the corporation and its workers.

In order to promote gender equality and to increase and retain women in game design, myths about masculinity also have to change. Since 1992, when the Childcare Leave Law was established, "Japanese residents have been entitled to take advantage of laws that provide for maternal and paternal leave at up to 60% of full salary" (Morrone and Matsuyama 2010, 372). Although men were not interviewed in this study, Morrone and Matsuyama's (2010) interview-based study on fathers taking paternity leave revealed that "most contemporary fathers expressed great enjoyment being in the physical presence of their children and family" (374).[8] However, they noted: fathers "often remarked that taking leave for a long period of time threatened to put them 'out of touch' with developments at work. They might run the risk of being considered irresponsible or incompetent, or just plain selfish" (Morrone and Matsuyama 2010, 373). In an auto-ethnographic study, Masaki Matsuda (2011) recounts the various forms of criticism he received from his colleagues and family members for choosing to become a "househusband." With respect to Japan's work culture, then, one's loyalty to the team reveals a competing stereotype: women *want* to quit so as not to harm the group, whereas men *do not want* to quit so as not to harm the group.[9] Loyalty, within the context of Japanese organizational culture, is a gendered concept that is premised on the stability of (heteronormative) roles.

When women are placed in positions of authority, they have the power to change corporate policies that will benefit other women. Other game companies in Japan such as iNiS Ltd. have started a program that allows working mothers to bring their child to work.[10] Moreover, programs offered by companies such as CyberAgent, Inc. provide working mothers with special vacations such as "F-day" that gives an extra day off during the month of January as well as pregnancy vacation that grant women with special leave to partake in parent-child excursions.[11] However, we should keep in mind that a simple inversion of existing paradigms of power will only reinstate a gendered hierarchy and that not all women seek to help other women.

To return to the question that I asked in the opening line of this chapter— is there a need to recruit and retain more women developers in the Japanese game industry?—the answer is that it depends. What was made clear in this study is that not all women work in the industry for their "love" of games. For some, game development is a full-time job, whereas for others it is part time or (serious) a hobbyist activity. Some were driven by their love of *mecha*,[12] while others not. Some knew from "the gecko" that they will become game developers, while others struggled to find employment and/or describe it as chance. Not all women are thinking about long-term career goals within the corporate game industry. However, it is important to dismantle the deep-seated gender biases that discourage some women from pursuing a career in SET, ICT, and/or game development simply because they are women. The central claim of this study is that gender segregation stems out of legislative policies that are intended to protect the patriarchal construction of femininity, which inform cultural perceptions about women in game development, but women currently in the industry are breaking the rules, per se, by challenging stereotypes and paving a way for aspiring women game developers in Japan.

**Acknowledgments** I would like to thank Dr. Geoffrey Rockwell and Dr. Mia Consalvo for their unwavering support and generous funding that made this project possible. I am also grateful to the editors for their guidance and many helpful suggestions.

# Notes

1. Translated from "CEDEC 2014 Women Creators Discuss 'Ways for Working Women in the Game Industry!'" Gpara.com, last modified September 4, 2014, http://www.gpara.com/infos/view/16023.
2. See also Shulamit Reinharz and Susan E. Chase (2002) and Pamela Cotterill (1992) for feminist implications of conducting interviews with women.
3. See Nakanishi Tamako (1983), Makoto Kumazawa (1996) and Tachibanaki Toshiaki (2010) on the paradoxes of protectionist discourses and further details on the equality vs. protection debates.
4. See for example, Takahara, Kumio. 1999. "Female Speech Patterns in Japanese" *International Journal of the Sociology of Language* 92 (1): 61–86. https://doi.org/10.1515/ijsl.1991.92.61; Okushi, Yoshiko. 1997. "Patterns of Honorific use in the Everyday Speech of Four Japanese Women." *Dissertation Abstracts International, Section A: The Humanities and Social Sciences* 58 (3): 1–273. http://repository.upenn.edu/dissertations/AAI9727271.
5. Translates to "easy" work for women or work that is not physically laborious.
6. *Angelique* was the first women's dating-sim game "for the Super Nintendo Entertainment System in 1994, published by Koei and developed by Ruby Party, an all-female team within Koei (Marfisa 1999)" (qtd in Kim 2009, 170).
7. Hobbyist groups, which consist mostly of women who create games, manga (Japanese comics) and anime by adapting popular or mainstream works.
8. Morrone and Matsuyama's study involved fathers who "worked for large, and thus prestigious, corporations with clearly stated policies for paternal leave" (374). See also comparisons made between fathers in Sweden, Korea and France.
9. I thank Mia Consalvo for pointing out this paradox in an earlier draft of this paper.
10. Translated from "CEDEC 2014 Women Creators Discuss 'Ways for Working Women in the Game Industry!'" Gpara.com, last modified September 4, 2014, http://www.gpara.com/infos/view/16023.
11. Ibid.
12. Pronounced as "meka," it generally refers to machines, technology, electronics and robots.

# Bibliography

Adler, Patricia A., and Peter Adler. 2012. Expert Voices. In *How Many Qualitative Interviews Is Enough? Expert Voices and Early Career Reflections on Sampling and Cases in Qualitative Research*, ed. Sarah Elsie Baker and Rosalind Edwards, 8–11. Southampton, GB: National Centre for Research Methods.

Aoki, Ted T. 1996. *Imaginaries of "East and West": Slippery Curricular Signifiers in Education*. Paper presented at the International Adult and Continuing Education Conference, 1–8. ERIC Clearinghouse. http://files.eric.ed.gov.login.ezproxy.library.ualberta.ca/fulltext/ED401406.pdf.

Assmann, Stephanie. 2012. 25 Years After the Enactment of the Equal Employment Opportunity Law (EEOL): Online Access to Gender Equality in Japan. *Asian Politics & Policy* 4 (2): 280–285.

———. 2014. Gender Equality in Japan: The Equal Employment Opportunity Law Revisited. *Asia-Pacific Journal: Japan Focus* 45 (2): 1–24.

CEDEC. 2014. Women Creators Discuss 'Ways for Working Women in the Game Industry!'" 2014. *Gpara.com*. Accessed September 4, 2014. http://www.gpara.com/infos/view/16023.

Consalvo, Mia. 2008. Crunched by Passion: Women Game Developers and Workplace Challenges. In *Beyond Barbie & Mortal Kombat New Perspectives on Gender and Gaming*, ed. Yasmin B. Kafai, Carrie Heeter, Jill Denner, and Jennifer Y. Sun, 176–190. Massachusetts: MIT Press.

Cotterill, Pamela. 1992. Interviewing Women: Issues of Friendship, Vulnerability, and Power. *Women's Studies International Forum* 15 (5–6): 593–606.

Diamond, Chris, and Gillian Whitehouse. 2007. Gender, Computing and the Organization of Working Time: Public/Private Comparisons in the Australian Context. *Information, Community and Society* 10 (3): 320–337.

Dwyer, Sonya Corbin, and Jennifer L. Buckle. 2009. The Space Between: On Being an Insider-Outsider in Qualitative Research. *International Journal of Qualitative Methods* 8 (1): 54–63.

Ezawa, Aya Elise. 2011. The Changing Patterns of Marriage and Motherhood. In *Transforming Japan: How Feminism and Diversity Are Making a Difference*, ed. Kumiko Fujimura-Fanselow, 105–120. New York: Feminist Press.

Fan, Jennifer S. 1999. From Office Ladies to Women Warriors? The Effect of the EEOL on Japanese Women. *UCLA Women's Law Journal* 10: 103–140 http://escholarship.org/uc/item/9cj8g2h3.

Faulkner, Wendy. 2001. The Technology Question in Feminism: A View from Feminist Technology Studies. *In Women's Studies International Forum* 24 (1): 79–95.

Flick, Uwe. 1998. *An Introduction to Qualitative Research*. London: SAGE.

Fujihara, Masahito. 2014. Career Development among Japanese Female Game Developers: Perspective from Life Stories of Creative Professionals. In *Gender Considerations and Influence in the Digital Media Gaming Industry*, ed. Julie Prescott and Julie Elizabeth McGurren, 110–124. Hershey, PA: IGI Global.

Fullerton, Tracy, Janine Fron, Celia Pearce, and Jacki Morie (Ludica). 2008. Getting Girls into the Game: Toward a 'Virtuous Cycle'. In *Beyond Barbie & Mortal Kombat New Perspectives on Gender and Gaming*, ed. Yasmin B. Kafai, Carrie Heeter, Jill Denner, and Jennifer Y. Sun, 161–176. Massachusetts: MIT Press.

Ganguin, Sonja, and Anna Hoblitz. 2014. Career Paths of Women in the German Games Industry. *The Journal of the Canadian Games Studies Association* 8 (13): 22–42.

Gubrium, Jaber F., and James A. Holstein. 2002. From the Individual Interview to the Interview Society. In *Handbook of Interview Research: Context & Method*, ed. Jaber F. Gubrium and James A. Holstein, 3–32. Thousand Oaks: Sage Publications.

Hara, Kimi, and Kumiko Fujimura-Fanselow. 2011. Educational Challenges Past and Present. In *Transforming Japan: How Feminism and Diversity Are Making a Difference*, ed. Kumiko Fujimura-Fanselow, 71–88. New York: Feminist Press.

Kameda, Atsuko. 2011. "The Advancement of Women in Sciences and Technology. In *Transforming Japan: How Feminism and Diversity Are Making a Difference*, ed. Kumiko Fujimura-Fanselow, 89–101. Translated by Malaya Ileto. New York: Feminist Press.

Kaneko, Sachiko. 2011. The Struggle for Legal Rights and Reforms: A Historical View. In *Transforming Japan: How Feminism and Diversity Are Making a Difference*, ed. Kumiko Fujimura-Fanselow, 3–14. New York: Feminist Press.

Kim, Hyeshin. 2009. Women's Games in Japan: Gendered Identity and Narrative Construction. *Theory, Culture & Society* 26 (2–3): 165–188.

Kumazawa, Makoto. 1996. *Portraits of the Japanese Workplace: Labor Movements, Workers, and Managers*. Edited by Andrew Gordon. Translated by Andrew Gordon and Mikiso Han. Boulder: Westview Press.

Labor Standards Act. 1947. *International Labour Organization*. Accessed September 24, 2016. http://www.ilo.org/global/lang%2D%2Den/index.htm. (Act No. 49 of April 7, 1947).

Leech, Nacy L. 2005. The Role of Sampling in Qualitative Research. *Academic Exchange Quarterly* 9 (3): 280–286.

Matsuda, Masaki. 2011. My Life as a Househusband. In *Transforming Japan: How Feminism and Diversity Are Making a Difference*, ed. Kumiko Fujimura-Fanselow, 138–144. New York: Feminist Press.

Morrone, Michelle Henault, and Yurmi Matsuyama. 2010. Japan's Parental Leave Policy: Has It Affected Gender Ideology and Child Care Norms in Japan? *Childhood Education* 86 (6): 371–375.

Nakanishi, Tamako. 1983. Equality or Protection? Protective Legislation for Women in Japan. *International Labour Review* 122: 609–621.

Prescott, Julie, and Jan Bogg. 2010. The Computer Games Industry: Women's Experiences of Work Role. In *Women in Engineering, Science and Technology: Education and Career Challenges: Education and Career Challenges*, ed. J. Prescott and J. Bogg, 138–158. USA: IGI Global.

———. 2011. Segregation in a Male-dominated Industry: Women Working in the Computer Games Industry. *International Journal of Gender, Science and Technology* 3 (1): 205–227.

————. 2013a. Stereotype, Attitudes, and Identity: Gendered Expectations and Behaviors. In *Gendered Occupational Difference in Science, Engineering, and Technology Careers*, ed. J. Prescott and J. Bogg, 112–134. Hershey, PA: Information Science Reference.

————. 2013b. Work Life Balance Issues: The Choice, or Women's Lack of It. In *Gendered Occupational Difference in Science, Engineering, and Technology Careers*, ed. J. Prescott and J. Bogg, 167–191. Hershey, PA: Information Science Reference.

Raskin, Patricia M. 2006. Women, Work, and Family: Three Studies of Roles and Identity among Working Mothers. *American Behavioral Scientist* 49 (10): 1354–1381.

Rawstron, Kristi. 2011. Evaluating Women's Labour in 1990s Japan: The Changing Labour Standards Law. *New Voices: A Journal for Emerging Scholars of Japanese Studies in Australia and New Zealand* 57: 57–77.

Reinharz, Shulamit, and Susan E. Chase. 2002. Interviewing Women. In *Handbook of Interview Research: Context & Method*, ed. Jaber F. Gubrium and James A. Holstein, 221–238. Thousand Oaks: Sage Publications.

Renshaw, Jean R. 1999. *Kimono in the Boardroom: The Invisible Evolution of Japanese Women Managers*. New York: Oxford University Press.

Simpson, Ruth. 1998. Presenteeism, Power and Organizational Change: Long Hours as a Career Barrier and the Impact on the Working Lives of Women Managers. *British Journal of Management* 9 (s1): 37–50.

Starich, Megan L. 2007. The 2006 Revisions to Japan's Equal Opportunity Employment Law: A Narrow Approach to a Pervasive Problem. *Pacific Rim Law & Policy Journal.* 16 (2): 551–578.

Tachibanaki, Toshiaki. 2010. *The New Paradox for Japanese Women: Greater Choice, Greater Inequality*. Translated by Mary E. Foster. Tokyo: International House of Japan.

Takahashi, Mayumi. 2014. Ideological Dilemmas: Constructing Motherhood through Caring Consumption in Japan. *Young Consumers* 15 (1): 84–93.

UN CEDAW. 2015. Consideration of Reports Submitted by States Parties under Article 18 of the Convention on the Elimination of All Forms of Discrimination against Women. *August 3*: 2015 http://tbinternet.ohchr.org/.

UN CEDAW. 2016. *Alternative Report of the New Japan Women's Association on the Implementation of the Convention on the Elimination of All Forms of Discrimination against Women in Japan for the Consideration of Japan's 7th and 8th Periodic Reports by the Committee on the Elimination of Discrimination against Women*. January 9. http://tbinternet.ohchr.org/.

Wajcman, Judy. 2006. Technocapitalism Meets Technofeminism: Women and Technology in a Wireless World. *Labour & Industry: A Journal of the Social and Economic Relations of Work* 16 (3): 7–20.

Yamada, Kazuyo. 2009. Past and Present Constraints on Labor Movements for Gender Equality in Japan. *Social Science Japan Journal* 12 (2): 195–209.

# 9

## Sexism and the Wow Girl: A Study of Perceptions of Women in World of Warcraft

Thaiane Oliveira, Reynaldo Gonçalves, Alessandra Maia, Julia Silveira, and Simone Evangelista

The purpose of this chapter is to discuss sexuality in the game World of Warcraft (WoW) and the female representation in specialized game reviews. For that, we focus on the WoW Girl website which is the main source of information about WoW in Brazil and is managed exclusively by women. Thus, this work investigates how Brazilian players perceive the relationship between in-game sexuality and women's participation in the spaces of opinion formation on games.

WoW has been in the market for ten years. In a revenue report referring to the second quarter of 2014 published by Activision Blizzard (Vieira 2015), the company revealed that WoW currently has 5.6 million active subscribers, with no indication of the percentage of male and female players. Women are a strong presence in this epic and engaging allegory through the image of heroines, cunning and charismatic warriors, powerful goddesses, and brutal villains. However, according to data collected during this investigation, the female representation found in the game does not exclude in-game male-dominant behavior, known as *machismo* in Brazil. This type of behavior is an archaic conduct, considered a sexist cult of aggressive masculinity, defined as

This chapter was translated into English by Patricia Matos, translator and PhD student at Federal Fluminense University, Niterói, Brazil.

T. Oliveira (✉) • R. Gonçalves • J. Silveira • S. Evangelista
Federal Fluminense University, Rio de Janeiro, Brazil

A. Maia
State University of Rio de Janeiro, Rio de Janeiro, Rio de Janeiro, Brazil

a type of sexual and physical conquest (Lancaster 1994). This hegemonic model of masculinity constructed from patriarchal values is a target of criticism and currently co-exists with more flexible models of male gender identity.

A study conducted by Avon Institute/Data Popular revealed worrisome data on sexism in Brazil. In a survey made with 1029 women and 1017 men, the results indicate that 96% of respondents consider that they live in a sexist (male-dominated) society, although deeply rooted and hidden in traditional practices (Gonzalez 2014) where independent women are seen as responsible for the housework and family financial support. This male supremacy attitude in Brazilian society is still predominant and this is believed to be linked to virile masculinity, competition, and violence. As an example, we can mention the studies by Fátima Cecchetto (2004), which focus on young people from Rio de Janeiro (Brazil) engaged in funk dances and jiu-jitsu fights. Based on this audience, she points out the intrinsic relationship between violence and male identity, which is reinforced through competitive practices.

In this context, games are configured as another relevant arena to the manifestation of sexism, despite (or because of) a growing increase in women's participation among Brazilian players. According to the Game Brazil survey (2015) conducted by Sioux consulting, women accounted for about 47% of Brazilian players in 2015. Therefore, the hypothesis discussed in this study is that sexuality in Brazil is a complex cultural issue in a period of transition and, therefore, the understanding of women's participation in the game and as specialist critics is controversial and reflects the multiplicity of views on the subject, both for men and women.

As Usva Friman (2015) stated in the article *The Concept and Research of Gendered Game Culture*, "the first step in this process and the study of gendered game culture in general is to clarify how the concept of gendered game culture itself is understood within the context of academic game studies" (Friman 2). Friman analyzed the titles and abstracts from over a thousand articles and papers published between 2001 and 2014 and found out that only 40 dealt with gender issues.

The competition in Massively Multiplayer Online Role-Playing Game (MMORPG) is one of the male's main motivations to engage in this game genre, as opposed to women's interest more focused on the sociability (Yee 2009). In this scenario, it is important to conduct further study on the *machismo* manifested within the game world, especially for players whose culture endorses this type of hierarchical behavior over women, as it is the case in Brazil. This study focuses mainly on the player's behavior which vary significantly, always reflecting the cultural essence of our society since, as

defended by Johan Huizinga (1996), the game is born of the culture and cannot be separated from it.

In his work, Huizinga points out that games have their own spatial and
temporal universe which determines the frontiers between the game world
and the common world or the rest of the world. This concept emerges in a
passage of the medievalist's book where he writes that "the special and extraor-
dinary feature of a game is illustrated in a notorious way by the aura of mystery in which it frequently involves itself... Inside the magical circle, the laws
and traditions of everyday life lose validity. We are different and we do different things" (Huizinga 1996, 15–16). The concept of magical circle has been
widely discussed in the field of games study, mostly regarding the frontiers
that separate the games from the common world. Recent theories consider the
magical circle a mediating tool between the two worlds in question. Juul
(2005) considers that the magical circle is formed not only by the structures
of rules built by the games, but it also needs the players to reaffirm the illusion
of the constructed world—the circle's edges are constantly negotiated and
defined by the players themselves. Therefore, we are talking about a negotiation between the game universe and the ordinary world, which does not represent an alternation of "worlds" where the laws and the mores of the everyday
life lose validity. On the contrary, what we have observed is precisely a reproduction of these costumes in the digital environment, as we'll learn throughout this chapter. Such questions match what Lori Kendall (2002) has also
observed through an ethnographic research in the multiuser domain (MUD)
BlueSky, which testifies the social dynamics, masculine cultures, and hierarchies of power reproduced in the digital environment.

As reported by Gray (2014), who analyzes gender and race issues as a hierarchical social structure—or a social fabric of social order—video games "have
manifested stereotypical manners that fit within the hegemonic notions of
what it means to be a person of color or what it means to be a woman" (4). The
author also mentions Omi and Winant's (1993) approach who define this logic
as "a schema wherein racialized ideas, bodies, and structures are constructed,
mediated and presented through a safe medium". Still according to her,
although these processes are a contemporary issue of study, the Gramscian
concept of hegemony can still be used to understand how the maintenance of
the dominant ideology is guaranteed through its reproduction in cultural institutions. In that sense, she seeks a perspective that does not look specifically at
masculinity, but focuses on hegemonic masculinity, seen as "a construction
process, not simply as a set of expectations or an identity" (Gray 2014, 19).
Thus, the dominant narratives in most video game constructs and maintains
this hegemony as a privilege, as a guarantee of power, that marginalizes other

gamers. In the specific case of video games, the social hierarchization of sexual differences begins when "heroines are few within video games" and "most female characters [...] are highly stereotypical" (Gray 2014, 17). Since we verify *machismo* in male players' behavior in WoW, the interest of this study is to understand what motivates it, both in-game and out-game, and its consequences to the players. Therefore, it is necessary to understand the origins of *machismo* in Brazil and its peculiar formation in Brazilian culture to analyze how it affects the contemporary representations and experiences of women in Brazil, in the digital or offline environment.

## Machismo and Women's Resistance in the Brazilian History

Historically, there is no concrete information on the origins of *machismo* in Brazil, but Brazilian society is born from the confluence of the Portuguese invaders, indigenous peoples, and Africans recruited and brought as slaves (Ribeiro 1995). Therefore, to understand the roots of *machismo* in Brazilian society, it is also necessary to understand the heritage of patriarchal patterns of these three basic influences of Brazilian culture. As pointed out by DeSouza et al. (2000), during the process of colonization, the Portuguese brought their cultural baggage of patriarchy and settled in Brazil through the domination of the land and of the women by force.

As well as supremacy of their strength and power, the colonizers had sex without consent with indigenous and later with African slaves, which produced a high miscegenation in the Brazilian people (Van Den Berghe 1967), an ethnic characteristic prevalent today. Also, according to DeSouza et al. (2000: 486), "when white women arrived during the Colonial era, they kept the archetypal model of Mary, they were asexual; their lives restricted to the limits of the house or the church. Women were stereotyped as weak, submissive, passive and powerless in the public sphere."

The Amerindian natives also have a patriarchal structure, as stated by Darcy Ribeiro (1995):

> The family is centered in patricentric and polygynic structure, dominated by the chief as a domestic group of people of various generations; essentially, the father, his wives with their offspring and relatives of them. The Indian women linked to the group as captives were concubines of the father and his sons. Only gradually, the religious marriage is imposed as sacredness of the mother of legitimate children. (Ribeiro 1995, 368)

Currently, this family and patriarchal structure has been gradually reformed. In indigenous villages, many women have begun to act in community decisions and have been holding important political positions in public spheres that were until recently unthinkable for Brazilian indigenous woman.

As one of the three ethnic and racial elements in the composition of Brazilian culture, African culture imposed traces of their structuring virility, including the *quilombos*[1] formed after the escape from the big senzalas.[2] However, due to the slavery model, black families were forced to reformulate their own cultural and symbolic structures. There was no gender distinction for the work carried out by slaves because everybody performed the same hard work and exploitation took away humanity from African men and women.

After Slavery Abolition in 1888, the spaces of action for the black women (and some stories of resistance) were strict to what their position allowed: household work and as a sex object. In addition, black African women, when freed from slavery, moved to the matrifocal role, being responsible for maintaining their cultural traditions from generation to generation, and are seen currently in cultural spaces, such as "trays of Bahia" (Dos Anjos 2007).[3]

In his work *O que faz o brasil, Brasil?* (What makes Brazil, Brazil?), DaMatta (1986) identifies as a remarkable feature of Brazilian culture a dichotomous separation between public and private space, or more specifically, between "home" and "street", understood not only as physical locations, but "spaces where we can judge, classify, measure, evaluate and decide on actions, people, relationships, and morals" (Damatta 1986, 33). Also, according to the author, each of these spheres imposes on individuals its specific values and visions and if analyzed together they allow us to understand Brazilian society more broadly.

The private space of the house corresponds to what is good, beautiful, and "above all, decent", in contrast to collective dwellings as "prisons, dormitories, apartments, hotels and motels" (Damatta 1986, 27). The transition between the public and private spheres is historically more difficult for females, either by moralist conventions or the overload of tasks and demands for women in the home. Thus, still according to the theory mentioned above, women "from the streets" are seen and hence treated differently, judged by a different value system than the notion of honor, decency, and purity household.

But all this analysis brings specificities according to race and class features. White women from the elite had a reputation to show. Lots of them were locked up in convents—or in hospices in extreme cases—where the purity and/or "honor" were guaranteed by institutionalized encasement. Married white women, in turn, used to live under the yoke of the spouse who controlled every aspect of her life and sociability. Black women, on the other hand, were seen as a collective property, belonging to the public space, the sphere of the street, work, pleasure, and sex—in opposition to the houses, churches, and convents. Since the beginning of the Portuguese colonization of Brazil, race and social class are intrinsically linked and this social heritage explains why black women still experience intersections of oppression.

The history of women's struggle for rights in Brazil is not linear, nor can it be understood from a unique perspective, class, or ethnicity. As an organized movement, feminism first appeared in Brazil in a more concrete form in the twentieth century, strongly inspired by women's movements in Europe and the United States, but with specificities, influenced by the nation's slavery past, landlordism system, and strong Christian religious conservatism as a political force and social control.

This first wave of feminism fought for the right to vote and was restricted to the typical middle class, the white bourgeoisie formed by more educated women, who had access to newspapers, travel, and/or foreign cultures (Toscano and Goldenberg 1992; Freitas 2016). Despite gaining the right to vote in 1932, through the Electoral Code consolidated in the 1934 Brazilian Constitution, the feminists of this first cycle have been criticized throughout history, especially by anarchist militants, for their "narrow agenda" and "elitist and exclusively white struggle".

According to a research made with the analysis of magazines and newspapers published in the first decades of the twentieth century, it was possible to observe the rise of a "sexist fury" in the Brazilian journalism at that time, due to the increase in feminist discussions in the agenda. In these articles from local magazines, it was normal to satirize and characterize feminist women as hysterical, ugly, mannish, or unloved. This behavior "resulted in a misidentification, mischaracterization and the dilution of the political nature of the movement" (Ferreira 1996, 158). Such events, also noted by other researchers like Ellen Carol DuBois (1999), show what Elizabeth Badinter (1997) claims about the social construction of the ideal manhood. Defined in opposition to femininity, this prevalence of the *machista* behavior occurs, especially, when some social changes in gender roles occur and they disrupt male references, resulting in the need for self-assertion among men. This can be explained by the idea of Social Drama, proposed by Victor Turner (1979). According to the author, in times of social transformation, there can be the emergence of practices that seek to subvert order through the inversion of roles manifested in grotesque and sense of humor. A "magical mirror" is established, a "mirror" that not only reflects reality, but also calls for a reflection on this projected reality (Dawsey 2005). Such assumption has an intrinsic relation with the idea of the magical circle discussed before.

The idea of gender hierarchies is also present in the digital world, in which sexist attitudes are reproduced through the technological apparatus and the use of mockery and insults (Abreu 2014). The relations, negotiations, and disputes held in the cyberspace are not immune to the sexist dynamics rooted in the Brazilian culture and women also face harassment and restrictions to their presence and actions in the digital environment. That happens because "diminishing individuals so they do not occupy the same space of power is still, online or offline, an aspect of a society that yet has not overcome many of its old social discourses" (Abreu 2014, 743).

Back to a historical approach, the second feminist wave, as identified by Freitas (2016), refers to the 1960s and 1970s and its motto is "the personal is political". In Brazil, this second wave was postponed and simultaneously contributed to the political resistance against the military dictatorship regime, even without a clear definition of what represented the female participation in armed struggle. As Cynthia Sarti points out that:

> The presence of women in armed struggle involves not only rebelling against the existing political order, but represented a major transgression with what was designate at the time for women. Without a deliberate feminist proposal, the activists denied the place traditionally assigned to women by take sexual behavior that put into question the virginity and the institution of marriage, "behaving like men," taking up arms and experiencing success in this behavior. (Sarti 1998, 3)

According to research conducted by the author, this gender equality was mostly rhetoric, and women found other causes to fight for, such as the one against the political system that made use of sexual violence. This rhetoric of equality began to turn into an effective struggle only in the late 1970s with the political amnesty, which allowed the return of some women exiled in Europe influenced by Marxist feminists such as Simone de Beauvoir.

The renewal of the literature on the subject, which began with the publication of the classic *Le Deuxième Sexe* (The Second Sex) by Simone de Beauvoir, influenced decisively the new conceptions and activist actions. In this context, an important dialogue emerged between political and feminist theories, sociology, psychology, anthropology, Marxism and some segments of philosophy (Biroli and Miguel 2012, 7). In addition to deepening the discussion on women and public and private spaces, issues such as reproductive rights and rights to the own body and sexuality gained visibility, especially due to the advent of the contraceptive pill, which in practice allowed the autonomy and separation among maternity, pregnancy, and female sexuality. That's when violence against women, mainly practiced by their partners, started to be questioned and discussed, represented by the slogan "the one who loves doesn't kill".

In the 1980s, according to the aforementioned author, women's movements were divided into groups: the ones who move away from state organizations and the segments that decide to dialogue with them occupying spaces, positions, and institutional responsibilities—under penalty of being criticized for an alleged co-optation. In this context, academic feminism gains visibility, as we can tell from the increasing number of research on the subject in Brazil (Freitas 2016). "Feminism was no longer something practiced in small and specific groups", becoming "something more diffuse, permeating many areas of society" (Toscano and Goldenberg 1992, 41).

Finally, from the 1990s onwards, a third wave comes, identified by Freitas (2016) as the "difference feminism". The distinctions between men and women are stated, but not seen as inequalities anymore. Amid the identity fragmentation processes, features such as class, race, gender identity, and sexual orientation began to be considered and addressed in collective struggles, creating temporary units and strategic coalitions. Feminists start to claim multi-thematic movements, dialoguing with other social demands, and are broken down into several sections with principles not always reconcilable. These reconfigurations and complex groups and disputes are reconfigured and amplified over the internet and cyberfeminist movements—that started in the 1980s and has become a fundamental part of contemporary activism in Brazil, mainly from the 2010s through the increasing use of new media. As it occurred before, self-affirming manhood manifestations also became stronger as feminist protests grew on new media, generating new ways of reassurance of the sexist culture still hegemonic in the country.[4]

## Sexuality in Game Culture and the Emergence of WoW Girl

Guided by social relations and structures that refer to colonization, gender relations in Brazil were strongly influenced by factors such as slavery and segregation of women to certain spaces in the public and private spheres. Despite the history of feminist struggles and increasing discussions related to *machismo*, sexuality is still a complex cultural issue in a period of transition. In this context, some useful insights may appear on reflections about how sexism is manifested in games, since game culture is also being questioned worldwide on this issue.[5]

Since the Gamergate controversy, there have been many discussions about gender relations within the gaming universe. Persecution of developers and of game writers, including rape and death threats, currently pervades the world of gaming, and consequently the specialized critique. These allegations point out to the existence of a movement that aims to prevent women's freedom of speech in the games industry by organizing themselves globally through threats and blackmail of women critics and developers in the video game community (Kendall-Morwick 2015). This movement has been successful and is growing around the world at a time when the active participation of women in search for their place in the technology industry becomes increasingly necessary (Chess and Shaw 2015).

In Brazil, this combative space against male hegemony resonates with some particularities in the specialist game reviews. One of these initiatives is the WoW Girl website, written exclusively by women, aimed initially at reviews of the game WoW. The page was created in 2007 by the gamer Lorraine Boyer, who used the pseudonym Lorie. At the time, there was not much information in Portuguese about the game, even with the Brazilian community growing. With this growing demand in Brazil, Lorie began to translate and produce unique content in this language. Quickly, the blog became a place of reference on the game in Brazil, as the mechanics of this genre of game exceed the gameplay and therefore the player needs a supportive off game community, participating in forums and many other interactive tools with the game world on the internet, to expand the experience (Yee 2009).

Since its creation, as the name suggests directly, WoW Girl is formed exclusively of women contributing to the production of content and administration of the site (though eventually it would welcome a man as a guest). Despite the many male requests in the comments of the forums, men are not allowed in the administrative body and among employees. However, the site is a reference especially for its contents about general issues of the game and not a space for the feminist militancy. Such a stand can be considered a marketing strategy in order to reach a wider audience, interested in any genre.

## Sexism in WoW Girl

Since its inception, as the name suggests directly, WoW Girl is composed exclusively of women, with regard to the production of content and administration of the site, eventually with a man as a guest. Although many male requests in the comments of forums, men are not allowed in the administrative body and between employees.

Despite this explicit targeting the editorial board of the site, it never demotivated the presence of male readers. There are 533 members subscribers in the site forum. Eleven percent (58) say they are female, 60% (320) were male, and 29% (155) did not identify the sex, or stand as the genre of characters, which already denotes that sexuality is not a matter of extreme importance since a significant portion does not present their gender, but by the character of the game.

The editorial staff and collaborators generate content through articles, game analysis, and views on various issues relevant to the game or other matters of interest to the community. A search based on keywords related to gender, it was identified only five posts content where sexism is showing evident on the site[6]:

- *Women in World of Warcraft*, posted by Lorie on June 2, 2008 (a *machist* strip that shows that women take 24 hours to build a character);
- *Rose does not give XP,* on International Women's Day posted by Alessandra on March 8, 2013, after gamergate case (and when Lorie went to Blizzard);
- *Because WoW is also something for woman,* posted by Milena, on May 9, 2013;
- *Guide to learn to lose to a girl and not cry,* posted by Milena in July 4, 2014;
- *Toxic player, Do not Be this guy!,* posted by Milena in August 20, 2015, in which he talks about toxic behaviors among them, a topic with the caption *"Your sexual organ is not license to be a jerk with the other"*.

Most of the content is about issues related to gameplay and game information using universal language without gender characterizations embedded in the construction of speech, except in isolated cases, such as the posts indicated above. The silencing regarding gender issues is the result of hegemonic social practices over the last centuries that led, through sexism, to the silencing of women in the society. To have a space to advocate in a men-filled environment would mean to call upon extreme reactions from readers and self-assertion from male player, especially because in the current social structure specialized critique is legitimized only by men, as pointed out by Elizabeth Badinter (1997). We can observe some of extreme reactions as from readers of Wow Girl, when the subject portrayed in posts refers to sexism, especially when the approach is feminist, the behavior of readers is completely changed, indicating a strong growing radical polarization:

*Nowadays, women, according to the feminist project, are not trying to be directly treated equal to men, but are trying to overcome men in many cases. (…) It does not mean that you are weak, but rather that biologically speaking, women are not prepared to adapt to the world of virtual games as men. (Fernando, reader of WowGirl)*

Despite the success and their relevance to the achievement of women in the gaming communities in Brazil, the WoW Girl's publishing guidelines have a clear concern not to reinforce some cultural myths surrounding the image and presence of women in the creation process and acceptance of the site from readers. For them, the intellectual impulse and content generation should not be linked to the gender for those who produce, so any reference to sexuality should not be exalted, even though in some posts such position is not clear, as we have argued in an interview attempt with the administrators.[7]

## Methodology

In order to investigate how Brazilian players understand the relationship between sexuality and gender in-game and how women's participation in the spaces of opinion formation on games is perceived by these players, this research sought to understand how the website WoW Girl, formed exclusively by women, became one of the biggest references about the game in Brazil. Hence, it was targeted only on its users and visitors and aimed at understanding the relations between gender and the WoW game. Therefore, there are questions focused on understanding not only the respondents' experience with the website, but also their interaction with the game, and four questions meant to analyze the users' profiles.

The respondents were told that their anonymity would be preserved, so they could have more freedom to answer the questions that could be considered controversial, related to in-game sexuality. In the questionnaire, the researchers' e-mail addresses were provided, for questions, suggestions and in case the respondents had further interest in the research.

Before implementation of the survey on the WoW Girl forums[8] and on social media, such as Facebook groups focused on the game's universe and RPGs generally, the surveys were pre-tested by four volunteers, among them were researchers and gamers, in order to adjust the questions to be as clear and direct as possible. By the end of the pre-test, and considering that the goal was to do a qualitative research and not quantitative, the questionnaire was rebuilt in a way that would provide more freedom to the answers. It had six open questions, four closed questions and one Likert scale with 16 questions. Seeking to understand the relation between gender, consumption and the in-game and out-game experience, the six open questions were divided in two themes: the gamers consumption regarding the WoW Girl website and their experience as a gamer when playing the WoW. On the theme part related to the website, the questions were focused on what type of content the gamers tend to read and comment, in order to find out how the consumption of information and users' engagement is structured in these spaces. We also asked about the respondents' opinions regarding the fact that the website in produced exclusively by women. About the in-game experience, the focus was to ascertain possible sexist and offensive behavior from other gamers due to the chart gender choices of the respondents from this research. So, we sought to explore the choices of the characters' gender in the game and their motivation, providing a space to report offensive in-game situations.

This being a qualitative study, the number of respondents necessary was not limited a priori but according to their availability, as it was considered to be important to explore the potential of the open answers, that is to say, it would be more useful for the research to be closed when it was found the repetition of the answers to the six questions. The survey was open for two weeks, from 15th to 22nd of September, 2015. In total, 26 people answered the questionnaire. However, one answer was voided because it was filled out incorrectly with random spelling and it made no sense.

## The Sexuality In-game and Out-game

Assuming that the MMORPG game experience goes beyond the magic circle of the game and includes out-game experience as participation (Yee 2009), our main goal is to identify the position of the players and readers of the site WoW Girl on the issue of gender and sexuality both in-game as well as in the critical spaces of the website. Therefore, we realize that, despite the fact that it is an important space for woman's representation, just a few female players are active in the spaces of in-game and out of the game, such as forums and game communities.

Among 25 respondents, only six were women. Of these six, four evaluated the website positively and exalted the aspect of representation of women, because "*as a woman and a WoW player I'm very happy to see that the WoW Girl is composed of women and has become one of the largest reference sites in Brazil*" (Respondent Eemya). One of the respondents considers the fact indifferent and thinks the website's stance is sexist because "*the other sites, even if it is made almost only for boys, don't prohibit girls to write, you see some girls in their teams. I do not like this segregation thing. It is good to have a feminine space, but not when it creates opposite sides, prohibitions, lack of inclusion … I think these things do not help. If we stay in this story of "girls talking to girls" and "girls only interested in girls talk", we only create more barriers*" (Respondent Elune).

In relation to the male audience (19 respondents), ten respondents considered women's participation in the game as positive and encouraging as well as being "*important to fight prejudice from the machismo that is present in all areas, including virtual games*" (Respondent Frozad). Nine male respondents consider it indifferent, because "*if the content was produced by murlocs, then yes I would think this otherworldly!*" (Respondent David), after all, "*we no longer live in the medieval age…*" (Respondent Null). Given these responses, we observed that the issue of representation is something evident, considering that the initiative is a political act of extreme importance to combat sexism in- and out-game, regardless of the respondent's gender. However, when asked openly about their opinion on the WoW Girl website, the issues of gender and sexuality were not even mentioned, with the words "information", "actuality", "reference", and "content", highlighted in the responses. Such fact shows the efficiency in the silencing of gender issues in the Brazilian specialized critique. Because gender issues are not evident in the speech and on the reports written by the collaborators, it allows the WoW Girl website to gain the public's recognition, formed mainly by men.

Regarding the performance in the game, the six women interviewed said they preferred to play with female characters, because "*it is a matter of identification and female empowerment, since I am a woman*" (respondent Suelen). On the other hand, among the male players, ten prefer to play with male characters because of gender identification in ordinary life; five of them said they were indifferent and played with characters of both genders; four said they prefer to play mostly with female characters, pointing out that the aesthetics of these are more pleasant and beautiful, reinforcing female stereotyped as aesthetical admiration object.

From the six female respondents, four stated they had felt offended in game situations, two related to sexism and two related to the gameplay without reference to gender. Among the 19 male respondents, 12 indicated that they had never felt offended during the game, six were offended in relation to their gameplay and the fact of being a *noob*, and only one claimed to have witnessed *machismo* and homophobia in the game. Of course, working with such a small sample does not open possibilities for further comparisons and the inflections proposed here does not lead to an understanding of the in-game experiences, but point to a discrepancy concerning offenses, especially when related to gender and sexual orientation.

Still seeking to build a comparative table on a Likert scale, in order to establish a filter by gender, we observed a significant difference when comparing responses between genders. One example is in relation to the term "rape the boss", a common term used among MMORPG players, the meaning of which is equivalent to destroying and annihilating an enemy. The term has been discussed in various spheres, including among gamers in various forums, in relation to <rape culture, as currently debated in Brazil in various spheres.

The notion of rape culture became popular recently in the country and defines a society that not only tolerates sexual violence against women but also encourages and reinforces it. The concept was coined by US feminists in the 1960s and has been used in Brazil by militancy, which criticizes the blaming of raped women for sexual violence from their behavior (Rost and Vieira 2015, 267).

As we can see in the chart (see Fig. 9.1), the term "rape the boss" widely used in the in-game affects more women than men. Sixty percent of the women interviewed relate the expression to gender, while 55% of men deny any allusion to the non-consensual sexual act (Fig. 9.2).

Still, in relation to safety, there is a relative difference between the responses compared by gender. While women are divided on this matter, only 5% of respondents agree that men prefer not to inform the gender in-game to avoid conflict with other players (Fig. 9.3).

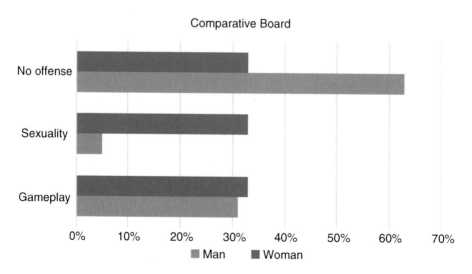

**Fig. 9.1** Comparative board between male and female respondents

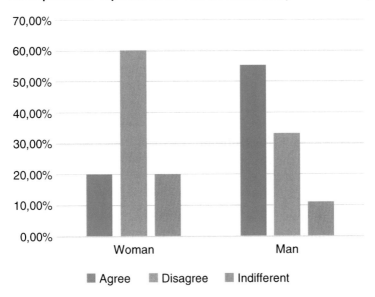

Fig. 9.2 Reactions to expression "rape the boss"

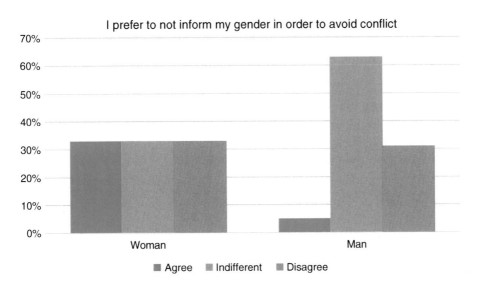

Fig. 9.3 Gender and safety

# Final Considerations

The issue is complex and there is still much to be unfolded from the in-game behavior on gender performance in Brazil, whose cultural values are reflected in the game. In-game *Machismo* is one of the cultural reflections of Brazilian society. In this sense, women point out feelings of insecurity and discomfort from terms and behaviors so widespread both in the game and outside of the game, as well as in ordinary life. We can see that there is not a separation between the physical and digital environments, like Huizinga suggested referring to the magical circle of the game, in which we are different and, therefore, we can do different things. Instead, oppressive behavior is reproduced and even going unnoticed and unchallenged. Women are often harassed and offended because of their gender or their ability in gameplay, but that doesn't make them give up their identity claims, choosing feminists charts, for example. In the same way, even if men do not acknowledge their in-game sexist attitude—an issue that requires further research—it is possible to notice men's indifference about everyday social practices that instigate offensive and sexist propagations, such as the expression "rape the boss" or even the objectification of women by the character's choices just to provide aesthetic pleasure to men.

As every culture is dynamic and societies are constantly changing, these issues have been discussed in several areas. In this sense, we believe that the critique is one of those possible performance spaces to reflect on the hegemonic behavior and deconstruct certain values taken as standard. However, as we have seen, the WoW Girl website, despite being a space exclusively produced by women and a place for female representation, does not take this political position, as the commercial interest in reaching a wide audience is larger than its political activities. In a way, the social dynamics from outside the magical circle of the game are reproduced in the ordinary world (Juul 2005). Part of this silencing is the result of centuries of oppression where women are not fit develop critical judgment in some fields socially recognized as male—by men themselves. Thus, the silencing of issues related to women and gender in these specialized critics fields indicates the naturalization of sexism in society as a way to avoid conflicts and gender dispute with the hegemonic public.

# Notes

1. This chapter was translated into English by Patricia Matos, translator and PhD student at Federal Fluminense University, Niterói, Brazil.
2. *Quilombos* were places of refuge for African slaves and African descents.

3. *Senzalas* were the accommodations that harbored the African slaves in old farmhouses or manor houses.

4. Being regarded as a slave commodity for 400 years, black Africans were decimated and, despite their high strength, were suppressed in Brazilian historiography. In 2004, a curriculum reform was proposed for the inclusion of African history in basic education, so far focused only on European history. This reformulation created the National Curriculum Guidelines for the Education of Racial-Ethnic Relations and the Teaching of African and Afro-Brazilian Culture. In 2011, public policies were established to fight racism still strongly present in Brazilian society.

5. An example of such attitude, the campaign #meuamigosecreto that exposed daily sexist behavior through testimonials on social media sites, which generated important debates, was appropriated by groups against feminism. In retaliation, the hashtag #minhaamigasecreta was created to vilify feminists on the same spaces. The hashtags #meuamigosecreto and #minhaamigasecreta (My secret friend, in Portuguese) refer to the Secret Santa tradition where usually people describe others without mentioning their names before giving them gifts. In this case, the use of the hashtags consisted of pointing out friend's and acquaintances' sexist or feminist behavior without mentioning their names.

6. Although sexist attitudes are not prevalent among all male players, it is not hard to see in-game statements imprint sexist, homophobic and racial (Higgins 2015). Statements such as "women do not know how to play" or "lost the game for a woman", among others, are very common in the game universe.

7. http://www.wowgirl.com.br/2008/06/02/mulheres-no-world-of-warcraft/, http://www.wowgirl.com.br/2013/03/08/dia-da-mulher-rosa-nao-da-xp/, http://www.wowgirl.com.br/2013/05/09/porque-wow-tambem-e-coisa-de-mulherzinha/, http://www.wowgirl.com.br/2014/07/03/guia-para-aprender-a-perder-de-uma-menina-e-nao-chorar/#comment-1469800052, http://www.wowgirl.com.br/2015/08/20/jogador-toxico-nao-seja-esse-cara/.

8. During the process of collecting data about the site, we contacted the managers in order to interview them and therefore gather more relevant information to this research. Also, we asked for permission and collaboration for the dissemination of a survey, which was designed to address gender issues in the WoW universe. One of the managers informed us about the editorial position with respect to this research, claiming that they would help us if we changed the term sexuality in the survey. Since one of the bases of feminist struggle lies precisely in gender equality, which meets the principles of what had been said to us by the manager, we agreed with the possible changes regarding the use of terms directly related to sexuality. However, we never got replies from members of the website, even after a few attempts. Later, our survey was taken down from the forum and our profile deleted without further explanation.

# Bibliography

Badinter, Elisabeth. 1997. *XY: On Masculine Identity*. New York: Columbia University Press.

Biroli, Flávia, and Miguel, Luis Felipe (Org.). 2012. *Teoria Política Feminista: Abordagens Brasileiras*. Vinhedo/SP: Editora Horizonte.

Cecchetto, Fátima Regina. 2004. *Violência e Estilos de Masculinidade*. Rio de Janeiro: FGV Editora.

Chess, Shira, and Adrienne Shaw. 2015. A Conspiracy of Fishes, or, How We Learned to Stop Worrying about #Gamergate and Embrace Hegemonic Masculinity. *Journal of Broadcasting & Electronic Media* 59 (1): 208–220.

DaMatta, Roberto. 1986. *O Que Faz o Brasil, Brasil?* Rio de Janeiro: Rocco.

Dawsey, John. 2005. Victor Turner e antropologia da experiência. *Cadernos de Campo (São Paulo, 1991)* 13 (13): 163–176.

de Abreu, Carla. 2014. Géneros y sexualidades no heteronormativas en las redes sociales digitales. 393 f. Tese (Doutorado em "Artes y Educación") – Facultad de Bellas Artes, Universitad de Barcelona, Barcelona, Spain.

DeSouza, Eros, Baldwin R. John, Da Rosa, and Francisco Heitor. 2000. A Construção Social dos Papéis Sexuais Femininos. *Psicologia: Reflexão e Crítica* 13 (3): 485–496.

Dos Anjos, Suelen Gonçalves. 2007. Cultura e Tradições Negras no Mesquita: um Estudo sobre a Matrifocalidade Numa Comunidade Remanescente de Quilombo. *Padê: Estudos em Filosofia, Raça, Gênero e Direitos Humanos* 1.1.

DuBois, Ellen Carol. 1999. *Feminism and Suffrage: The Emergence of an Independent Women's Movement in America, 1848–1869*. New York: Cornell University Press.

Ferreira, Verônica. 1996. Entre Emancipadas e Quimera – Imagens do feminismo no Brasil. *Cadernos AEL* 2 (3/4): 153–200.

Freitas, Rita. 2016. *Feminisms and Social Movements*. Class of extension course, Federal Fluminense University. Class notes.

Friman, Usva. 2015. The Concept and Research of Gendered Game Culture. In *Proceedings of DiGRA 2015: Diversity of Play: Games – Cultures – Identities*.

Gonzalez, Débora de Fina. 2014. Entre Público, Privado e Político: Avanços das Mulheres e Machismo Velado no Brasil. *Cadernos de Pesquisa* 44 (151): 239–243.

Gray, Kishonna L. 2014. *Race, Gender, and Deviance in Xbox Live: Theoretical Perspectives from the Virtual Margins*. London: Routledge.

Higgins, Alexander. 2015. *Cuties Killing Video Games: Gender Politics and Performance in Indie Game Developer Subculture*. PhD dissertation, Ohio University.

Huizinga, Johan. 1996. *Homo Ludens: O Jogo como Elemento da Cultura*. São Paulo: Perspectiva.

Juul, Jesper. 2005. *"Half-real." Video Games between Real Rules and Fictional Worlds*. Cambridge, MA: MIT Press.

Kendall, Lori. 2002. *Hanging Out in the Virtual Pub: Masculinities and Relationships Online*. Berkeley: University of California Press.

Kendall-Morwick, Joseph. 2015. The Need for Voices in CS to Address the# GamerGate Controversy. In *Proceedings of the 46th ACM Technical Symposium on Computer Science Education*. New York: ACM.

Lancaster, Roger N. 1994. *Life Is Hard: Machismo, Danger, and the Intimacy of Power in Nicaragua*. Oakland: University of California Press.

Omi, Michael, and Howard Winant. 1993. On the Theoretical Status of the Concept of Race. In *Race, Identity and Representation in Education*, ed. Cameron McCarthy and Warren Crichlow, 3–10. New York: Routledge.

Ribeiro, Darcy. 1995. *O Povo Brasileiro: Evolução e o Sentido do Brasil*. São Paulo: Companhia das Letras.

Rost, Mariana, and Miriam Steffen Vieira. 2015. Convenções de Gênero e Violência Sexual: A Cultura do Estupro no Ciberespaço. *Contemporanea – Revista de Comunicação e Cultura* 13 (2): 261–276.

Sarti, Cynthia A. 1998. *O Início do Feminismo Sob a ditadura no Brasil: o Que Ficou Escondido*. Paper presented at the XXI Congresso Internacional da LASA, Chicago, May 24–26, 1998.

Toscano, Moema, e Goldenberg, Mirian. 1992. *A Revolução das mulheres. Um balanço do Feminismo no Brasil*. Rio de Janeiro: Revan.

Turner, Victor. 1979. Frame, Flow and Reflection: Ritual and Drama as Public Liminality. *Japanese Journal of Religious Studies* 6: 465–499.

Van den Berghe, Pierre L. 1967. *South Africa, a Study in Conflict*. Oakland: University of California Press.

Vieira, Márlon. 2015. Activision Blizzard fatura us$ 850 milhões com 'Hearthstone' e 'Destiny' em 2014. *MMORPGBR*. Accessed February 2, 2015. http://mmorpgbr.com.br/activision-blizzard-fatura-us-850-milhoes-com-hearthstone-e-destiny-em-2014/.

Yee, Nick. 2009. Changing the Rules: Social Architectures in Virtual Worlds. In *Online Worlds: Convergence of the Real and Virtual*, ed. William Bainbridge, 213–223. London: Springer.

# 10

# With Great Power Comes Great Responsibility: Video Game Live Streaming and Its Potential Risks and Benefits for Female Gamers

## Lena Uszkoreit

Within the past five years, video game live streaming on Twitch and other streaming platforms has become a popular phenomenon that draws millions of viewers to their web browsers and mobile phones. Given the novelty of live streaming, few research projects have begun to tackle what could be the next big thing in media. Video games and the gamer community are notorious for skewing heavily male and are often referred to as toxic and misogynistic environments (Williams et al. 2009; Yee 2006; Taylor 2006).

This chapter aims to explore possible opportunities and risks video game live streaming ('streaming') might bear for the perception of female gamers as well as esports and gaming in general. The chapter will begin with a short overview of what streaming is and how Twitch, the most successful platform in Europe and the Americas, works. After this general introduction, the chapter will attempt to outline potential theories for framing and understanding Twitch and the perception of female streamers and gamers in online spaces. Three case studies will describe the channels of three female streamers in more detail. These case studies are specific examples which cannot be extrapolated to the general population of Twitch streamers. They can, however, provide a more detailed look at a few different types of streamers. The chapter will conclude with a final discussion of the risks and opportunities live streaming could have for the perception of female gamers and esports.

L. Uszkoreit (✉)
University of Ontario Institute of Technology, Oshawa, ON, Canada

© The Author(s) 2018
K. L. Gray et al. (eds.), *Feminism in Play*, Palgrave Games in Context,
https://doi.org/10.1007/978-3-319-90539-6_10

Given that there is little research on streaming, this chapter will provide the reader with an overview of the topic in question, as it is common for book chapters. It will, however, leave the reader informed about what streaming is, what role female streamers play, how the three streamers in question are perceived by the community, and what implications this might have for the perception of female gamers in the gaming community and esports. On Twitch, it is quite common to imitate strategies successful streamers employed to grow their channels' popularity. The three selected case studies are rather successful and have helped shape certain 'archetypes' of female streamers by creating strategies often copied by aspiring newcomers.

## How Does Streaming on Twitch Work?

A video game live stream or live broadcast on Twitch consists of four major elements: the screen showing the video game being played, a live audio or audio-visual commentary, a real-time stream chat, and the so-called 'stream overlay'. In addition, each channel also provides a static description often including additional information about the streamer hosting the channel, what games they play, their streaming schedule, and other social media profiles. Most recently, Twitch also added the option for streamers to publish channel updates to their community so that the channel profile becomes more similar to a Facebook or Twitter wall. While streaming happens live, recordings of broadcasts can be saved on the streaming platforms themselves or uploaded to YouTube and other video sharing platforms. All live streams are structured into categories. These are usually organized by the game being played on stream. In addition to video game live streaming, Twitch now also offers a 'Creative' stream category and the 'IRL' category. Both of these do not require streamers to provide gaming content. As the name implies, channels listed under the 'Creative' category mostly stream artistic or crafting content. 'IRL' is short for 'in real life' and is used to by gamers to designate the life outside of games. Hence, streaming under this category allows for any kind of content that doesn't fall under the categories of gaming or creative and usually entails streamers simply chatting with viewers or them streaming their every day life.

Twitch Interactive Inc., acquired by Amazon in 2014, started out running the broadcasting platform Justin.tv in 2011. In 2014, Twitch first crossed the 100 million unique monthly user mark (Twitch 2014) and on August 23rd, 2015, the number of concurrent viewers watching two major esports events streamed simultaneously peaked at 2,098,529 (Twitch 2015, 2016). According to numbers provided by Twitch to potential advertising clients,

75% of their viewers are male and 73% of them are between the ages 18 and 49 (Twitch 2015). These numbers demonstrate that watching people play video games has become a mass phenomenon.

Everyone can watch streams on Twitch without being registered or logged in to the site. However, only registered users can chat, follow, subscribe, and stream themselves.

Streamers who manage to build a large enough community around their channel can apply to the platform for 'partnership'. Viewers can subscribe to partnered streamers for five dollars per month. In general, the streamers receive approximately 50% of the subscription fees while the platform takes the other half. In addition, streamers get a certain percentage of advertising revenue generated by running ads on their channel. On top of receiving a percentage of advertising revenue, as well as their share of subscriber revenue, streamers can also be tipped by their viewers. Most streamers also accept donations from their viewers. These can range from small tips of a few dollars to large donations of thousands of dollars. As Twitch streamers attract larger amounts of recurring viewers, commercial partners often become interested in them as well. Some hardware companies and online game stores enter sponsorship contracts with successful streamers for promoting their products on stream.

## Trying to Get a Theoretical Handle on Twitch

As mentioned previously, there has not been a lot of research published about streaming, especially with a focus on gender. First, this section will provide a very brief discussion of previous research on Twitch and then go into more detail where it is more relevant to this chapter.

In 2012, Kaytoue et al. presented the first analysis of large-scale Twitch data and found that channel growth and popularity of streamers evolve in a predictable way. They also described mechanics for explaining why certain channels peak at specific number of viewers. Kaytoue et al.'s (2012) paper was the analysis of large-scale data on streaming on Twitch. Nascimento et al. (2014) successfully studied a large sample of data from Twitch channel chats to model chat activity, stream hopping, and churn, which describes how many viewers quit watching the specific stream. Pires and Simon (2015) presented analyses of a large Twitch dataset including broadcasters and viewers as well as what games were played. However, these analyses remain very much on the technical and descriptive side perhaps because many of them are published in the proceedings of network and multimedia systems-based conferences focusing on the technological aspects of video game live streaming platforms rather than social scientific perspectives.

It seems like there is a fascination with the opportunities the behavioral data collected through Twitch might offer but less of an interest into the quality of social interaction. One recent study on Twitch investigates the motivations behind watching Twitch from uses and gratifications perspective (Sjöblom and Hamari 2016). In a survey of $N = 1097$ Twitch viewers, the authors find a positive correlation between tension release as well as social integrative and affective motivations and the number of hours participants watch Twitch streams. Social integrative motivations, on the other hand, best explain subscription behavior. In other words, socializing with other viewers and the streamers seems an important motivation to take the step from being a viewer to becoming a subscriber and supporter of a specific stream. Despite the authors' efforts to explain motivations for watching Twitch, the lack of distinction between different channels and respective motivations to watch them appears to diminish the explanatory power of this study. Given the wide range of content provided by different Twitch streamers and what aspects of entertainment they focus on, it seems unlikely that motivations can be explained without specifying which channels viewers choose to watch, follow, and subscribe to. Even the highlighted streamers in this chapter feature such a broad range of content and possible distinct motivations to watch them.

Another recent study was conducted on comments by Twitch users in channel chats (Nakandala et al. 2017). The researchers found that comments on female identifying streamers' channels often included words unrelated to gaming such as 'boobs', 'babe', 'smile', or 'omg'. Viewers commenting in channels hosted by male identifying streamers, however, often used words such as 'melee', 'glitch', 'shields', or 'reset' that refer to the gaming content the streamer engages with. The researchers' sample is rather dated and lacks control over alternative explanations for why the investigated streams might encourage or punish certain words. Nevertheless, the overrepresented words on female identifying channels are clearly pointing toward an objectifying image of female streamers and demonstrate a lack of interest for their gameplay. These results resonate with a preliminary study conducted by the author of this chapter in 2014 which surveyed Twitch viewers. The study found that assumed criteria for success heavily differ for male and female streamers. Viewers believe that skill at the games played and an interesting personality are important factors for male streamers' success while physical attractiveness is the most important criterion for a female streamer's success (Uszkoreit 2015).

Another relevant paper studies Twitch as a place for community. Hamilton, Garretson, and Kerne (2014) explored Twitch streams and their communities.

The authors took a qualitative approach to an in-depth analysis of several Twitch streams and the communities they fostered. Hamilton et al. (2014) apply Oldenburg's conceptualization of the 'third place' to Twitch. Third places can be characterized as a place that is neither the home (first place) nor the workplace (second place) but rather a space which is meant first and foremost for conversation, communication, and community (Oldenburg 1997). One of the major characteristics of third places is that the status a member holds in the first and second places, such as age, affluence, educational degrees, is of no importance when conversing with other members. Third places level status. The authors argue that Twitch channels, with their particular subcultures formed around them, can be described as third places for the gaming community. In stream chats, members of the community come together to converse in a playful manner, their outside status does not play a role. If Twitch channels can be characterized as third places for the gaming community, the inclusion and representation of female streamers and viewers is essential for them playing a part in negotiating the rules, codes, and norms of the community. Participation requires women to be affected by the leveling function that ensures members' societal status in the real world to be of minor or no concern. However, by categorizing and quantifying the content of chat comments, Nakandala et al. (2017) demonstrate that, at least, streaming women are not perceived as just another member of the community.

## What Is Different About Female Streamers?

In an earlier study of Twitch streamers, I analyzed 32 streams at different times and found that the observed male and female streamers chose to present themselves quite differently on stream (Uszkoreit 2015). They also employed different strategies for attracting and retaining viewers. Not only did the female streamers in the study have larger camera feeds in relation to the size of the gameplay screen, they also provided more personal information in their profile, and put more effort into their appearance—make up, clothing, hair—as compared to the male streamers (Figs. 10.1 and 10.2). The perks for subscribing to a female streamer's channel included cosplay or playing a dancing game on stream as rewards for reaching global subscriber goals. Other rewards offered were access to voice chat exclusive to subscribers or the streamer promising to follow her loyal subscribers on Twitter and share her Snapchat with them. The rewards for subscribing can generally be described as dedicating more time and attention to subscribers which results in a feeling of exclusiveness that viewers (at least that is the plan) will then desire. Obviously, this

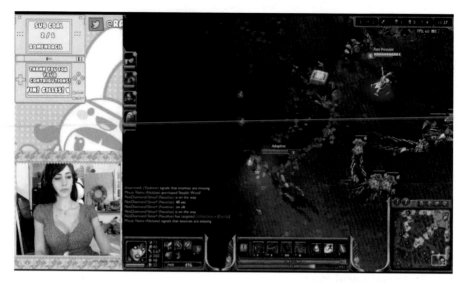

**Fig. 10.1** A female streamer playing League of Legends

**Fig. 10.2** A male streamer playing League of Legends

study was not representative for all Twitch streamers. However, the study looked at the streams with the most viewers for different types of popular games, and in many cases, newcomers try to imitate successful strategies. Therefore, studying the most successful streams will most likely be representative of a larger portion of streamers than actually observed.

In a second quantitative part of the study, I also found that there is a strong negative correlation between what viewers think to be important for a female streamer's success: personality or attractiveness. The same negative correlation was found for attractiveness and good gameplay as criteria for success (Uszkoreit 2015). This leads to the conclusion that many viewers either watch because they are interested in a female streamer's personality or her looks. Given the way the question was phrased, the results also imply that women on Twitch can either be attractive or have an entertaining personality but not both. This gives reason to believe that female Twitch streamers are often objectified—viewers perceive their bodies and especially their sexual body parts as disconnected from their personality and their person as a whole (Gervais et al. 2012). Heflick and Goldenberg (2009) found that sexually objectifying women can lead to perceiving them as less competent as well as less moral and warm. In a community, in which mastery over technology and increasing one's skill level at gaming become the main criteria for assessing and validating members, being perceived as less competent automatically revokes access to membership (Taylor 2015). Women are either tolerated for being attractive but not appreciated for their gaming skills and personality, or vice versa (Uszkoreit 2015).

Due to a plethora of reasons and mechanisms systematically excluding women from gaming and preventing them from improving their skills as well as professionalizing their gameplay (Taylor 2015), female gamers often struggle to compete on the same level with male gamers. Blatant sexual harassment, commonplace in gaming (Gray 2012; O'Leary 2012), is one of the more obvious puzzle pieces contributing to excluding women from gaming. If a woman cannot stream top level game play, she could likely be inclined to take the other route and be accepted into the community for her looks and sex appeal rather than her gameplay. However, with entering the male-dominated gaming community, women often assimilate to behavioral patterns more accepted within this community. Levy (2006) describes the rise of a new type of empowered woman within Western culture: the 'female chauvinist pig'. While the term might sound appalling at first, a closer look in Levy's reasoning provides a solid foundation for her claim. According to Levy (2006), female chauvinist pigs can be characterized as feeling empowered by the allegedly open public discourse on sexuality, the female body, and gender equality. Levy urges the reader to take caution, though, since in her opinion, these young women showing nudity and embracing crude sexual images are likely stuck in a trap. For example, a trap that provides only the illusion of empowerment and choice. The author iterates that our hypersexual society does not really offer women the choice to willingly engage in these behaviors but rather makes the 'choice' for them (Levy 2006). A similar phenomenon has been summed up into the 'cool girl' trope. To some degree, the women described by Levy (2006) appear to be stuck in the 'cool girl trap'—an expression coined by author Gillian Flynn in her novel *Gone Girl* and applied to the tech world by Cooke-Garza (2015). Flynn describes the 'cool girl' archetype as the woman who essentially fulfills all of men's desires. Women who strive to live up to this fantasy are caught in the 'cool girl trap'. The 'cool girl' is of stunning beauty while still performing as the best buddy with whom guys like to catch a game and later maybe have a threesome.[1] The cool girl is 'hot and understanding' and never angry. In an environment that is so full of men with so few women, being a 'cool girl' appears to be a valid strategy for survival. In terms of Butler's (1988) theory of performative gender constitution, the 'cool girl' might be constituted through repeating acts of masculine gender performances (burping, playing video games, or watching football) while sexually performing and looking hyperfeminine. However, as one can imagine, this involves quite a balancing act that might not be maintainable for long. On Twitch, the cool girl can often be seen as a beautifully dolled up streamer who just waves off viewers' sexist and objectifying commentary while eating chips, drinking beer, and playing a video game.

## Case Study: Spotlight on Three Female Streamers

In the larger context of media studies, live streaming is a novelty. However, within the five years of its existence a set of rules, norms, and codes have been established by the community. A quite impressive illustration of just how far these codes have developed is the secret language of Twitch emoticons. The undefeated king of Twitch emoticons is *Kappa*, a little smirking image of a former Twitch employee which has become a symbol indicating sarcasm. Whenever a *Kappa* shows up in Twitch chat, the reader can assume the statement is denoted as sarcastic or ironic. Similar to the language on Twitch, certain norms and codes have emerged for denoting the kind of stream to expect from the way a profile looks, the way the stream overlay is designed or the title of the broadcast. While the signs and codes might be subtle at times and blatantly obvious in other cases, they indicate that viewers have certain expectations.

The three streamers highlighted in this section are by no means a representative sample of all female streamers and the analysis has no intention to derive generalizable statements. All of them are trendsetters for other streamers due to their success. However, the reasons why they are successful are unique to each streamer.

## Alinity

Alinity was one of the first female streamers on Twitch. She is a Colombian but lives in Canada. She started streaming in 2012 and has been playing *World of Warcraft* ('*WoW*') for over ten years. On her Twitch profile she mentions that she has been gaming since she was a little kid and that she was rather successful as a *WoW* 'raider', that is, she has participated successfully in playing the end-game player versus environment content. She also plays *Hearthstone* on stream regularly and has reached the highest level ('legendary') in this game. Since she streams daily for several hours, it can be assumed that streaming is her main occupation (Fig. 10.3).

Her Twitch profile provides the viewer with information about herself and her gameplay, as well as with information on subscriber perks, how to donate money or gifts (the profile features a link to a quite extensive Amazon wish list), links to other social media profiles and sponsors. Her channel has received a total of 16,588,812 views and as of February 2016 has 255,372 followers. The subscriber perks she mentions on her profile include 'a super special Dance by the one and only Alinity when the sub goal is reached'. Every subscriber receives her Snapchat, chat emoticons, and a special subscriber icon next to their name in chat as well as the ability to post links in chat. Alinity also performs a daily 'sub-dance' for her subscribers. There is no mention of it

**Fig. 10.3** Alinity's Twitch profile

on her profile but she also used to blow up a balloon with a little pump for every new subscriber and write their name on it. While Alinity probably has many monthly supporters, she also receives quite a lot of donations. Her profile offers a link to PayPal for donations as well as a PO-box address in case fans want to send her a gift. Every received package will be opened on stream. She also honors her highest donators on her profile. The three highest donators of all times donated $9406.77, $4825.98, and $3558.00. The list includes well over 20 names and is limited to donations above $200.

Alinity's Facebook page has more than 18,000 likes. She has 26,600 followers on Twitter and roughly the same amount of Instagram followers. There is an incredible amount of photos on her social media profiles: Alinity dressing up to go out at night, Alinity on vacation, Alinity interacting with her subscribers, Alinity dancing for her subscribers. In many pictures, she wears crop tops and shorts. Some pictures show her with a bikini on the beach. Many photos are of her cosplaying. Recently, a photo she shared on social media provoked excitement within the streaming community: a donator has given her Keith Haring-themed underwear for Valentine's Day and she modeled them, topless, covering her chest with an arm.

Alinity is very successful. Because of her success many other streamers have started to adopt similar strategies for gaining and retaining viewers. A special dance for reaching a subscriber goal or a special cosplay event is frequently found as incentives other female Twitch streamers offer in return for subscriptions. Obviously, it is impossible to tell whether Alinity was the only streamer establishing these strategies for success within the community but she is one of the more successful female streamers who has set trends for many years. She is, of course, also setting trends for what is expected of a female Twitch streamer. Whether it is uploading bikini photos or dancing in front of a camera for her subscribers, not every female Twitch streamer wants to show as much skin and provide as much information about herself as Alinity does.

## Hafu

Hafu is 24. She is a Chinese-American and lives in California. On her Twitch profile Hafu mentions that she has been playing games since she was 14. She is one of the few women who made a name for themselves in esports. These days, she mainly plays *Hearthstone* but she used to play *WoW* competitively as a 'player versus player' champion. While Hafu has been a star within the gaming community for quite some time she just gained wider recognition through an interview in which she discusses her 'trials as a female esports champion' (Roose 2016). During the interview, Hafu can hardly hold back her tears when she talks about her experience with harassment. At a *WoW* tournament she participated in when she was only 17, a competing team named themselves 'Gonna Rape Hafu at Regionals' (Roose 2016). In Hafu's case, the harassment does not only happen online. She is confronted with it whenever she attends esports events offline and online (Fig. 10.4).

There is not a lot of personal information about Hafu on her Twitch profile. She does not disclose her real name or where exactly she lives. Most prominently displayed are the chat rules for her channel. Hafu makes it very clear that she does not tolerate any spam, hate speech, or disrespect toward anyone. Next to the rules, she lists her esports achievements. She competed in and won several *WoW* and *Hearthstone* competitions as well as reached one of the highest levels in Blizzard's *Diablo III*, a very popular role-playing game. In addition to linking to social media profiles, play lists, and her streaming schedule on her website, she has a list of her gaming equipment on her profile. There is also a button for donations and every donation above $2 will show up as part of her stream overlay. However, there are no subscriber perks listed or a list of her top donators. Hafu's channel has a total of 44,362,554 views and 392,920 followers.

**Fig. 10.4**  Hafu's Twitch profile

More than 76,000 people like Hafu's page on Facebook and she has 63,400 Twitter followers. She does not link to Instagram. Most of the pictures on her social media profiles show her sitting in front of her computer, playing and streaming, or at esports events. Some pictures show her with her friends or her boyfriend, out for dinner or at a bar.

Hafu, as she says in the interview mentioned earlier, wants her stream and her fans to be about her gaming. Sometimes, she says, the harassment is so bad that she asks herself why she is even doing it (Roose 2016). While part of the reason might be that streaming and gaming has become more than a hobby and is her main profession now (she left college to stream and game fulltime), Hafu also simply wants to do what she loves. Her follower numbers show that she is by no means less successful than Alinity and although she has not been setting trends in regard to how a Twitch channel profile should look like and what subscriber rewards could be working well, Hafu is one of the few successful and widely renowned female esports athletes.

## SeriouslyClara

SeriouslyClara is a self-proclaimed 'Asianese' living on the Canadian west coast. She is the only real 'variety gamer', that is a streamer who broadcasts a variety of games rather than specializing in one game or game genre, in this list of streamers. She plays and streams games on her personal computer (PC) and on gaming consoles. Her frequently asked questions (FAQ) page on her Twitch profile links to an extensive collection of websites about SeriouslyClara and her gameplay. While SeriouslyClara might not be as popular within the gaming community (possibly due to her playing multiple kinds of games and not playing on a competitive level), she has made a name for herself through social media and her store, in which she sells merchandise, such as t-shirts, phone cases, and more. SeriouslyClara is very interested in creating a community around her hobby and leads a Vancouver nerd and gaming community (Fig. 10.5).

SeriouslyClara's profile is full of links to social media, her shop, other shops, sponsored links, her patreon site, and her website. There is only little information about what games she plays or her gameplay in general on the profile but she links to a spreadsheet that her viewers can use to request games she should be playing on stream. A little picture of herself with a Minecraft foam sword and the caption 'This is a no pants stream so take those suckers off' shows her upper body but is cut off right below the waistline. What exactly the meaning

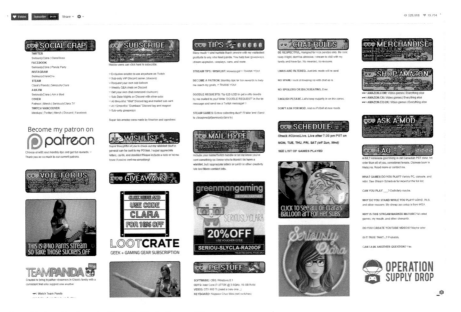

**Fig. 10.5**  SeriouslyClara's Twitch profile

behind this picture might be difficult to guess but it links to her Instagram feed. In addition to her announcing she would like to get more involved with cosplaying (a picture that again links to her Instagram) and some information about her computer, her profile also features a link to pictures of balloon art she created for her subscribers. Clicking the link leads to hundreds of photos with SeriouslyClara and balloons she is holding up. Her channel has a total number of 526,668 views as of February 2016 and 19,704 followers.

Two links on her profile take you to two different Twitter accounts: one is her actual account while the other one is for giveaways: follow, retweet, or favorite in order to participate in a giveaway of mainly games. She has about 10,000 Twitter followers, 2000 Instagram followers, and 569 people like her Facebook page. Overall, SeriouslyClara tweeted more than 30,000 times with this account and uploaded almost 4000 photos and videos.

SeriouslyClara also has a website on which she provides extensive information about herself and the community of gamers and streamers she is trying to foster in her local area.

On her websites, she explains how she started streaming on Twitch.

Whatever successes I've had on Twitch were mostly accidental. I was sort of tricked into streaming once to start in December 2013.... Streaming in general was bizarre and brand new information to me. I'd hosted a 2v2 PvP tourney prior, but still had no idea what streaming was really about. After a week or two hanging out in a Guild Wars 2 channel, I was coerced into streaming for an hour while that streamer was on nom break (it was for in-game gold, don't judge 𝘀𝘂𝗮𝗴 🔲 ). A few days after that, I was offered more gold to stream again. I hated it.

It took months of on again off again streaming—with days to weeks between each cast—before I actually enjoyed it. The only reason I even did it at all was because I was bugged to constantly 🐼 and sometimes it was fun to play with my core friends. After some weird fucking incidents, including this crazy internet asshat involving the police and several unrelated death threats when I said I was leaving GW2, I finally got into streaming.

According to SeriouslyClara herself, she was more or less coerced into streaming by her community in the game *Guild Wars 2* but now she really started to love it and therefore wants to share it with a community of people. This rather confusing message demonstrates how conflicted SeriouslyClara seems to still be about streaming. Having other people watch you in your home while playing a video game and giving them the option to interact with you, even harass you, is a very intimate experience. SeriouslyClara goes into much detail about her history with Twitch and streaming. A complete account of her story would be beyond the scope of this chapter; however, she seems to have overcome the adversities streaming first presented her with and returned stronger. This feeling of empowerment and learning to love herself and what she does is what she wants to share with her community. Her goal is to provide a safe space for gamers and streamers to come together and discuss.

# (Mis)Representation Matters?

For media scholars, the case study of female streamers serves as an enticing example of how media representation and misrepresentation can matter for how female gamers perceive themselves and are perceived by other members of the community and the general public. The underrepresentation of women in the gaming community, as Taylor (2006, 2015) and Shaw (2014) argue convincingly, has been and continues to be problematic in many ways. The perception of gaming and esports as a male-dominated, hostile environment casts a very negative light on the gaming community as a whole in the eyes of the larger public and therefore complicates the process of moving esports and gaming from the fringes to the center of society (Roose 2016). In addition, future generations of female gamers have hardly any female esports athletes or popular gamers to look up to. No female players rank among the current top 50 *Hearthstone* players[2] or the current top 20 *League of Legends* players, both widely popular esports games. When esports tournaments are broadcast via Twitch or even on ESPN, they hardly ever feature even a single female player. Within gaming culture, one thing leads to another to create a reinforcing and self-reproducing system: women are often not motivated to play games or reluctant to expose themselves to harassment. Therefore, there are not many opportunities for them to master the games they are playing. As Taylor (2015) notes, competing against players of slightly higher skill levels is important in order to improve. However, even young boys refuse to play with girls because they are afraid of losing against a girl.

As a result of these and other factors, hardly any women compete in esports tournaments and women remain underrepresented. Twitch, however, has the power to slowly but steadily change this and break out of this cycle. The presence of female streamers can help generate a broader audience and acceptance for gaming and esports. Alinity, Hafu, and SeriouslyClara all have comparable amounts of followers. Hafu can certainly be described as a celebrity in the esports scene and Alinity is widely popular in the streaming community. When Hafu streams her viewer numbers usually range from 1000 to 5000 or even up to 10,000. Streaming to these large numbers of viewers creates a lot of visibility for female streamers and gamers. The created visibility can help reduce the perceived pervasiveness of the white male gamer stereotype. If the image of gaming women stops being a rare occurrence and becomes normalized, female gamers would be perceived as less of a minority and therefore be less marginalized. It also creates opportunities for the many women who excel at gaming to showcase their skills to a broader audience and could therefore help to mitigate the most common sexist stereotypes in gaming, such as the misconception that women are generally bad at video games (Fox & Tang 2014).

Another positive development that can be observed within the larger gaming and streaming community is women banding together and watching out for each other. '#WCW' or '#womancrushWednesday' is a very popular Twitter phenomenon. Men and women alike will send a tweet with #WCW addressed to a woman they have a crush on. Female streamers often mention each other and send affirmative and empowering messages to other female streamers. According to her website, SeriouslyClara spends a great deal of her time and energy to create an inclusive and safe community for gamers and nerds within her local area.

However, wherever there is an in-group, there will also be an out-group. Not every female streamer will want to tweet out selfies of herself on the beach or comment on how great someone else's selfie on the beach looks. There is a lot of pressure on female streamers to keep up with the amount of skin others show and to reaffirm each other's strategies for attracting viewers to their channels and social media profiles. Hafu mentioned in an interview that a lot of expectations the community has for what she is supposed to deliver on and off stream stem from how other female streamers present themselves (Roose 2016). The audience for Twitch streams is mostly male. There is high demand for beautiful 'cool girls' showing cleavage.

There are also downsides to this new visibility. Out of the three streamers discussed, only Alinity does not openly discuss incidents of harassment on her profile or social media sites. Both Hafu and SeriouslyClara tell stories about problems arising from not being cool with being the 'cool girl' anymore.

Additionally, there is also need for caution in regard to perpetuating new and existing stereotypical perceptions of female gamers and streamers. Steven Asarch, a writer for gaming and esports outlets, made a list of the best *League of Legends* streamers. Toward the end of his list, he also mentions the 'gamer girls' who only play video games to make money showing cleavage:

> I would be amiss if I did not mention the bane of the Twitch community, the "gamer girl." Now I don't mean girls who play the game normally, like the Hearth-stone streamers Hafu and Eloise. I mean girl gamers who flaunt massive cleavage and play League of Legends poorly to anger the people watching. My advice is to avoid any streamer whose camera on screen is bigger than the actual game (though you'll check them out anyway.). (Asarch 2016)

While it is awful to see this incredibly sexist generalization published online, it still reflects a widely held and popular opinion. Do female streamers have the power to defy these stereotypes and make it big without creating sexually objectified presentations? I would argue they do but likely at a price: the most successful streamers in terms of viewers and subscribers on Twitch are still men. Not emphasizing her femininity and using it to her advantage, will put a female streamer into direct competition with male streamers who have other advantages (e.g. the male majority of viewers likely has an easier time to identify with a male streamer). In addition to simply normalizing female gaming and streaming through sheer numbers and visibility, female streamers have the power to not engage in slut shaming behaviors and to accept, respect, and support each other. No matter how they choose to present themselves on their channels, the community of female streamers is currently engaging in the work of supporting and respecting fellow women as opposed to shaming each other. So rather than implying that women on Twitch have the responsibility to promote a non-sexualized image of female gamers, I would suggest they have the power (and the responsibility) to promote a supportive and positive community whose members accept all types of streamers as fellow content creators and gamers.

For many women whose primary occupation is streaming, creating a brand and a channel that meets the demands of viewers is crucial. Still, it is tempting to classify some female streamers as complicit in further perpetuating and reproducing negative stereotypes of female streamers and gamers. After all, some women willingly, and consciously create promiscuous and fun streaming personas—one could describe them as 'cool girl streamers'—who appear to repel any sexist and objectifying commentary. However, it is important to remember that most of these personas are solely created for the purpose of making money on Twitch. As scholars, we should also remind ourselves that empowerment comes with choice. Despite the choice to market oneself as a 'boob streamer' probably being more illusion than actual choice, failure to credit solidarity and acceptance within this community and instead condemning it as being complicit, will likely lead to an overly simplified and one-sided perspective on femininity in streaming and gaming.

# Notes

1. Flynn writes: 'Men always say that as the defining compliment, don't they? She's a cool girl. Being the Cool Girl means I am a hot, brilliant, funny woman who adores football, poker, dirty jokes, and burping, who plays video games, drinks cheap beer, loves threesomes and anal sex, and jams hot dogs and hamburgers into her mouth like she's hosting the world's biggest culinary gang bang while somehow maintaining a size 2, because Cool Girls are above all hot. Hot and understanding. Cool Girls never get angry; they only smile in a chagrined, loving manner and let their men do whatever they want. Go ahead, shit on me, I don't mind, I'm the Cool Girl'.
2. Rankings are available based on different measures and they will slightly vary but the rankings used here are available on http://www.gosugamers.net/hearthstone/rankings?page=1 and http://www.lolesports.com/en_US/featured/top20.

# Bibliography

Asarch, Steven. 2016. Here's the Best Twitch Streamers Playing League of Legends in 2016. *idigitaltimes*. Accessed March 21, 2017. http://www.idigitaltimes.com/heres-best-twitch-streamers-playing-league-legends-2016-514216.

Butler, Judith. 1988. Performative Acts and Gender Constitution: An Essay in Phenomenology and Feminist Theory. *Theatre Journal* 40 (4): 519–531.

Cook-Garza, Kennedy. 2015. The Cool Girl Trap: Or, Why Sexism in Tech Isn't Going Away. *Medium*. Accessed March 2, 2016. https://medium.com/absurdist/the-cool-girl-trap-or-why-sexism-in-tech-isn-t-going-away-825b9a7642f5.

Fox, Jesse, and Wai Yen Tang. 2014. Sexism in Online Video Games: The Role of Conformity to Masculine Norms and Social Dominance Orientation. *Computers in Human Behavior* 33: 314–320.

Gervais, Sarah J., Theresa K. Vescio, Jens Förster, Anne Maass, and Caterina Suitner. 2012. Seeing Women as Objects: The Sexual Body Part Recognition Bias. *European Journal of Social Psychology* 42 (6): 743–753.

Gray, Kishonna L. 2012. Intersecting Oppressions and Online Communities: Examining the Experiences of Women of Color in Xbox Live. *Information, Communication & Society* 15 (3): 411–428.

Hamilton, William A., Oliver Garretson, and Andruid Kerne. 2014. Streaming on Twitch: Fostering Participatory Communities of Play within Live Mixed Media. In *Proceedings of the 32nd Annual ACM Conference on Human Factors in Computing Systems*, 1315–1324. ACM.

Heflick, Nathan A., and Jamie L. Goldenberg. 2009. Objectifying Sarah Palin: Evidence that Objectification Causes Women to be Perceived as Less Competent and Less Fully Human. *Journal of Experimental Social Psychology* 45 (3): 598–601.

Kaytoue, Mehdi, Arlei Silva, Loïc Cerf, Wagner Meira, Jr., and Chedy Raïssi. 2012. Watch Me Playing, I Am a Professional: A First Study on Video Game Live Streaming. In *Proceedings of the 21st International Conference on World Wide Web*, 1181–188. ACM.

Levy, Ariel. 2006. *Female Chauvinist Pigs: Women and the Rise of Raunch Culture*. New York: Free Press.

Nakandala, Supun, Giovanni Luca Ciampaglia, Norman Makoto Su, and Yong-Yeol Ahn. 2017. Gendered Conversation in a Social Game-Streaming Platform. In *Proceedings of the Eleventh International AAAI Conference on Web and Social Media, Montréal, Québec, Canada, May 15–18, 2017*. Palo Alto, CA: The AAAI Press.

Nascimento, Gustavo, Manoel Ribeiro, Loïc Cerf, Natália Cesário, Mehdi Kaytoue, Chedy Raïssi, Thiago Vasconcelos, and Wagner Meira. 2014. Modeling and Analyzing the Video Game Live-Streaming Community. In *Web Congress (LA-WEB), 2014 9th Latin American*, 1–9. IEEE.

O'Leary, A. 2012. In Virtual Play, Sex Harassment Is All Too Real. *The New York Times*. Accessed October 30, 2014. http://www.nytimes.com/2012/08/02/us/sexual-harassment-in-online-gaming-stirs-anger.html?_r=0.

Oldenburg, Ray. 1997. *The Great Good Place: Cafés, Coffee Shops, Community Centers, Beauty Parlors, General Stores, Bars, Hangouts, and How They Get You through the Day*. New York: Marlowe & Company.

Pires, Karine, and Gwendal Simon. 2015. YouTube Live and Twitch: A Tour of User-Generated Live Streaming Systems. In *Proceedings of the 6th ACM Multimedia Systems Conference*, 225–230. ACM.

Roose, Kevin. 2016. She's Been Called 'the Michael Jordan of Video Games.' And She Has a Message for Sexists and Trolls. *Fusion*. Accessed March 2, 2016. http://fusion.net/video/269318/real-future-hafu-female-esports-champion/.

Shaw, Adrienne. 2014. *Gaming at the Edge*. Minneapolis, MN: University of Minnesota Press.

Sjöblom, Max, and Juho Hamari. 2016. Why Do People Watch Others Play Video Games? An Empirical Study on the Motivations of Twitch Users. *Computers in Human Behavior* 75: 985–996.

Taylor, T.L. 2006. *Play Between Worlds: Exploring Online Game Culture*. Cambridge, MA: MIT Press.

———. 2015. *Raising the Stakes: Esports and the Professionalization of Computer Gaming*. Cambridge, MA: MIT Press.

Twitch. 2014. Audience. *Twitch Interactive, Inc.* Accessed March 1, 2016. http://twitchadvertising.tv/audience/.

———. 2015. Two Thousand Moreteen. *Twitch Interactive, Inc.* Accessed March 1, 2016. http://www.twitch.tv/year/2014.

———. 2016. Welcome Home. The 2015 Retrospective. *Twitch Interactive, Inc.* Accessed March 1, 2016. http://www.twitch.tv/year/2015.

Uszkoreit, Lena. 2015. *Girl Playing <3: Video Game Live Streaming and the Perception of Female Online Gamers*. Presentation, Annual Convention of the International Communication Association, San Juan, Puerto Rico, May 2015.

Williams, Dmitri, Mia Consalvo, Scott Caplan, and Nick Yee. 2009. Looking for Gender: Gender Roles and Behaviors Among Online Gamers. *Journal of Communication* 59 (4): 700–725.

Yee, Nick. 2006. The Demographics, Motivations, and Derived Experiences of Users of Massively Multi-user Online Graphical Environments. *Presence: Teleoperators and Virtual Environments* 15 (3): 309–329.

# Part III

## Beyond Feminization: Gaming and Social Futures

# 11

# Doing/Undoing Gender with the Girl Gamer in High-Performance Play

## Emma Witkowski

Kat "Mystik" Gunn and Anna "uNcontroLable" Prosser are on stage, dressed in a portrait of "emphasized femininity"[1]: sequinned cocktail dresses, hair ironed or curled, looking sleek and made-up. Tonight they're on stage at a pro-league event for *League of Legends* and *StarCraft II* (SC2), being questioned by fellow gamer and esports host Rachel "Seltzer" Quirico. They're all esports regulars who perform in various roles including community managers, event hosts, and as high-performance players.[2] It's a similar production to the previous year's event, with host and participants wearing "what the event designers requested" (Partin 2013). In this interview, Gunn and Prosser are brought on-stage to talk about why they enrolled in the Maxim Gamer Girl contest.[3] As a former Miss Oregon, Prosser puts her pageantry experience on show, framing her entry as a way of enhancing the image of the thing she loves, competitive games: "… as female gamers, owning whatever it is that we are and we have to offer is going to be the most positive way to impact not only our community but the world" highlighting that she'll "use what I may have been given, whether that's looks or personality" (CyberSportNetwork 2012). Quirico is clearly unconvinced about the here-and-now vision of broader community support for empowered female gamer subjectivities, especially where emphasised femininity is a part of the equation. She rattles off some of the contradictions women experience within cultures of high-performance gaming, from receiving acceptance in maintaining a feminine—"pretty, cute, and relatable"—performance-persona, to hostility when

E. Witkowski (✉)
Royal Melbourne Institute of Technology, Melbourne, VIC, Australia

© The Author(s) 2018
K. L. Gray et al. (eds.), *Feminism in Play*, Palgrave Games in Context,
https://doi.org/10.1007/978-3-319-90539-6_11

presenting oneself more glamorously. Or as Quirico creepily paints it, that image of being someone's "special little girl" is unsettled and met negatively, framed as "attention seeking and distracting." Gunn follows another pathway to the contest, she states "… it calls for gamer girls, so that to me seemed kind of obvious, because I've been gaming all my life." But Gunn also pinpoints a catch-22 surrounding participation and representation for many women as marginalised actors in high-performance play cultures, noting the community "keep assuming that Maxim is not going to choose a gamer girl [a player who adheres to a conservative community-driven notion of 'real gaming'], so if I don't enter then they won't choose a gamer girl." Gunn's opt-in suggests collusion to the social feminisation of women in games at the institutional and community level of esports, reifying women in games as eye-candy for mostly male consumption. Though, Gunn simultaneously confronts that position. She enters herself to represent one of the "real" gamer girls, a player who engages with games as a serious part of her lifestyle, in other words she's a player first. In less than ten minutes on-stage, three women with careers in esports lay bare some of the structures, variability, and quicksand surrounding the term "gamer girl" in high-performance play (a construct here-on referred to as girl gamer); from individual orientations to gender performativity and desired/produced leisure representations within networked media sports[4] communities, to issues of embodiment, gendered marketing economies, and institutional power. The interconnections between doing gender and doing esports are clearly complex. As such, Bordo's work on the reproduction of femininity is particularly useful here. Her work provides a scaffolding to explore the layered and networked gender productions within high-performance play by calling for attentiveness to the "… network of practices, institutions and technologies that sustain positions of dominance and subordination within a particular domain" (1992, 15). Such powerful stories of individual player processes expose the newly established infrastructures and cumbersome cultural underpinnings of high-performance play cultures for many women, alongside of highlighting the significance of assembling holistic accounts of player practices (as contrasted to single-sited data information points). As career professionals, where expertise is claimed and performed on a daily basis, Gunn, Prosser, and Quirico make it very clear: the trappings of "girl gamer" are hard to escape on existing multi-sited foundations of high-performance play, underscoring that the term, and even the terms of play itself are simply not cultivated alone.

The young women in this study explicate the nuanced ways in which gender is activated as a part of their esports lifestyle and career orientation, a mix of professional, amateur, and serious leisure pursuits (Stebbins 2007).[5]

Through qualitative fieldwork, the daily performances of women engaging in various esports scenes are traced, with players expressing how they are reminded and regulated, through tacit and explicit practices, of the gendered frames arranging full participation in their preferred site of serious leisure. As dedicated players, they reveal what involvement means for many women participating in and around esports, where femininity is toyed with and managed.

This chapter takes its lead from research on women who have their high-performance computer gameplay broadcast from tournament events or via Twitch—a dominant game livestreaming platform. As participants, many of these women have experienced being positioned on the outer edge of organised scenes of competitive computer game tournaments and institutions, which are channels towards financial and alternative socio-cultural benefits (N. Taylor 2009). Benefits include acquiring prize-winnings or sponsorships, realising a recognisable public personality (and monetising it), or transitioning from piecemeal competitive players to career (regular wage-earning) administrators—otherwise seen as pathways to a career in esports. Not all players necessarily see the full spectrum of these benefits, nor desire them. Though, when women at the high-performance level of play regularly communicate how they run the gauntlet as a gendered object in their path towards serious esports competition, these profitable opportunities and career possibilities are worth considering. The passages towards high-performance play, complete with subtle and overt discrimination, highlight the disparity in pathways, everyday experiences, and eventual accessibility to career positions in esports on a foundation of difference in which the construct of the girl gamer is a foundational piece (T.L. Taylor 2012).

Ten in-depth interviews, alongside of ethnographic material on high-performance players (conducted between 2010 and 2015), and secondary documents with mid-to-high level players lay the foundation for this exploration on how the girl gamer is lived and produced[6]: zooming in on the players' reflections and listening to their accounts on what the mainstream surface of gender dualism means for their everyday leisure, career opportunities, and identity production. These diverse player/performers help to convey a deeper understanding of how players embody the construct of the gamer girl. As such, this exploration ties some of the voices and actions of women in-and-around esports who have been confronted by and have contested this moniker, offering a textured view of the environment in which women both drive and derail the construct to make new meanings and mobilities in this career/lifestyle.

# Productions of Femininity and the Gendering of High-Performance Play

Women's participation in high-performance play has been discussed in pioneering work on player practices (Kennedy 2006), serious team/guild membership (T.L. Taylor 2006; N. Taylor 2009), embodiment and expert involvement (T.L. Taylor 2012; Witkowski 2012), and resistant (but often complicated) gender performances in competitive networked game spaces (Gray 2013; Beavis and Charles 2007; OMGitsfirefoxx 2015). Alongside the rapidly progressing media sports industry, sociological research on esports has grown in recent years with individual, interactional, and institutional gender productions in focus (see Taylor et al. 2009; T.L. Taylor 2012; Witkowski 2013). Within these studies, visual and embodied traces of normative Western femininity linger as a culturally recognisable category persistent in esport scenes, and while out of the scope of this chapter, such productions can't simply be detached from broader histories around gender and identity production, game and networked cultures.

## Doing Femininity in Esports

Doing femininity can be thought of as a sense-making and ongoing identity production, which is "… produced through personal and cultural messages about what clothing, figure, comportment, life course, and values are expected of women"—the dominant forms of which are associated with white cisgender bodies (White 2015, 5).[7] In this regard, a mainstream projection of girl gamer femininity is well located by Quirico, when she jests that one represents as "Completely, attractively female, and completely attractively good at games" (CyberSportNetwork 2012). But doing femininity doesn't sit in a void, which media sports—as places of high risk, high-tech, and high reward—provide numerous examples (see N. Taylor 2009). For women engaging in such expert gaming endeavours, their gender performances (while varied), are made alongside productions of hegemonic sporting masculinity as a gender performance that is locally dominant, associated to traditional sports, and aligned to male body skill superiority, antagonistic competitiveness, and heterosexual virility (see T.L. Taylor 2012; Messner 2007; Christensen 2006). Thinking with Connell and Messerschmitt's framing of gender as, "… always relational … [where] patterns of masculinity are socially defined in contradistinction from some model (whether real or imaginary) of femininity" (2005, 848). We can start to grasp the disruptive work involved by those women who participate as experts, as they do the heavy lifting of undoing traditional gender relational patterns on their given scene. And while we should remind ourselves here that there is no singular category or experience of Woman; gender is still systematically deployed on many esports scenes on a dualistic foundation of female/male, woman/man, and femininity/masculinity. This is in part where the girl gamer is entangled. Caught in the imaginary (but also regularly claimed) categorical framing of essentialism, while also doing everyday expert play and identity work in their own way, where gender expressions across various esports scenes are varied and carefully curated. With the fluid range of gender performances and disparities across scene contexts in mind, writing a linear text with femininity in focus is tricky (White 2015). This study attempts to explore the nuanced spectrum of gender expressions, which deepens the experiential knowledge of women who engage at the top level of play, while teasing out key issues that relate to running the gauntlet towards esports as girl gamers.

## On Serious Networked Gender Trouble

Before moving into more particular and tacit issues affecting those performing around the construct of the girl gamer, a shared key issue (which extends to game cultures more broadly) is the serious business of talking about gender itself. Better characterised by esports commentator Lauren Scott: it's "a dangerous topic" (ESL 2015). In their critical work on the production of gender in-and-around games, feminist scholars convey the hazardous structures and marginalising cultures that often get tangled around women who cultivate a serious and visible gaming lifestyle (Chess and Shaw 2015). These include exclusive/exclusionary institutional practices,[8] pervasive communication of sexist, as well as racist and homophobic, language directed at women during play "and on social media, and regular scrutiny of women, femininity, and geek legitimacy as a player/performer (Gray 2013; Taylor et al. 2009). From individual and community practices to institutional interpretations of women and their "place" in high-performance play, these piecemeal experiences build up a gendered dossier of play. All participants share some familiarity with this dossier. It underpins the work involved in being a woman, and doing gender in interlocked relationships with other existing systems of inequality, in this particular space of play. In the following, esports participants walk through some of the serious work which happens through three frames: behind the scenes (tacit safety-work practices), during the scenes (doing expertise and doing gender), and as scene productions (institutional productions of gender) in high-performance spaces of play.

# Behind the Scenes: Tacit Safety-Work Practices

Twenty-four year old Rumay "Hafu" Wang has been on the high-performance scene for nearly a decade, her first major championship wins taking place during 2008 at the Major League Gaming (MLG) tournament in *World of Warcraft—Arena 3v3 Tournament*. She shifted her esports presence into regular livestreaming as an early Twitch partner, and maintains a robust social media presence maximising/monetising her reach. Hafu is a historical figure in esports; a top-level player and an early voice in the era of broadcast gaming who has regularly slighted dialogues that fixate on women who play as requiring gender focused media attention. During *The New Meta Women in Esports* panel, Hafu reflects on what's at stake for the expert player who is tangled in the production of femininity at game events, and her experiences post-event of being placed as a gamer girl,

> ... I stepped into my first MLG and it was kinda crazy, you'd see all these like really beautiful women, and then just a bunch of dudes, and then me. So, I just felt really out of place ... once you play though, you kind of lose yourself in the game and nothing else really matters. To me my gender didn't matter, more so being at events and being judged because I didn't look like everyone else. And even when I won, I feel like all my achievements are overshadowed by the fact that I'm a girl ... Every time I did an interview, it would be What's it feel like to be a girl who won? It's like, Well, ... just like it would feel like for a guy to win. (GGVogue 2014)

Despite Hafu's ongoing efforts to "lose herself" sans gender, femininity and the girl gamer are palpably wrapped up in the history of performance around her play, and perhaps her last sentence, which speaks to embodied expertise ("... just like it would for a guy to win"), offers a launching point to talk about other everyday embodied practices that are particular to women who play to win.

# Playing as Others: On Difference and Techniques of Erasure

Women in esports cultures report of high levels of animosity directed at their mere presence as performers, in particular when enmeshed with signs of hegemonic sporting masculinity such as expressed or desired gamer expertise read from a female body. Team Siren exemplifies how marks of hegemonic sporting masculinities surrounding broadcast esports—which on many main-stream esports scenes includes arrogance, authority, and competitiveness—are freely available, though with gendered consequences for many women looking to operationalise this professional frame. Team Siren's 2015 promotional YouTube video looked to market their entry into the *League of Legends* competitive scene as a new all-female team (looking to harness sponsors on a model of difference). Their video quickly garnered over 2 million views (Team Siren 2013). But perhaps it is the 28,000 dislikes and more than 18,000, mostly disparaging, comments that speak to how the neologisms of girl gamer or female gamer are going through a visible and ongoing process of pejoration. One of the original Team Siren members reflects on their promotional video:

> We already knew the hate was going to come [from, she notes, the "cheesy" video] … so we made a buddy system … if we couldn't keep up with the stress of all the hate overload kind of thing, we would talk with each other to try and relieve the stress. It was working for a little bit. (YoonieS2 2013)

Women are persistently derailed as authentic participants of this serious leisure activity via both personal and community attacks alongside of institutional positioning and dismissal (Klepek 2012; Taylor et al. 2009), often leaving it to the individual players to tough it out and devise methods to self-protect in her positioning as a woman who plays. Team Siren gives us a peak behind the often veiled scenes, and a measure of the safety work that women in esports engage in, which ranges from everyday personal network security (including high risk-management techniques for their online presence to avoid ddosing[9]) and welfare attentive buddy-systems (a victim-oriented safety measure historically suggested to women in order to "prevent" harassment).

Over the years, I have encountered numerous high-performance players who regularly mask their voice-communications in order to access "normal" competitive play (using software to lower the voice tone, see Witkowski 2012),[10] and who engage in tight concealment and management of, and being "discreet" in, their critical commentary towards the esports industry/communities writ large ("MissFlynn," esports pro/am livestreamer, personal communication). These last two issues are important to highlight, as they resonate with the invisibility of women's everyday labour on high-performance scenes, and just as noteworthy, how women are participating in their own erasure as expert actors in growing and global serious leisure activities. The muting of voices (for normal play or to participate and embody a culture tilted towards sporting masculinity) has a direct relationship with how gaming expertise and visibility is "given" as a male/masculine pursuit. But when individuals encounter and challenge gendered spaces, they become acutely aware that a personal attack is always just around the corner, only one comment or tweet away (ESL 2015). As such, full visibility is understood as treacherous terrain.

## Esports for All, Accountability, and Networked Caretaking

Singular subjects are bearing much of the weight of gender equity in high-performance gaming cultures today. With the ease and ferocity that hostile networked actions can take place against an individual actor (as seen through regular offensive chat commentary to aggressive mistreatment across networks), institutions require deeper consideration and infrastructural transformation around safety issues, which may shift some of the burden of "self-preservation" from those just trying to play games. Responsiveness and, more importantly, a proactive stance to such detailed gender inequities requires both commitment and incorporation by the dominant institutions themselves—as structural faults can be paved otherwise.[11] Ultimately moving mainstream institutions beyond mere instrumental organisation (such as superficially implementing gender parity frameworks from legacy sports institutions) to incorporating reflective practices towards networked caretaking. Networked high-performance arenas of play have deep inequalities regarding who and how one can participate; they are increasingly well documented and show a range of serious impacts on participant lives. As such, networked caretaking is a requirement of high-performance institutions claiming to act on promises of gender inclusivity in the esports era (Kamen 2014). Safety measures and caretaking, for those on the field as well as behind the scenes, require institutional energy and persistence which tackle the massive work of educating on equity from players to managers, shoutcasters to fans, if indeed this new industry is striving towards a "sports for all" model of serious leisure/career, where the practice of discrimination-free sport is understood as a human right (IOC charter 2015). Such experiences highlight some of the regular work of women who play, and the careful curation and production of self, where gender-oriented risks and burdens can extend and solidify in public networked cultures and codes of high-performance play spaces.

## Complicating the Girl Gamer and Extending Athletic Beauty

The experiences and productions of those positioned as girl gamers offer some perspective on how women are often "coded and dismissed in Internet settings" (White 2015, 9). For many women, being visible as expert players is in tension with erasing parts of oneself (dismissing aspects of voice, identity, and outlook) in order to persist "normally" in their leisure space. Though these are regular practices of many women who play, they are certainly not the only way gender and relationships to femininities and masculinities in high-performance play is produced. Hafu, Sasha "Scarlett" Hostyn (*SC2* player with South Korean esports team *Dead Pixels*), and Madeleine "Maddelisk" Leander (former *SC2* player with *Millenium* esports and shoutcaster) offer a glimpse of other everyday productions of and against the girl gamer construct, from their place as elite level competitors, including career longevity in competitive play and economic success through regular high-performance broadcasting (Hafu). Scarlett's multiple achievements in open and all-female tournaments (dismantling how sex-segregated tournaments don't match up to gendered lifestyles) and her total disregard of media inquiry around her gender as a transgender woman dominating in an arena of cisgender men, stating that "it has no bearing on her role in gaming" (McGrath 2014). Swedish player and esports media representative Maddelisk also confronts the normative construct of the girl gamer. In particular, through her play within the imaginary of traditional masculinity which includes her serious engagement with muscles (competitive street-workout athlete), maths (PhD in mathematics), and regular competitive tournament participation—a trifecta of supposed contradiction to traditional femininity. Riffing on Judith Butler's *Bodies that Matter*, Hans Gumbrecht situates how the athletic beauty and player intensity (aesthetic appeal and maximum emotional/physical effort formed through high-performance play) that these players regularly perform is a part of the fascination we have with sports. These players' daily networked performances move us beyond "the shapes that already exist" for men and women in esports, as they create new forms "that move bodies beyond traditional male-female types" through their actions in organised, competitive, play practices (Gumbrecht 2006, 156). As esports participants, these players' are both beautifully fascinating and beautifully mundane, as their everyday actions disrupt hegemonic sporting masculinities and traditional notions of femininity in the production of play across networked domains.

For those engulfed in the mainstream terminology of the girl gamer, playing to win might really mean to engage in substantial performance management in order to preserve basic mobility and safety on a high-performance gaming scene, while simultaneously chipping away at entrenched modes and forms of gendered participation therein. Though the question remains, how are such intense efforts shifting the bedrock that supports difference itself?

## During the Scenes: Doing Expertise, Doing Gender

In mainstream esports cultures, dominant forms and substructures supporting traditional femininity are comparable to performances and undercurrents found within traditional media sports. While muscles are not required as a function of traditional masculinity in esports (though as a form of cultural capital, it doesn't hurt to have them), technical expertise, and embodied knowledge of the sport itself are claimed, marketed, and institutionalised as "for young men" (Taylor et al. 2009; Witkowski 2013). Femininity is in service of—not a part of—the "main agenda." Where hand-eye coordination and clicks per minute are celebrated motor skills in esports, sporting expertise is equally feted in the tactical acuteness of its players, whether that is through trash-talking or pinpoint decision making during fast paced play (N. Taylor 2009). The productions of (media) sports and performances of technical expertise persist as actions deeply entrenched as male pursuits (Christensen 2006). For those women demonstrating virtuosity in networked high-performance play, the situation is paradoxical. In her personal (practice) domain, expertise is local and distinguished, and in the case of Twitch (live) broadcasters personalised, and moderated to her rules. In the public space of networked play, however, her expertise is frequently challenged with gendered inscriptions despite ongoing and demonstrated capability. What is established and celebrated locally is often dismissed through the infrastructures laid out in the networked public.

A snippet of dialogue captured between Hafu, playing on the channel of popular/professional male streamer "Destiny" (destiny.gg), offers a glimpse of public push back on gendered expertise in non-local settings, in particular where embodied knowledge and tactics are in focus. With 1700 spectators on Destiny's stream, Hafu is cursing regularly, and disputing the team's tactical calls. The following is a snippet of live-chat weaved in with Hafu and Destiny's voice-communications, taken from a period of *League of Legends* gameplay on Twitch:

| Hafu: | "When you smart cast[12] you cast on impulse, and this game is about precision" |
|---|---|
| Destiny: | "But isn't it about training that impulse?" |
| Subscriber A: | her logic is crazy as fuck |
| Viewer 1: | tell her to play ryze and try to not smartcast and see how different it is |
| Viewer 2: | worst logic ever … smartcasting is WAY better |
| Destiny: | "Put it back on smartcast, don't worry" |
| Hafu: | "No, it's buggy" |
| Viewer 3: | is that a grill!?! .o.^_^_^_^:3:3:3 [grill is slang for girl] |
| Viewer 4: | best grill ever |
| Viewer 5: | is he playing with that 3/10 chick hafu? [referencing Hafu by physical appearance. Her face-cam is turned off]. |

Hafu's history as an expert player across multiple games places her as a compelling virtuoso player who highlights a personal practice that involves extreme attention to the details of the rules of play and an individual play style. As she framed her practice in a public interview at an MLG LAN event, "I like to learn it myself … And so I mean, it's kind of bad, but at the same time I really push myself to be on top and learn it my way." Tactical acuity is personal in expert play (Witkowski 2012), and Hafu displays her command of numerous games where she has reached the top level of competition. Yet, her personalised style is regularly questioned—not "logical" even—and regularly elided to her gender (delimited here as "a 3/10 chick"). Regular commentary towards women as players/personalities by male competitors "putting them in their place" draws direct correlation to gender power relations revealed in sports studies, where "intrusions" into the male dominated space of sports disrupt "certainties about gender relations and sex differences that sport serves to guarantee" (Disch and Kane 1996, 282). Hafu is a far superior player than most in her chosen game, and tied to her tactical acuity she unravels those certainties around mastery and gaming expertise as a male preserve. Though, her regular public re-positioning as a "grill/girl" highlights the frictional distance from the local/inside (such as her own Twitch channel) to the public/ outside as an expert player categorised as a girl gamer.

## Doing Gender in Public: Teams

Moving from local to more public contexts can have particularly striking impacts for women who play in larger teams as expert teammates. High-performance *World of Warcraft* player "Saxo" exemplifies how her expertise is simultaneously diluted and celebrated through her positioning as a girl on the otherwise all-male guild "Exalant" (pseudonymed, a guild with a roster of over 100 players), where equity marketing generates one of the thorniest dilemmas to navigate for the individual involved.

As a top ranked guild (involved in world-first progress raids),[13] Exalant is invited to numerous events and conventions to "live-raid" as an on-stage performance, broadcast to thousands. It's a renumerated gig for the players on show, often entailing a trip abroad and accommodation for a small number of guild representatives, and the chance to be on-stage as a part of the spectated mega event. Saxo is often on-stage at these events. In the following, she explains how event organisers approach the guild:

> Well, usually they hope that Exalant will take the girl ... they've said that it would be nice if she could come. Every time it has been, you can bring anyone you would like to, but it would be nice if you brought one tank, one DPS (damage per second), one healer, and one girl.

In these moments, her everyday team status is temporarily rearranged. Her hard earned expertise is relocated—no longer a team role of tank, healer, or DPS, but rather her proficiency is stated as her gender, where "girl" is the singular marker of gender being done at all in such an expert team. As high-performance gaming institutions mature in their awareness of inclusivity in organised and promotional sporting leisure, Saxo offers a pointed case study, and feminist geographer Gillian Rose delivers the vital question to think with: "... how to represent women as social subjects without referring to the figure of Woman" (2013, 235). It is a challenging problem, but one to be asked more frequently, as women in esports repeatedly point towards the (negative) tacit actions of institutional bodies, marketing, and community or event management as going unchecked on deeper gender politics, in particular around issues such as organisational administration and inclusivity, reification of difference models, and participant care.

There are a growing number of players who highlight what this last subject of participant care means as a woman moving into traditionally male dominated spaces and established or emerging models of esports events. Maddelisk, for example, highlights the arrangements concerning participant care, which point directly to the institutional management of high-performance play.

## Doing Gender in Public: Single-Player Games

On receiving a wildcard invitation to a pro/am tournament, Maddelisk blogged about her hesitations in moving into this high-profile event, citing the elite player roster and all-male line-up as grounds to baulk on participating in the SC2 (1v1) competition. After seeing that the tournament regularly used wildcards, she accepted the invitation. During her first game, her opponent chose to trash-talk her in a contextually gendered and non-inclusive affront via another platform (on Twitter). As Maddelisk writes on the incident, "'Going to rape some girl soon #fragbitemasters' that's the tweet my opponent sent right before his match vs me. I'm the girl. He is one of the best StarCraft 2 players in Europe" (Leander 2014). The game was stopped mid-match, highlighting that while there is a varied integration of platforms that players are involved in during play, that these public expressions are traceable and localised by those watching and organising events. In inviting players as diversity or marketing wildcards, tournament management necessitates active consideration and preparedness towards participant care—which might include working towards a (proactive) code of conduct, setting potential wildcards (and their coaches) up with embedded and supportive mentors, or appropriate consideration of the local cultures surrounding the event and how participants can manoeuvre within them, online and offline. Participant care starts with the institution holding sway over participants' presence, not left exclusively to the players moving into that space. Maddelisk's attentiveness to institutional responsibility around participant care segues into the final section which tackles the girl gamer as a segregated entity, in the format of all-female esports tournaments.

## Scene Productions: All Female-Tournaments and Institutional Practices

Maddelisk's experience of international match participation (mixed and all-female) brings us full circle to the institutionalisation of all-female gaming tournaments. I have many hesitations about gender segregated tournaments, though none of these relate to the equitable grounds for including them, which includes scene diversification, a parity model working towards a more representative cultural and economic industry, and role-model presence. My concern rather lingers on the end-game. All-female tournaments have various guises, from marketing to promotional-equity work, and are often arrangements to clearly address "mistakes" that have occurred along the way in the making of high-performance play. Though in correcting mistakes, new ones are readily made, which is where my major discomfort lies. It must be asked: do segregated tournaments do more institutional and systemic work to seed those sporting-esque "certainties" about gender relations than the personal "level-up" development it attempts to leverage? Or as Messner identifies: do "… equal but separate opportunities for women in sport … leave men's sports largely intact and able to continue to reproduce hegemonic masculinity, replete with its traditions of violence, sexism, homophobia and militarism" (2007, 4). It is a lingering concern for many involved, and one not to take lightly. As we can see in this exploration and elsewhere, toxic practices are well facilitated by such binary gender distinctions (Connell & Messerschmidt 2005, p. 840) is well facilitated by such binary gender distinctions. To round off this tricky area, there are two valuable points to consider on how all-female tournaments can be read, in their present form, as valuable structures.

Primarily, there is praise to be given in taking the weight out of gendered play itself: Saxo and Hafu are players who represent the united participation ideal of play, where success in the local space is regularly achieved. However, both highlight the pressures that come with public play, where high-performance play can often be experienced as "representing" all women. Esports personality "RoseHigh" explains,

> Live streaming … motivated me to get better, play very regularly and keep going through hard times. I think it does the same for the other female streamers. I feel like we want to prove ourselves to the community and show what we can do, show that we are striving to improve and break the stereotype that we are there for the attention rather than the game … [but] there is more at stake with my gender being on display. I feel like I have to prove that girls can be good at StarCraft and motivated to improve so it feels like I am failing all of the women if I fail a game, or many games in a row, and that I am proving the stereotypes to be right.

Segregated tournaments paradoxically offer many of those entering esports a space where their presentation is not elided to doing gender, despite the "all-female" casing. In mainstream tournaments, women are playing to win, but also playing and positioned "to prove" women can play. The strategic essentialism of all-female tournaments releases players from the demands to represent for all women, opening other avenues to experience and do expertise, sans gender, in high-performance play.[14] Not having the pressures to do gender, or to feel gender, brings a sense of weightlessness. It is the everyday weightless experience available to a majority of (nonminority) male players, and a fuller experience which benefits all players in their holistic practice of play.

The value of all-female tournaments extends far beyond the players. These event spaces offer more than a stepping stone for players to compete in top end tournament events, as the backdrop of all-female tournaments initiates recruitment of a more equitable team including women as shoutcasters and team managers, as well as challenging marketing teams and background administrators to think about how they produce gender as a major esports institution (Taylor 2016; ESL 2015). Guaranteed missteps will (and have been) be made,[15] some of them excruciatingly reminiscent of the making of the Modern Olympics, whose history provides an entire century's worth of edification on gender and elite competition of which esports would do well not to recreate. Fresh opportunities are certainly cracked open through the introduction of all-female tournaments. And continued introspection of the cultural work these institutions engage with is a step towards improved dialogues (inclusive of diverse women who play) and deeper institutional engagement towards what parity in serious career/lifestyles means in practice.

## Conclusion

Susan Brownmiller writes on femininity as a "tradition of imposed limitations" (1984, 14). In networked game cultures, such traditions surrounding femininity are highly visible and nearly inescapable (though regularly confronted) as a player of computer games in competitive arenas. As Jones points out, "… feminism has long acknowledged that visuality (the conditions of how we see and make meaning of what we see) is one of the key modes by which gender is inscribed in Western culture" (Jones 2003, 1). This chapter is a fossil record of how the girl gamer identity has been positioned (visually and vocally by others) and wrangled with (viscerally and embodied by women who play) during 2010–2015 across mainstream platforms of high-performance play. It unfolds how women navigate and perform across interrelated play topographies; spaces and practices of expert level play where gender is deeply entrenched across networks and cultures.

Notwithstanding the taxing extras and additional measures taken by women as high-performance players (safety routines, self-assurance and mobility management, and the weight of playing as a gendered object), the players' everyday expert presentations perforate the construct of girl gamer as something distant and distinct from the mainstream esports star projected onto the field of play.

At the end of an in-depth interview on Saxo's serious, daily, high-performance play, she neatly sums up her passion: "It's a lifestyle." The doing and undoing of femininities in esports has deep relationships that span across individuals, communities, infrastructures, and institutions. To move towards equitable lifestyle possibilities for all those who partake, renewed efforts towards inclusivity, from the top down, means treating wayfinding participants' interests and welfares thoughtfully, and taking their varied productive processes seriously (White 2015, p. viii). An "esports for all" institution might do well to consider the lives and styles of play of those who already engage in the abundant pleasures of high-performance play, while also interrogating its laddish bedrock, to fully recognise the depth and intensity of personal labour involved for women to just play games seriously.

## Notes

1. Connell refers to emphasised femininity a form of "women's compliance" in their subordination to men, by way of "accommodating the interests and desires of men" (1987, 183).
2. High performance players are those participating at an elite level of computer game play and are involved in expert communities of practice.
3. Maxim is an international men's magazine whose front page customarily displays scantily clad images of prominent women.
4. Media sports refer to a slice of a high performance sports cultures which are maintained by the interrelationship between mainstream media, advertising/ sponsors, and professional sporting institutions.
5. Stebbins' concept of serious leisure, while sitting within positive taxonomy of leisure, usefully highlights the pleasure of a dedicated and systematically pursued activity "… that people find so substantial, interesting and fulfilling that … they launch themselves on a (leisure) career centred on acquiring and expressing a combination of its special skills, knowledge and experience" (2007, 6). While such conditions are dimensions of an esports career, so too are what Rojek describes as "the real conditions of human striving" (2010, p. 116), which includes less celebratory aspects of a serious leisure lifestyle tied to for-profit corporations.
6. The interviewees taking part in this research are all fluent English speakers (first or second language), located in North American or Northern Europe, and identify as cisgender, White or Asian American.
7. During 2010–2015, there were few women of colour represented on esports scenes in visible roles.
8. Such as traditional media sports masculinity upheld at esports events and the employment of booth babes.

9. Ddosing is a Distributed Denial-of-Service attack. An attack disrupts a personal computer/user by flooding it with multiple requests, leaving the machine unavailable for networked use.

10. Gray's ethnographic work in Xbox Live, which requires voice communication, reveals how voice impacts on racial and gender equality within play, "… this mere technological advance [voice communication over traditional chat function] creates the most havoc in their virtual lives—racial and gendered inequality based of how they sound" (2013, para. 6).

11. See for example the diversity in esports advocacy organisation "AnyKey."

12. Smart cast is a keyboard shortcut that casts an ability on the nearest enemy target, instead of mouse targeting.

13. World-first raiding involves select teams of 10–25 players attempting to be the first in the world to defeat newly released game content.

14. This is certainly not to say that gender is disregarded completely, either positively or negatively. As Quirico notes, not "doing gender" while playing at all-female tournaments doesn't omit sharing gendered experiences with those who struggle with the same issues, and as such make playing "feel normal" (ESL 2015).

15. Which include gender policing (as seen at the Garena eSports tournament, Philippines); limited fields/events of participation for women (such as the IeSF HearthStone tournament held at The Assembly, Finland); and narrow diversity within governing institutions.

# Bibliography

Beavis, Catherine, and Claire Charles. 2007. Would the 'Real' Girl Gamer Please Stand Up? Gender, LAN Cafés and the Reformulation of the 'Girl' Gamer. *Gender and Education* 19 (6): 691–705.

Bordo, Susan. 1992. The Body and the Reproduction of Femininity: A Feminist Appropriation of Foucault. In *Gender/Body/Knowledge: Feminist Reconstructions and Being and Knowing*, ed. Alison M. Jaggar and Susan R. Bordo, 13–33. New Brunswick, NJ: Rutgers Press.

Brownmiller, Susan. 1984. *Femininity*. London: Hamish Hamilton.

Chess, Shira, and Adrienne Shaw. 2015. A Conspiracy of Fishes, or, How We Learned to Stop Worrying about #Gamergate and Embrace Hegemonic Masculinity. *Journal of Broadcasting & Electronic Media* 59 (1): 208–220.

Christensen, Natasha C. 2006. Geeks at Play: Doing Masculinity in an Online Gaming. *Reconstruction: Studies in Contemporary Culture* 6 (1).

Connell, Raewyn. 1987. *Gender and Power: Society, the Person, and Sexual Politics*. Stanford, CA: Stanford Press.

Connell, R.W., and James Messerschmidt. 2005. Hegemonic Masculinity: Rethinking the Concept. *Gender Society* 19: 829–859.

CyberSportNetwork. 2012. Kat Gunn & Anna Prosser at IPL4. April 16. http://www.youtube.com/watch?NR=1&feature=fvwp&v=unzO2waeVqE.

Disch, Lisa, and Mary Jo Kane. 1996. When a Looker Is Really a Bitch: Lisa Olson, Sport, and the Heterosexual Matrix. *Signs: Journal of Women in Culture and Society* 21 (2): 278–308.

ESL. 2015. Women in eSports – Intel Panel Katowice. March 14. https://www.youtube.com/watch?v=u_S7vZCaqic.

GGVogue. 2014. The New Meta Women in eSports Panel (Coverage). May 26. https://www.youtube.com/watch?v=b-sQKZbNHJA.

Gray, Kishonna. 2013. Collective Organizing, Individual Resistance, or Asshole Griefers? An Ethnographic Analysis of Women of Color in Xbox Live. *Ada: A Journal of Gender, New Media, and Technology* 2.

Gumbrecht, Hans Ulrich. 2006. *In Praise of Athletic Beauty*. New York: Harper Perennial.

IOC Charter. 2015. Olympic Charter. August 2, 2015. http://www.olympic.org/Documents/olympic_charter_en.pdf.

Jones, Amelia. 2003. Introduction: Conceiving the Intersection of Feminism and Visual Culture. In *The Feminism and Visual Culture Reader*, ed. Amelia Jones, 1–8. London and New York: Routledge.

Kamen, Matt. 2014. Hearthstone Gender Ban Is More Complex than It Seems. *Wired*, July 14. http://www.wired.co.uk/news/archive/2014-07/04/esports-and-gender-still-not-a-recipe-for-equality.

Kennedy, Helen W. 2006. Illegitimate, Monstrous and Out There: Female 'Quake' Players and Inappropriate Pleasures. In *Feminism in Popular Culture*, ed. Jonanne Hollows and Roberta Pearson, 183–201. Oxford: Berg.

Klepek, Patrick. 2012. When Passions Flare, Lines Are Crossed [Updated], February 28. http://www.giantbomb.com/articles/when-passions-flare-lines-are-crossed-updated/1100-4006/.

Leander, Madeleine. 2014. [ENG]Going to Rape Some Girl Soon. *Aftonbladet*, November 21. http://esport.aftonbladet.se/esport/enggoing-rape-girl-soon-frag-bitemasters/.

McGrath, Ben. 2014. Good Game: The Rise of the Professional Cyber Athlete. *The New Yorker*, November 24. http://www.newyorker.com/magazine/2014/11/24/good-game.

Messner, Michael. 2007. *Out of Play: Critical Essays on Gender and Sport*. New York, NY: SUNY.

OMGitsfirefoxx. 2015. Twitchcon Women in Gaming Panel! October 4. https://www.youtube.com/watch?v=jKQr3N4bYP4.

Partin, Will. 2013. Get to Know: Anna "uNcontroLable" Prosser Robinson. November 5. http://evilgeniuses.gg/Read/185,Get-to-Know-Anna-uNcontroLable-Prosser-Robinson/.

Rojek, Chris. 2010. *The Labour of Leisure: The Culture of Free Time*. London: Sage.

Rose, Gillian. 2013. *Feminism and Geography: The Limits of Geographical Knowledge*. Oxford: Wiley.

Stebbins, Robert. 2007. *Serious Leisure*. New Brunswick, NJ: Transaction Publishers.

Taylor, Nicholas. 2009. *Power Play: Digital Gaming Goes Pro*. PhD dissertations, York University.

Taylor, Nicholas, Jen Jenson, and Suzanne De Castell. 2009. Cheerleaders/Booth Babes/Halo Hoes: Pro-gaming, Gender and Jobs for the Boys. *Digital Creativity* 20 (4): 239–252.

Taylor, T.L. 2006. *Play Between Worlds*. Cambridge, MA: MIT Press.

———. 2012. *Raising the Stakes: The Rise of Professional Computer Gaming*. Cambridge, MA: MIT Press.

———. 2016. E-Sports and Cyberathleticism: European Edition (2010), Communities & Spectatorship Panel. January 25. https://www.youtube.com/watch?v=X3dkxGcuQvo.

Team Siren. 2013. Introducing Team Siren. May 30. https://www.youtube.com/watch?v=_Gz9um3wV1o.

White, Michele. 2015. *Producing Women: The Internet, Traditional Femininity, Queerness, and Creativity*. New York, NY: Routledge.

Witkowski, Emma. 2012. *Inside the Huddle: The Phenomenology and Sociology of Team Play in Networked Computer Games*. PhD dissertation, IT University of Copenhagen.

———. 2013. Eventful Masculinities: Negotiations of Hegemonic Sporting Masculinities at LANs. In *Sports Videogames*, ed. Mia Consalvo, Konstantin Mitgutsch, and Abe Stein, 217–235. New York, NY: Routledge.

YoonieS2. 2013. Why Siren Disbanded. August 24. https://www.youtube.com/watch?v=FLrqPoiUn3w.

# 12

# The Magic Circle and Consent in Gaming Practices

Emma Vossen

## Play as Sex/Sex as Play

At some point in my young adult life, I realized that it took more vulnerability on my part to play video games with men then to have sex with them. I was terrified to play games with almost every man I knew, even those I was having sex with. This strange epiphany raised a lot of questions about myself and gamer culture that I felt suddenly forced to confront. Why was I more afraid to pick up a controller than take off my clothes? Why did it take so much vulnerability to play games with or in front of others? Why was it so hard to find any situation where I could enjoy playing games with men?

The purpose of this chapter is to discuss the intersections between gender, game play, games culture, consent, and sex in order to examine how Johan Huizinga's 1944 definition of play and concept of the "magic circle"[1] still function in our lives when we play video games. Huizinga's requirements for what constitutes "play" apply easily to video game play almost 80 years later but as Bonnie Ruberg has pointed out in their article "Sex as Game: Playing with the Erotic Body in Virtual Worlds" (2010) Huzinga's requirements also apply to sex. Ruberg elaborates that Huizinga's definition of "play" consists of an act that is voluntary, doesn't produce anything useful, takes place outside of "real life" in a "temporary sphere of activity", is repeatable, is freeing, has tension that can be resolved, can sometimes involve "special clothing", and has rules (18–25). When these requirements are all in place, Huizinga argues

E. Vossen (✉)
University of Waterloo, Waterloo, ON, Canada

K. L. Gray et al. (eds.), *Feminism in Play*, Palgrave Games in Context,
https://doi.org/10.1007/978-3-319-90539-6_12

that a type of "magic circle" is formed where the voluntary participants find themselves immersed within "temporary worlds within the ordinary world" (10). Without actually using the word consent Huizinga's theories create a model where consent is integral to maintaining the magic circle and creating a state of true "play". Beyond Huizinga's definition, thinking about sex as a type of "play" or "game" with roles, rules, and goals to achieve is not uncommon in contemporary conceptions of sex especially when thinking of BDSM (Bondage Dominance Submission/Sadism Masochism) play or sexual role playing.[2]

But, unfortunately, because of contemporary practices surrounding game play, most video game play I have participated in has contained practices that were not consensual or enjoyable, such as harassment, gender-based insults, or trash talk that forced me outside of the magic circle and led me to wonder if I was truly "playing" at all. Jesper Juul has argued that "the magic circle is best understood as the boundary that players negotiate" (2008, 56) and while this is indeed the ideal state and use of the magic circle, that boundary is rarely negotiated by all players. Most frequently those boundaries are defined by the dominate players in games culture, while marginalized players find themselves outside the boundaries of the circle.

This chapter uses my personal experiences with games and sex as a young female gamer to demonstrate how difficult it is for young women like myself and other minority players who are subject to harassment and other unenjoyable play practices to join the magic circle and take part in immersive game play in social scenarios. Full participation in gameplay is frequently inaccessible to women and other marginalized players because of a disregard for their consent, comfort, and well-being. Contemporary discussions of consent surrounding sexual practice can inform how we think about issues of consent when it comes to practices of competition, trash talk, or harassment in contemporary video games play spaces both online and in person. Lastly, I argue that as social interaction becomes more constant in game play the magic circle is formed less by the rules of the game itself and almost entirely on the social contracts of pervasive gamer culture. It is in this culture, which is not only male dominated, but frequently abusive to women and other minorities, that I spent my formative years.[3] The section that follows is an autobiographical passage that outlines my experiences playing video games with boys and then with men and repeatedly attempting, and failing, to form a magic circle around game play with members of this culture that is so steeped in the subjugation of women.

# "I'll Just Watch"

I started playing games at the age of 5 on an old Commodore 64 my parents got at a garage sale for me and my brother. From then on we were hooked and we always played as a team. We didn't have a lot of money so we usually got consoles and games a few years late but that didn't stop us from becoming rabid gamers. Everything changed around the age of 13 when I realized that it wasn't the same to play games with or around boys who were not my brother. My brother and I had always worked together in order to play games that were too hard for children. Two heads were better than one when trying to uncover the mysteries of *Myst* (1993) or help Indiana Jones discover the *Fate of Atlantis* (1992). Conversely, when I played games with other boys they made fun of me, they got angry, they got overly competitive, they got defensive when I beat them, or as an affront to my young identity they would express disbelief that I even liked playing games at all. Even boys who were quite nice to me still considered it strange that I would rather go home to play video games than hang out after school and therefore they called me (affectionately) "Nintendo Girl."

All of these experiences led me to a conclusion that many young girls come to: post-puberty things were different, boys were allowed to keep playing games into their teens years but girls were not. As a teen I would mostly only play games if there were no men in the room, which was difficult as my brothers' friends became a regular fixture in our household. I remember taking my gamecube from the living room and into my father's room and locking the door in order to play *Wind Waker* (2002) on his tiny bedroom TV. I knew that I needed total privacy if I was to maintain my magic circle and enjoy playing the game. Later in high school I was that girl who would "just watch" while her boyfriend and guy friends played multiplayer games. I didn't have to play to know I didn't want to join in as I sat there listening to them berate, humiliate, and insult each other while I quietly played on my Gameboy in the corner. I could feel that there was a magic circle in place, and that the insults flying around the room were a part of it, but I was not. As the only girl in the room I was the lowest in the hierarchy of gamers and was therefore constantly the focus of jokes that reduced me to my gender, my body parts, or to my role as "girlfriend". Within our "friend" group I was considered at worst a constant annoyance who was taking up valuable space in the car or basement and at best and I was considered unintelligent, unfunny, and unskilled but "one of the guys" nonetheless.

As an adult the fear was still there. I would find myself waiting for boyfriends and roommates to go to school or work so that I could camp out on the couch playing games blissfully alone until about ten minutes before they would come home. When *Skyward Sword* (2011) came out, I completed my familiar ritual by unhooking the console from the living room television and hiding away from my roommates to play all weekend in my room behind a locked door. I *did* try playing with other people to push my boundaries or confront my fears but it never ended well. These experiments would almost always lead to someone forcefully telling me what to do in the game, critiquing my skills, making comments about the difficulty mode, trying to take the controller away and do it themselves, or even throwing the controller across the room if I beat them. The magic circle was sometimes there but almost always broken. For example, once in an academic setting I was having a great time until I refused to kill another player in a co-op Mario game and was called "a typical girl gamer" to howls of laughter from a large group constituted of entirely male grad students. Most memorably, I once beat the highscore of my ex-boyfriend in an on-rails shooter we both liked and it was the first time I outperformed him in a game. That night I laid in our bed staring at the ceiling of our shared apartment listening to the sounds of the same level ringing out countless times, the same shots being fired, the same music being played, until eventually around 3 am I fell asleep without him. The next morning, I woke up to find my score beaten and we never spoke about it again. We played games together frequently, but for our magic circle to stay intact he had to always be the winner.

## Scoring

As a woman who played video games I frequently felt a very specific type of disrespect and objectification where I was sexualized for my gamer identity while also being disrespected as the lowest in the hierarchy of gamers. Comments about my gaming skill, or about me being a "fake gamer girl", were frequent but attempts to sleep with me simply because I was a "gamer girl" were just as frequent—as a female gamer I somehow felt adored and deplored by male gamers all at the same time. Despite this, when I did meet someone I was interested in, sex was nothing like my gaming experiences outlined above. Not that I didn't have a few negative experiences, or experiences of highly questionable consent, I did (and unfortunately most women have) but with my repeat partners who I trusted in bed I felt very strongly that my body and my pleasure were my own and I easily demanded autonomy over it. Consent was extremely important in sexual play; I felt like my rights were respected and that my magic circle was always intact. But this same logic and enjoyment did not extend to playing games together. I didn't feel safe and respected in the same way. Mutual enjoyment didn't seem to be as important, and therefore a magic circle was frequently broken. The following sections will investigate how consent functions (or doesn't function) in contemporary play practices in order to enquire what makes forming a magic circle within contemporary social gaming so difficult.

# The Magic Circle

Play, sexual or otherwise, requires an intense amount of trust and vulnerability and Huizinga was well aware of this when writing about play as a concept in his now classic text *Homo Ludens* (1944). When establishing what makes play *play*, Huizinga emphasizes "first and foremost ... all play is a voluntary activity. Play to order is no longer play: it could at best be a forcible imitation of it" (7). Huizinga goes on to explain that play is "never a task" and is "free, [it] is in fact, freedom" (7). If we put the free and voluntary nature of play at the forefront of how we define play, we can see how it has much in common with the way we define sexual play which must be consensual for all participants to be considered sex or play and not assault. Huizinga coined the term "the magic circle" to describe the "space" in which this type of consensual, voluntary, and free play took place. Huizinga explains that play "moves and has its being within a play-ground marked off beforehand ... The arena, the card-table, the magic circle ... All are temporary worlds within the ordinary world" (10). The magic circle Huizinga describes has boundaries, but these boundaries are both flexible and liminal. During both sex and gameplay, you are vulnerable simply because you are participating in a type of play with boundaries that are unclear unless made explicit beforehand. In single player play, the boundaries are usually easily determined between the game and the player making it simple to sustain the magic circle. But, when you play with someone else (in the same room or online) those boundaries become more blurred.

# Bursting the Bubble

Huizinga, like many others after him, notes that constraints in the form of rules are what make a game *a game* and what make play *play*. He explains that "all play has its rules. They determine what 'holds' in the temporary world circumscribed by play" (11). In pleasurable sexual encounters or positive game play sessions where rules are followed, we don't notice that the magic circle is in place. But when something goes wrong for us, or the rules are not followed, the magic circle becomes highly visible. Huizinga explains that inside the magic circle

> an absolute and peculiar order reigns. Here we come across another, very positive feature of play: it creates order, is order ... Play demands order absolute and supreme. The least deviation from it "spoils the game", robs it of its character and makes it worthless. (10)

"Spoiling the game" is an act that I will refer to as "bursting the magic circle" throughout this chapter. The bursting of the magic circle is the moment which makes game play worthless to the player. That moment is based entirely on a player's own perception of the shared magic circle. In other words, when you play with someone else the magic circle could ideally ebb and flow nicely between two people's comfort zones until the play is finished but often what we see instead are scenarios where order is disrupted and the magic circle "bursts" due to interfering elements that compromise the comfort, or enjoyment of a player. Most importantly, what is "order" to one player *is not always* order to the other; therefore, players will either re-negotiate what is and is not allowed, or one person will continue to play while the other person is taking part in the game but is left on the outside of the magic circle. Furthermore, the "order" that Huizenga insists play "creates" is now frequently based less on the rules of the game itself and is instead based on which social behaviors and play practices are considered part of hegemonic masculine gamer culture. Therefore, women and other minorities frequently find themselves left out of the magic circle of many games due to contemporary play practices that disrupt the order of their play.

## Contemporary Play Practices and the Magic Circle

Instances where the magic circle "bursts" will vary greatly from player to player. This is especially apparent in multiplayer games with open channels of communications and large groups of players with varying amounts of privilege. It is easy to imagine a situation where two players "playing together" have competing play practices and magic circles that do not overlap. This problem begs many questions: are these people with different motivations for playing still "playing together"? Furthermore, if both players are inside different magic circles that do not overlap are they both playing the same game? And lastly, how do we play with other players who have conflicting magic circles? (Fig. 12.1)

**Fig. 12.1**   Author's chart

This diagram illustrates three hypothetical overlapping magic circles. Imagine these three people are playing a massive multiplayer online role-playing game (MMORPG) separately and are matched up based on class to play through a dungeon together. Player #1 is totally okay with trash talk and using/hearing racist and sexist slurs and insults while they game but is annoyed by role players. Player #2 likes to role play while they play the game and they spend a lot of time and effort constructing their characters persona but they are not in anyway okay with trash talk or slurs. Player #3 also likes role playing but unlike person #2 trash talking is part of their character's persona. All these people have different play practices; in an ideal world they would be on different servers with other players who are interested in getting the same things out of the game. But is separating people completely based on play practice really the only solution to these problems?

This *is* the logic we use when picking sexual partners though. If your magic circle didn't overlap at all with someone else's (sexual orientation, kinks, personal preferences), you would be considered sexual incompatible. With sex we require consent before playing rough, role playing nonconsensual situations, or inflicting pleasurable pain. If our partners are not within the magic circle of our sexual encounter, it is no longer enjoyable for us. Gaming on the other hand is fraught with play practices that purposely make the experience unenjoyable for other players such as griefing, trolling, or general trash talking. Trying to ruin the game for others is frequently what makes gaming fun for some.

## Talking Trash

When is trash talk "just talk" and when is it harassment? The answer seems simple to some, and much more complicated to others. For example, when professional gamer Aris Bakhtanians was asked "can I get my Street Fighter without my sexual harassment" he replied: "You can't. You can't because they're one in the same thing. This is a community that's, you know, 15 or 20 years old, and the sexual harassment is part of a culture, and if you remove that from the fighting game community, it's not the fighting game community" (Klepek 2012). In this interview, Bakhtanians' also demonstrates the commonly held belief that banning trash talk and harassment in games or tournaments is actually seen as *oppressive* to gamers. He has explained that there is no reason someone shouldn't yell, for example, "rape that bitch" at a female player while playing or competing because "we're in America, man, this isn't North Korea. We can say what we want" (Klepek). Harassment during gameplay is seen by many gamers as both a part of the game itself, part of participating in games culture, and an exercise in "free speech". While these practices have become an everyday normalized part of play for participants in gaming communities, they are not a *necessary* part of play. In fact, these practices make it impossible for some people to be included in the magic circle.

On the other side of the issue, gamer Jenny Haniver advocates for gender equality in online gaming by recording reactions to her presence in online gaming spaces and uploading them to her website "Not in the Kitchen Anymore". In her various posts and interviews, Haniver outlines the ways in which game play stops when she enters the virtual room and uses her voice as people need to acknowledge that there is a woman present by insulting or hitting on her (Sun-Higginson 2015). In order for Haniver's play to take place without interruption in an online space within the magic circle, she would need to not speak and not have a username or avatar that easily identified her as female. While the rules of gameplay itself do not indicate this or create this impenetrable magic circle, the rules of games culture do. If women cannot speak or listen to voice chat in online gameplay for fear of being harassed, they are not enjoying the full experience of being able to communicate with other players.

Importantly, trash talk was not always part of gaming practice and wasn't always welcomed by male gamers. In David Kushner's *Masters of Doom* (2004), Kushner gives a narrative description of John Romero, one of the creators of *Doom* (1993), and Shawn, one of his employees, attending a tournament in 1994:

> It was silent except for the sounds of fingers rattling on keys. But all that changed as the id guys began to play. Romero hurled a few shotgun blasts into an opponent and yelled, 'Eat that, fucker!'. The sheepish guy on the computer looked up in fear. Shawn knew that look—the look of a gamer who had never heard true, unbridled smack-talk, just like he'd been the first time he had heard Romero insult him during a game. But now Shawn was a pro and joined right in. "Suck it down, monkey fuck!" he called, after firing a few blasts from his BFG. The gamers cowered. They would learn (140).

Romero's behavior was the same when playing *Doom* in the office. He was known for:

> hurling insults like a trash-talking jock after school. The most aggressive thing people usually did when they played video games was roll their eyes. But *Doom*, Shawn realized, called for something more. After winning the next round, he punched the wall back and screamed, "Eat that, motherfucker!" Romero cackled approvingly. This was how games were meant to be played (Kushner 2004, 131).

These two quotations show the early development of games culture in its current aggressive rendition. Multiplayer games became more competitive and more violent in the late 1990s and the male-dominated LAN (local area network) parties and pro gaming communities soon grew to include this type of trash talk as part of their practice. For many people, including in this case Romero and Shawn, trash talk was part of "*how games were meant to be played*". For these two men, trash talking became a consensual practice and part of their magic circle. Trash talking *can be and frequently is* part of game play, it can be consensual, and it was *originally* a type of subversive play. But, these behaviors are no longer subversive; they have become quite dominant and are now used to police the spaces of games culture to ensure that marginalized players stay out.

# Subversive and Deviant Play

In *Critical Play*, Mary Flanagan outlines the practice of "subversive play" for players who step outside the boundaries of what is expected of them:

By moving and playing within the structures of work and play systems, users interact and experience the pleasure of creating play culture. The digital "magic circle" that players enter is an open environment focused on experimentation and subversion. (61)

In this quotation Flanagan is discussing play at large but more specifically she is investigating the ways players use games to "reveal anxieties and uncertainties about domestic roles" in a type of subversive or critical play (61). But, this quotation about subversive pleasure also applies to the scenario described above in in *Masters of Doom*. At the time, the trash talking Romero and his employees participated in was highly unconventional and therefore very subversive when done outside of their offices. But these practices spread and grew throughout the next few decades and are no longer subversive within gamer culture. Trash talking has gone from "subverting online cultures norms of interaction" (Flannagan 2009, 61) to becoming an online norm in and of itself. Even if you don't yourself trash talk, many would argue that you need to learn how to not "let it get to you" in the same way you would need your poker face not to be read even if you chose not to bluff. Therefore, without it being coded into the game, trash talking has become part of many games and therefore is not being used to subvert any dominant norms. In fact, as was the case with the example I gave at the beginning of this section (see the comments of Aris Bakhtanians) asking someone *not* to trash talk would actually be considered a deviant behavior within most of gaming culture.

In her book *Race Gender and Deviance in Xbox Live* (2014), Kishonna L. Gray explains that deviant behavior is an act that, "does not conform to socially accepted norms established by rules" of a certain community (35). Therefore, what is considered deviant in larger culture frequently is not considered deviant in certain subcultures. Sexism and racism in the context of Xbox Live are not considered deviant: it is within the magic circle of gameplay and has become normalized. Bigoted statements are arguably helpful to winning as they will make your competitors uncomfortable or maybe even make them quit the game. While acts of sexism and racism "should be viewed as deviant" within online gaming spaces they are not (Gray 2014, 35). In fact, because those who lack power are more likely to have their behaviors be labeled deviant (Gray 2014, 35), we see a model where deviant behavior has been reversed and those of us drawing attention to sexism and racism within games and games culture are the ones that are considered deviant and disruptive to the established magic circle around online gaming. Gaming spaces adopt what Gray calls a "relativist approach" where "no behavior or person is inherently deviant; deviance emerges through a labeling process where some behaviors are identified as bad, undesirable, or unacceptable on the basis of rules made by those in positions of power" (2014, 36). The behaviors that have been identified as deviant by the gamer community range from taking any sort of offense at bigoted speech or trash talk, to simply participating in the game world as "other". The presence of a woman or person of color is often identified through vocal patterns in Xbox Live or sometimes by their screen names and therefore "marginalized gamers within Xbox Live have been constructed as deviant bodies, undeserving of the full status of gamer by the default white male" (Gray 2014, 47). Any presence of marginalized gamers is therefore policed with sexist, racist, and homophobic speech by the dominate players so that the marginalized players won't remain and "ruin the game." While you can report the harassment, the reporting system is often used by the harassers to get the victim themselves banned.

# Rape

Maybe the most nefarious way in which dominate players ruin the game for marginalized players is through experiences of in-game rape as outlined in Julian Dibbell's classic "A Rape in Cyberspace" and also documented by the authors of the anthology *Violation: Rape in Gaming* (2012). Many of the participants and authors experiences outlined in this book involve a scenario where rape is sprung on a female player without their consent in the middle of either a online, live action, or tabletop role playing game (Dibbell 1999, 25–44; Moore 2012, 45–56; Laurenson 2012, 81–90). In-game rape has sadly become a common magic circle bursting experience for women who play role playing games as their frequently male dungeon masters often do not consider the traumatizing effects having to role play the rape of their character might have on them (Dibbel 1999, 25–44; Moore 2012, 45–56; Laurenson 2012, 81–90). As Clarisse Thorn puts it in the introduction to *Violation: Rape in Gaming* "when picturing the typical mostly-male gamer group, it's hard to imagine a situation in which a character would be raped that would feel easy or innocent for any women involved. Implicit threat is *built into* that situation" (11).

But it's not only role played rape that can burst the magic circle for women, it is also the language of rape and domination used during trash talk. Not only are descriptions of rape and sexual assault often used during trash talk but the language of sexual domination, while empty of its significance to many of the men who use it, can mean something else entirely to female players. In her article "Three Words I Said To The Man I Defeated In Gears of War That I'll

Never Say Again" (2012), Patricia Hernandez explains that while for many years she attempted to use the common gamer refrain "I raped you" (meaning I won) but she eventually realized that it didn't mean the same thing to her as it did to male players and frequently male players would laugh at her in response. She, as a rape survivor, wanted the words to represent domination, she wanted the words to hurt her opponents the way the words hurt her but Hernandez concludes that her words do not affect her male opponents because "trash talk makes it obvious that the implicit understanding of the language of domination isn't just sexualized. It's gendered" (126). There is a disconnect between the way that male players and female players view and experience game play situations and contemporary gaming practices and that discontent is caused by a lack of consent in our gaming communities as well as a general lack of respect for women.

## Conclusion: Developing Critical Consent for Gamers

This disconnect was visible when game developer Patrick Harris gave an anti-harassment talk at the Game Developers Conference in 2016 in which he used a personal "experiment" harassing an unconsenting woman in a virtual reality setting (by grabbing her body parts) as evidence that harassment is very upsetting for women and will be a larger problem in VR worlds. While in the presentation he insisted on game developers doing something to stop this type of harassment, he did not seem to see the ethical concerns of doing it himself and then showing a video of himself harassing this woman to the world in the name of "progress" (Sampat 2016; Frank 2016). This is just one example of how the consent and bodily rights of women are often not considered in games culture even when they are the topic of conversation. Women don't have to purposely experience or perpetrate harassment to know that harassment (sexual or otherwise) is and will continue to exist in gaming spaces as we have become accustomed to having our consent either pushed aside or violated when we game. So much of the language used in gaming communities is that of domination both sexual and physical but no one asks you if you enjoy being threatened or yelled at. No one asks for your consent by saying "is it okay if I yell at you? If I tell you that I'm going to own you? To murder you? To rape you?"

In her book *Queer BDSM Intimacies* (2014), Robin Bauer discusses how even within the larger BDSM community, there is often a very black and white definition of consent that does not consider the ways in which people sometimes give verbal consent in sexual situations but not of their own free will. Simple "yes" consent can be given out of fear, out of exhaustion, or because one feels that it is what they are "supposed" to do. While verbal yes/no consent is very important, we also need to complicate our ideas of consent further in order to make sure that there is enjoyment, pleasure, and *play* taking place to indicate full consent. Enthusiastic consent, negotiated consent, or working consent are all types of "critical consent" that through their respective modifiers explain that legal consent alone is not enough (Bauer 2014, 75). Unfortunately playing any sort of multiplayer game is the equivalent of giving a "yes" to the harassment that takes place during game play and not playing is the only surefire way to say "no." Consent should be an evolving process and not a static "yes" or "no" to whatever is about to happen in a space. Within online gaming spaces women sadly have very little access to any type of negotiated consent. Their only options are to stop playing and/or report harassment—neither of which are a solution to the core problem of systemic sexism in the gaming community.

BDSM play, rape play, and rape fantasies, while controversial to many, are perfectly normal to others but this play must be constructed in a way that is totally safe, consensual, and *enjoyable* to both parties. Arrangements like this do exist in gaming culture; there are friends who insult and trash talk each other for mutual pleasure but there are other circumstances where the trash talking is only enjoyable for the perpetrator *because* it is unconsented. In conclusion, while trash talk may sometimes be a type of pleasurable pain for all involved, if others don't consent to this behavior then it's violence and harassment. As Huizinga explained all those years ago, for play to be play it must be voluntary, and many of us do not voluntarily participate in being insulted as part of gaming practice—it is forced upon us and it is forcing us out of the magic circle.

Those of us who play games need to think critically about our own consent and boundaries as well as that of others during game play online and in "real life". I've frequently heard the advice, from gamers and non-gamers, that if the harassment bothers someone, they shouldn't play video games. But I've also experienced this harassment from gamers on Facebook, Twitter, and YouTube—are women consenting to harassment simply by being present online? When playing games online I sometimes wonder if what I'm doing is really "play" if I'm not enjoying myself because of the words and actions of other players. Has game play, at that point, become work? Is it what Huizinga called a "forcible imitation" of play? (7). Will my magic circle never overlap with others online because of our differing play practices? Lastly, shouldn't game play, like sexual play, be pleasurable for all involved?

# Notes

1. The existence, relevance, and use of the magic circle as a concept has been hotly debated by scholars. Many see Huizinga's division between play spaces and "ordinary life" to be problematic. See Cindy Poremba's (2007) "Critical Potential on the Brink of the Magic Circle" for comprehensive discussion of this topic. Within this article I am attempting to bring issues of "ordinary life" (such as sexism, racism, harassment and consent) to bare on the magic circle while focusing in on the idea of worlds within (and not separate from) worlds or "temporary worlds" that are "within the ordinary world" (Huizinga 1944, 10). For a comprehensive overview of these debates please see Jaakko Stenros' (2012) In Defence of a Magic Circle: The Social and Mental Boundaries of Play.
2. It should be noted that Huizinga himself didn't feel that his rules for play could be applied to sex in 1944 as it was seen as an activity that was primarily for the purpose of reproduction. Although, Huizinga *did* say that the label play could be "specially or even exclusively reserved for erotic relationships falling outside the social norm" (43). In other words, I would argue that Huizinga's definition of play now easily adheres to what is considered sex within the "social norm" in 2018 (i.e. sex for purposes other than reproduction).
3. For more on the abuse of women in games culture see Mia Consalvo's (2012) "Confronting Toxic Gamer Culture", Shira Chess and Adrienne Shaw's (2015) "A Conspiracy of Fishes", Kishonna Gray's (2014) *Race Gender and Deviance in Xbox Live*, Lisa Nakamura's (2012) "Queer Female of Color: The Highest Difficulty Setting There Is?", and Katherine Cross' (2014) "'We will Force Gaming to be Free': On Gamergate & The Licence to Inflict Suffering".

# Bibliography

Bauer, R. 2014. *Queer BDSM Intimacies: Critical Consent and Pushing Boundaries.* London: Palgrave Macmillan.

Chess, Shira, and Adrienne Shaw. 2015. A Conspiracy of Fishes, or, How We Learned to Stop Worrying about# GamerGate and Embrace Hegemonic Masculinity. *Journal of Broadcasting & Electronic Media* 59 (1): 208–220.

Consalvo, Mia. 2012. Confronting Toxic Gamer Culture: A Challenge for Feminist Game Studies Scholars. *Ada: A Journal of Gender, New Media, and Technology* 1 http://adanewmedia.org/blog/2012/11/11/issue1-consalvo/.

Cross, Katherine. 2014. 'We Will Force Gaming to Be Free': On Gamergate & The License to Inflict Suffering. *First Person Scholar*, October 8. http://www.firstpersonscholar.com/we-will-force-gaming-to-be-free/.

Dibbell, Julian. 1999. A Rape in Cyberspace. In *My Tiny Life: Crime and Passion in a Virtual World.* New York: Holt Paperbacks.

Flanagan, Mary. 2009. *Critical Play: Radical Game Design*. Cambridge, MA: MIT Press.

Frank, Allegra. 2016. Online Harassment in Virtual Reality Is 'Way, Way, Way Worse'—But Can Devs Change That? *Polygon*. March 16. https://www.polygon.com/2016/3/16/11242294/online-harassment-virtual-reality-gdc-2016.

Gray, Kishonna L. 2014. *Race, Gender, and Deviance in Xbox Live: Theoretical Perspectives from the Virtual Margins*. London: Routledge.

Haniver, Jenny. 2010. About. *Not in the Kitchen Anymore*. http://www.notinthekitchenanymore.com/about/.

Hernandez, Patricia. 2012. Three Words I Said to the Man I Defeated in Gears of War That I'll Never Say Again. In *Violation: Rape in Gaming*, ed. Clarisse Thorn and Julian Dibbell. Lexington, KY: CreateSpace Independent Publishing Platform.

Huizinga, Johan. 1944. *Homo Ludens: A Study of the Play-Element in Culture*. Boston: Beacon Press.

Juul, Jesper. 2009. The Magic Circle and the Puzzle Piece. In *Conference Proceedings of The Philosophy of Computer Games 2008*, ed. Stephan Günzel, Michael Liebe, and Dieter Mersch. Universitätsverlag Potsdam.

Klepek, Patrick. 2012. When Passions Flare, Lines Are Crossed. *Giant Bomb*. February 28. https://www.giantbomb.com/articles/when-passions-flare-lines-are-crossed-updated/1100-4006/.

Kushner, David. 2004. *Masters of Doom: How Two Guys Created an Empire and Transformed Pop Culture*. Reprint ed. New York: Random House Trade Paperbacks.

Laurenson, Lydia. 2012. How to Deal with Rape in Roleplaying Games. In *Violation: Rape in Gaming*, ed. Clarisse Thorn and Julian Dibbell. Lexington, KY: CreateSpace Independent Publishing Platform.

Moore, Anne C. 2012. Women in Gaming: Conversation on Roleplaying Game Rape. In *Violation: Rape in Gaming*, ed. Clarisse Thorn and Julian Dibbell. Lexington, KY: CreateSpace Independent Publishing Platform.

Nakamura, Lisa. 2012. Queer Female of Color: The Highest Difficulty Setting There Is? Gaming Rhetoric as Gender Capital. *Ada: A Journal of Gender, New Media, and Technology* 2: 1 http://adanewmedia.org/blog/2012/11/11/issue1-nakamura/.

Poremba, Cindy. 2007. Critical Potential on the Brink of the Magic Circle. In *Situated Play, Proceedings of DiGRA 2007 Conference*.

Ruberg, Bonnie. 2010. Sex as Game: Playing with the Erotic Body in Virtual Worlds. *Rhizomes Cultural Studies in Emerging Knowledge* 21. http://www.rhizomes.net/issue21/ruberg.html.

Sampat, Elizabeth. 2016. Here's How We Failed Women at GDC 2016. *Gamasutra*. March 21. https://www.gamasutra.com/blogs/ElizabethSampat/20160321/268527/Heres_How_We_Failed_Women_at_GDC_2016.php.

Shaw, Adrienne. 2015. Circles, Charmed and Magic: Queering Game Studies. *QED: A Journal in GLBTQ Worldmaking* 2 (2): 64–97.

Stenros, Jaakko. 2012. In Defence of a Magic Circle: The Social and Mental Boundaries of Play. In *Proceedings of DiGRA Nordic 2012 Conference: Local and Global – Games in Culture and Society.*

Sun-Higginson, Shannon. 2015. *GTFO: Get the F&#% Out.* [Documentary].

Thorn, Clarisse. 2012. Reflections on Game Rape, Feminism, Sadomasochism, and Selfhood. In *Violation: Rape in Gaming*, ed. Julian Dibbell and Clarisse Thorn. Lexington, KY: CreateSpace Independent Publishing Platform.

# 13

# Shoot the Gun Inside: Doubt and Feminist Epistemology in Video Games

## Elyse Janish

The identity "feminist academic" has recently come under explicit attack by some gamers. In late 2014, the so-called Gamergate scandal broke when game designer Zoe Quinn was falsely accused by her jilted ex-boyfriend of having sex with journalists, executives, and producers in order to ensure her indie game's success. Although proven false within hours, the accusations became a rallying point for anti-feminist backlash against women in video game spaces. In the months following the slander of Zoe Quinn, a full-fledged anti-feminist hate campaign ensued. Some of the backlash even came to focus on feminists who write about video games academically, much to the surprise of feminist games studies scholars—a subject position that both I and my good friend Holly, who figures prominently in this autoethnographic study, occupy. When Gamergate finally began to die down, it had the following accomplishments under its umbrella: bullying Intel into dropping advertisements for *Gamasutra*, which published the work of a despised feminist (Johnston 2014); three women forced to flee their homes due to bomb, rape, and death threats (Frank 2014; Arce 2014); the cancellation of a keynote address by long-time feminist critic Anita Sarkeesian due to gun threats (Hern 2014); the withdrawal of feminist critiques by several scholars from journals and conferences (Chess et al. 2014); and widespread, mainstream media attention, including coverage by CNBC, Fox News, *The Telegraph*, *the Christian Science Monitor*, *Businessweek*, *the New York Business Journal*, and many others (an uncommon feat for the video game industry, excepting times when people pick up the cry of anti-violence after school shootings).

E. Janish (✉)
University of Colorado, Boulder, CO, USA

© The Author(s) 2018
K. L. Gray et al. (eds.), *Feminism in Play*, Palgrave Games in Context,
https://doi.org/10.1007/978-3-319-90539-6_13

**221**

In the wake of Gamergate, I found myself sucked back into gaming after some time away. The researcher in me, perhaps masochistically, saw Gamergate's explicitly anti-academic and inherently anti-female commitments as a point of departure for better understanding how feminist scholars who study games experience gaming for pleasure and/or for work. This study was designed around that exigence—in an often explicitly hostile environment, how do I, as a woman and feminist academic, experience playing video games? In this chapter, I argue several key points for consideration when studying gender and gaming. First, and most obviously, women's experiences when playing games are linked inextricably to their larger life environments, such as social, cultural, work, home, and political arenas. When we try to account for and/or change gender inequity in gaming, we must remember that our experience of gender in our non-gaming lives weighs directly on the way we interact with games, gamers, and games studies (see: Jenson & de Castell 2010; Terlecki et al. 2011). Second, I argue for the methodological relevance of narrative autoethnography within games studies. As a method, narrative autoethnography opens doors of understanding and empathetic engagement, which in turn forward the work of making games more hospitable to people of diverse identities. Finally, this study shows how doubt functions as a feature of my/our/an epistemology; it is, in other words, an integral part of how I know and learn things about myself, my work, and my gaming. Doubt is the pivot point around which the first two arguments circle. The narrative structure is intended to help the reader experience this epistemological feature, perhaps even opening a new way of understanding how the larger forces of patriarchy and misogyny that sometimes seem disconnected from gaming practices are in fact relevant and present in women's gameplay.

But how could I enter game space again, given the overwhelming dread Gamergate successfully inspired in me? My identity as a scholar *and* a gamer had evolved since I had last tanked for a World of Warcraft (*WoW*) team as an axe-wielding troll (finesse characters, as I learned the painful way, are not my forte). Since then, I had stopped playing most multi-player games, adopted feminism as a lifestyle, taken up the label "queer," and aligned myself with radical feminist rhetorical critics. The desire to play and study games directly clashed against my disgust for all Gamergate stood for: the explicit dismissing, marginalizing, and punishing of feminist activists, among other marginalized groups. Grappling with questions of being true to myself, of balancing philosophical and political commitments with relationship maintenance, I waded into the waters of online gaming again slowly, and with reinforcements.

*Early in the conception of this project*: Holly, a fellow feminist academic who studies games, and I mostly talk about the project on Facebook chat, of all places. The project was born out of the death of another, permissions having fallen through in preliminary stages. However, a trusted mentor urges me toward using a video game as the site for study instead, and my excitement for the project takes over. I tell Holly immediately, since we had already been throwing around the possibility of doing a study on video games together. We talk that night and debate about choosing *League of Legends* (*LoL*) as our site, as it is one of the most popular multi-player online games, but we both have reservations.

"If there's any game full of rampant sexism, it's *LoL*," Holly says. "I don't play it myself, it's too intense. Everyone gets harassed." We shy away from *LoL* because the learning curve is too high. Novices are too hated in *LoL*, and neither of us is experienced enough with that style of game to make headway on track with my timeline for the project. It would take so long just to reach a high enough level of competency to be accepted by other players, let alone feel comfortable doing a study. I don't tell Holly, but I'm a little relieved; I've heard and read horror stories of women playing *LoL* and the harassment they face. I am also full of self-doubt. I tell myself that *LoL* is too much for me to handle. The last time I played a hardcore game like that, I was used as sniper bait by my teammates because I spent most of the time running in circles, an easy target for the enemy. It was a laugh at the time, and still a story I love to tell, but it undermined my confidence as a player of hardcore games thoroughly. Such games became offlimits.

We decide on *Project Zomboid*, a post-apocalyptic zombie thriller all about survival. "These are End-Times," the loading screen says. "This is how you die." Ironic, since part of our reason for choosing it was self-preservation.

## Method and Theoretical Basis: Taking Up Space Through Feminist Narrative Autoethnography

While Holly and I struggled to pick a game as the project's site and wait for approvals, I was similarly struggling with conceiving the endgame of my project. What would it look like? How could I connect the experience of playing *Project Zomboid* to my larger goals as an academic, and to Gamergate as a whole? While exploring these questions, I became increasingly attracted to the idea of narrating my experience as an academic means to open new avenues for knowledge-seeking. To convey my experience, to dig into the question of what makes my experience as a woman—academic—game player significant or meaningful, narrative autoethnography became an increasingly compelling choice of method.

Autoethnographers seek to not only create the thick description of ethnography, but also relate personal and interpersonal experiences (Ellis et al. 2011). Bochner (2012) suggests that as scholars of human experience, we write about "contradictions, emotions, and subjectivities;" yet although these "may be recognized as concrete lived experiences, ... [they] are usually expressed in forms of writing that dissolve concrete events in solutions of abstract analysis" (159). This abstraction, the typical mode of relaying information academically, has the effect of "distancing readers from the actions and feelings of particular human beings" (Bochner 2012, 159). But this distancing, a practice which has become conventional in the social sciences, "[confines] inquiry to a limited range of researchable experiences represented in a narrow domain of recognizable texts" (Bochner 2012, 160). Video games are often outside of the "domain of recognizable texts" for academia, yet provide ample ground for the study of culture, communication, interaction, and other important social constructs. The autoethnographer upsets convention and foregrounds *experience* not in its distilled abstractions that turn into theory, but in the narrative form that confronts the reader with subjectivity and, sometimes, discomfort.

As a method, autoethnography entails much of the same work as other forms of ethnography. An autoethnographer, however, begins with the self as the subject of research, usually within the context of a subculture she already participates in—such as gaming. Chang (2013) suggests that autoethnography "uses the researcher's personal experiences as primary data," in order to "expand the understanding of social phenomena" (108). Although the actual procedure may vary depending on the goal of the researcher, data collection occurs in much the same way as other ethnographic endeavors, through participant observation, interviews, and document analysis. Berger (2001) points out that the autoethnographer is "not a detached observer, taking portions of interviews and analyzing them in the context of grand theory" but rather that the work done by such a researcher is intricately tied to her personal history and experiences (512). Field notes and reflective journaling are also an important element of the process, capturing immediate reactions and secondary reflections on the proceedings of the site of study. The narrative element is designed to close the affective gap between the researcher and the reader as much as possible; this pursuit treats subjective and emotional experiences as critical knowledge-building tools, rather than prioritizing analytical abstraction.

For this project, I chose to extend the study beyond myself to include Holly, in part due to the remarkable similarities between us: we are both feminist academics who love to play, work, and think together about games and interaction. I also chose this collaborative approach because it parallels *how* I play games: I enter game worlds socially, for the purpose of maintaining and enjoying my friendships. Holly and I play together far more often than I play by myself, so to include her from the beginning as an insider participant made sense. She participated not only in the recorded game sessions but also in short debriefs after each session, as well as a longer interview at the end of data collection. Since the end of data collection, she has consulted from time to time about the presentation of certain elements in my writing; however, as per our original design, she did not co-author this piece. It is with her consent that she remains anonymous.

Notably, the use of narrative autoethnography as a means of taking up space stems from the work of especially feminist scholars of color, who have laid the foundations for narrative as a scholarly endeavor. Calafell and Moreman (2009) remind us of the power of narrative and using one's voice: "Feminists of color have long argued for the importance of listening to the experiences of women of color and attending to the politics that underlie these voices. These scholars understand that not all voices are granted equal power or access, nor are they always welcome" (124). The idea of unwelcome voices with limited access or power rings true to my experience as a white woman who studies gaming culture, especially given recent developments with Gamergate, which served as the initial exigence for the study. My goal, then, is to narrate my subject position within games, and invite readers to understand it, without suggesting it is an essential experience for all women in games.

Within the Gamergate movement, proponents acknowledged neither race nor gender as pertinent to their goals, but did direct explicit and negative attention toward feminist academics who study games. In a series of tweets, Gamergaters rallied around the hashtag #OperationDiggingDiGRA. DiGRA stands for the Digital Games Research Association, an international academic and professional association dedicated to researching "digital games and associated phenomena" (DiGRA 2014). The tweet thread starts with one Gamergater identifying the objective of the "game" #OperationDiggingDiGRA: "Fact-check, verify all of feminist papers in DiGRA." Others respond to him using phrases that indicate a warlike, combative stance, such as "hit them where it hurts most" and "fight them in academics." One reply suggests that "they" (feminist scholars investigating digital games) will "fear us in their sleep" because of #OperationDiggingDiGRA. The original post's author responds to questions and comments by giving instructions on the proper way to dig DiGRA, explaining the importance of choosing publicly available articles to fact-check and that the Gamergaters can play the academic game and win at it (whatever that means). Chess and Shaw (2015) wrote about their inadvertent involvement in the Gamergate witch-hunt. They point out how Gamergaters were quick to jump to conclusions about people being academics and feminists with little actual understanding of the practices and institutions of academia, and how this opacity and misunderstanding served as support for a conspiracy theory that feminist academics were attempting to ruin gaming. Normal academic procedures, when applied to the study of video games, became themselves a way of bolstering outsider malice.

Besides blatantly mistrusting academia, Gamergaters also targeted non-academic feminist activists in gaming such as Anita Sarkeesian, proving how precarious a position it is to be a feminist in gaming culture at all. The men of Gamergate have done their best to silence the voices of women who were asking for, even demanding, better representation and treatment of women in video games. As a response to silencing tactics, Rachel A. Griffin (2012) once again issues the call for narrative:

> While our voices will sound different at the intersections of our identities and be negotiated by the privilege (if any) we have access to, we have got to speak up at home, work…, everywhere, all the time. We need to get used to the sound of our own voices demanding space and respect because each one of us deserves it, and we must understand that we are all worthy of the energy of another. (149)

Audre Lorde (2009) similarly encourages the researcher to bring herself into her work, stating, "If I do not bring all of who I am to whatever I do, then I bring nothing, or nothing of lasting worth, for I have withheld my essence" (182–183).

These women, although addressing a different oppression that cannot and should not be conflated with the sexism of video game culture, explain the very condition of womanhood and doubt. Can I take up this space? Is my voice worth hearing? Autoethnography is one approach to answering with a clear and resounding *yes*.

## Subversion, Doubt, and Gaming: Two Narratives

The following two narratives occurred at quite different moments in the project's development: the first happened during the data collection period in which Holly and I were recording our game sessions, and the second took place after data collection had concluded and I had volunteered to present preliminary data and analysis to a group of my peers in an academic setting. The final section will mesh these two narratives into a discussion on doubt and womanhood—but first, I invite you, the reader, to suspend academic expectations for a moment and experience the closing of the affective gap between my experience as researcher and yours as reader.

\*   \*   \*

*The fourth time we record:* Two hours and fifteen minutes into the game, Holly and I find ourselves teamed up with two other players, "Sam Johnson" and "Ramu" to our "POSSUM ARMOR" and "Basket Case." In local chat, so only the four of us can see, I say, "Hey Ramu, wanna find out what happens when you shoot a gun inside?"

In our private voice chat, Holly and I giggle about the proposition. We've taken shelter in a warehouse for the night, at Sam's urging. It's easy to get hypothermic and sick at night, he insists, so the best option is to wait out the night in the warehouse. Sam has already advised against shooting the gun in general as it attracts hostiles—the sole reason I suggested firing it inside, to be honest.

Ramu doesn't answer while Holly and I sass privately, but Sam tells us in local chat, "Zombies will still hear it." Seconds later, probably before he had a chance to register Sam's warning, Ramu answers me, too. "Sure?" he says, the question mark indicating his uncertainty at my proposal.

"Yeah man live on the edge!" I reply in local chat. As I type the words, Holly tells me in voice chat, "I really wish I knew what this person was, you know?" She means that she wishes we knew Ramu's gender and age. Despite our best intentions as gender-conscious feminists, we had immediately assumed Ramu's player was male, and probably young given the uncertainty of his demeanor. About Sam's gender, I have little doubt.

Sam asserts himself as our leader within minutes of teaming up; he senses, probably correctly, that he has the most experience in the game and with no ceremony whatsoever begins issuing commands: "This way," "I know the best place," "now over here," "smash the wall with your sledgehammer." When we take a little too long to hop a fence, Sam urges us quicker with a "guys?" sent to local chat. As Holly types "dude chillll" in chat, I animate Sam's command over private voice chat to her, mimicking him by saying "guys? Guys?" in the same voice I use to animate my dog's urgency when she wants to go on a walk. We mutiny with cigarette breaks while he urges us to the warehouse before nightfall, successfully enticing Ramu to light up with us, to Sam's annoyance.

Later, at the warehouse, I drop the ammo I collected early in the game for Ramu to grab. He has the gun, and it would be far more taboo for me to ask for that valuable item than for him to ask for my ammo, but either way one of us has to give something up for my plan. Can't shoot the gun without the ammo. It takes Ramu quite a while to find it, despite the fact that I have positioned Basket Case next to it and am shouting "hey! Over here!" (hotkey: Q) again and again.

Eventually it becomes clear Ramu cannot fire the gun, and strangely enough, Sam decides he'll just do it. He has warned us about bringing down a "war of worlds," attracting all of the zombies (or "zeds" as he sometimes calls them) nearby to our little haven. To this Holly and I recklessly responded "ALL THE WARS OF WORLDS" and "bring itttt." Ramu agreed with a "let's try." So overruled, Sam ended up being the one to fire a gun inside the warehouse.

Nothing happened. No *zeds* nearby, I guess. We make our excuses and exit the game not long after. Holly drops her leftover cigarettes for Sam, typing, "left you some ciggies" just before disconnecting.

*   *   *

*After data collection has ended:* I am standing before my peers presenting preliminary data analysis, watching Holly's and my avatars (this time, our usernames are "Dorito HANDS" for Holly and "CAKE" for me) run around on screen and listening to Holly and myself react to global chat interactions.

"Oh my God," CAKE/I say to Holly in the video, as our avatars check coat pockets in an abandoned shop for possibly useful items (strangely, we find nails, concrete powder). "Every time someone joins this server, they're like, 'hi!'" A pause to check another pocket (cigarettes), then I make a shushing sound privately at Holly but mockingly directed at the people saying hi, and chastise them: "Don't be friendly!" A lot is happening here, of course; Holly and I have a long-standing acknowledgment of each other's tendency toward anti-socialness, and our dislike for interacting with strangers. At the point that I jokingly shush the other players (who cannot hear me), I have not yet used global chat even once. I have no real desire to interact with players besides Holly.

In the present, my peers laugh a little at this recorded interaction, and I begin to explain about how I reflected on my unease at other players' friendliness. I tell them that I read the chat as gendered, even though at this particular juncture no one is making gendered comments. I tell them how I think this is a result of my experiences playing before, in other games, where global chat is often an overtly toxic and hostile language environment for women and LGBTQ individuals. "I raped that boss!" is as common and unexamined as calling something "gay" in gaming speak. Microaggressions like these against anyone who doesn't fit hegemonic masculinity are so frequent and ubiquitous, I tell my classmates that the absence of them was notable to me. I saw the "niceness" of people greeting each other, asking for friendly advice and even, on occasion, getting it, as anomalous and immediately read it as a feminine form of communication, perhaps even a queering of game space norms.

As I say this to my classmates, I hear myself begin to dig a hole, hedging that I read this as gendered because of my expectations, but that my expectations actually clouded my judgment. I essentially say that I have made something out of nothing, that my reaction that "this conversation is gendered" came about because I was *looking* for gendered language. I doubt myself, doubt my experience, doubt my right to make this claim, publicly, in front of the whole class. Even as I say it, I am mad at myself. It is so typical, such a classic internalization of the silencing effects of a sexist and anti-feminist culture. Doubt is a most effective tool for anti-feminists, because it is instilled in us, and we use it against ourselves without prompting. I hear myself make a subtle and complicated claim, and I stop myself, hold myself back from occupying that space. Don't make claims you can't support, says the inner monologue.

## Advancing a Reframed Narrative: Doubt as a Filter for Future Feminist Knowledge-Seeking

However, these *are* claims I can support; I've known the research on the gendered nature of communication types, both digital and non-digital, for years now. I know that in fact, online, women are more likely to use polite language while men are more likely to engage in combative language that purposefully aims to irritate others (Herring 1994). I know that online spaces are traditionally conceived of as male spaces, and thus men feel comfortable "flaming" while women have to ask permission, say please and thank you, use politeness tactics to be heard (Herring 1994, 1999). Many other studies have confirmed this finding, suggesting that women are more likely than men to use politeness tactics online (see Guiller & Durndell 2006; Taylor 2006; Martey & Stromer-Galley 2007; Massanari 2017). More specific to games studies, I'm familiar with studies about masculine forms of communicating in video games. Moreover, research has shown that video game culture fosters a competitive, masculine environment where femininity is not only discouraged but also actively attacked (Salter & Blodgett 2012; Bell, Kampe, & Taylor 2015). Thus, if it is feminine to be polite online, we can conclude that politeness is a norm discouraged by hypermasculine video game culture. It is, in short, my conclusion that the polite talk between the server users was anomalous, even gendered, is not only perfectly reasonable, it is well supported by the work of scholars before me.

I was familiar with this scholarship when I doubted myself while presenting my research. I nonetheless felt obligated to soften my stance, hedge my position as though I really did not have the right to speak about gendered norms of communication in video game spaces. Perhaps I picked up on the doubt of my non-gamer peers, who might have looked at the "hi" "hi" "hei" of the global chat and thought that it didn't look gendered at all. Perhaps I felt their skepticism and backed down for fear of—of what? Upsetting someone? Making myself look like the radical feminist I am? A moment of self-doubt, self-skepticism, of bowing to non-experts in something about which I can claim relative expertise, because I fear being labeled that which I label myself?

This moment, perhaps ironically, became the turning point in my data analysis. Presenting my data and experiencing this dissociated moment became part of the data itself, integral to how the rest of the project unfolded. I went into the project looking for some kind of conclusions to be drawn about the intersection of game player, academic, and woman, and it wasn't until I heard myself backing down on a reasonable claim about gendered interaction online, that I really learned something about that intersection. Looking back at the playful insubordination of the Sam and Ramu episode, I suddenly see not the snide comments made to Holly in private chat but the complete lack of such comments made in local or global chat. Despite finding Sam's overtly controlling mannerisms grating and even a little insulting, I never once spoke up, never asked him to back off, never even leveled any of my mocking commentary *at* him, only privately to Holly. My mutinous actions consisted of indirectly encouraging Ramu to engage in behavior Sam found annoying. Where I previously saw subversion, now I saw doubtful behavior, avoidance techniques, and, sure, maybe some subversion, too. Not every form of resistance must be overt.

With this reframing in mind, the research process from its very beginnings and on through writing and revising is seeded with doubt. The choice of site based on the urging of a mentor, with my own hesitation built in because, could I really do autoethnographic work on video games and have it be accepted for publication? The choice of *Project Zomboid* instead of *League of Legends*, since I doubted I could learn the skills fast enough to be able to learn anything useful about the community. The presentation of data wherein I undermined my most interesting claims at the first sign of someone in the audience possibly disagreeing. Doubt pervaded every element of the project, from its inception to its design to its data collection to its data analysis to its public presentation. This was not merely the doubt of either a younger academic looking to break into a tough field, nor merely that of a game player with less experience than the other players. Instead, it is a worldview, a way of interacting and knowing that seeps into everything I do.

The point, then: if doubt pervades, we become subjects which people like proponents of Gamergate can easily influence and control. Take the example of #OperationDiggingDiGRA, mentioned earlier. When Holly and I first talked about #OperationDiggingDiGRA, we laughed about it. "It's so ridiculous," she said. "It's still hilarious to me that they decided to fact check academic papers." But now I wonder, what if my papers were "fact-checked" by these men? In the face of peers whom I trust, I doubted my claims. How would public scrutiny from an anti-feminist mob have affected me? I am accustomed to responding to the typical kind of anti-feminism, which is so often grounded in vitriolic hate speech or dismissive behavior. But for someone to pick apart my academic writing in an anti-feminist, cold and reasonable way? Could I have found my voice to speak up again, to reclaim that space?

When the #OperationDiggingDigra organizer said to "hit them [feminist academics] where it hurts most [our research]," I laughed it off. Yet now I feel that maybe he was right for the wrong reasons. I do not fear that they can actually dismantle the sound scholarship of other feminists. I fear that if they try, my internalized guilt over *taking space*, over asserting my *experience*, will resurface, and I won't even recognize it.

This doubt is a filter through which I play, I write, and I interact. It is not debilitating for me, in most ways—I still play, write, and interact. Yet, doubt is often limiting and insidious. The open-ended qualitative nature of this study meant that I approached playing with only a rough guiding inquiry: to look at the way two important but sometimes conflicting identities—game player and feminist scholar—interacted. Through this process, I came to a better understanding of how doubt pervades my life, sometimes productively (overconfidence must be tempered with something, after all), but always in the background, filtering and sorting my world and how I understand my place in it, from the way I take up physical space and digital space in gaming and academic settings.

Ultimately, however, I do not think this doubt which colors my knowledge-seeking endeavors is only detrimental. It certainly has negative aspects, which have been discussed at length, and its basis in a patriarchal understanding of gender and knowledge ownership cannot be put aside. However, doubt is also what pushes us to ask questions, to double-check our work, to take a moment to consider before asserting a claim. In many contexts, these are in fact beneficial to the pursuit of knowledge; doubt can help us resist the urge to treat our scholarship as a product which must be mass-produced with cold efficiency, and instead embrace a slower and more thorough examination of our objects of study. If this is the case, then we must begin to navigate the line between pervasive, insidious doubt that acts upon us due to oppressive forces in our life worlds, and instrumental doubt that can be honed as a tool of inquiry. The first step in navigating this divide is to recognize that doubt born of oppression as it happens, to name it for what it is, to see it as connected to patriarchy (racism, homophobia, and so on). In order to make doubt an effective tool for knowledge-seeking, we must first see it for what it is, and then be able to evaluate it as it occurs, to assess how it is impacting our work. While it may end up being useful to our decision-making processes, doubt cannot be what drives our actions.

For now, I find it impossible to separate my doubt from my womanhood. In all things, I am a woman; therefore, in all things, I doubt. Still I love my womanhood, doubt and all. Doubt is part of the package, and I can work with that, especially in the context of narrative scholarship which cultivates a closer relationship between my experience of doubt and the reader of my work. As I put my personal narrative into the academic ether, I am putting myself, my essence, into that space and saying, this experience belongs here, it is relevant, it is important, it matters. It is to shoot the gun inside, to make the noise and risk the consequences, even if they turn out to be nothing.

# Bibliography

Arce, Nicole. 2014. Gamergate Continues: Female Video Game Developer Flees Home After Receiving Chilling Death Threats on Twitter. *Tech Times*, October 15. http://www.techtimes.com/articles/17901/20141015/gamergate-continues-female-video-game-developer-flees-home-after-receiving-chilling-death-threats-on-twitter.htm.

Bell, Kristina, Christopher Kampe, and Nicholas Taylor. 2015. Of Headshots and Hugs: Challenging Hypermasculinity through the Walking Dead Play. *Ada: A Journal of Gender, New Media, and Technology* 7 http://adanewmedia.org/blog/2015/04/01/issue7-bellkampetaylor/.

Berger, Leigh. 2001. Inside Out: Narrative Autoethnography as a Path Toward Rapport. *Qualitative Inquiry* 7 (4): 504–518.

Bochner, Arthur P. 2012. On First-Person Narrative Scholarship: Autoethnography as Acts of Meaning. *Narrative Inquiry* 22 (1): 155–164.

Calafell, Bernadette Marie, and Shane T. Moreman. 2009. Envisioning an Academic Readership: Latina/o Performativities per the Form of Publication. *Text and Performance Quarterly* 29 (2): 123–130.

Chang, Heewon. 2013. Individual and Collaborative Autoethnography as Method: A Social Scientist's Perspective. In *Handbook of Autoethnography*, ed. Stacy Holman Jones, Tony E. Adams, and Carolyn Ellis, 107–122. New York: Left Coast Press, Inc.

Chess, Shira, and Adrienne Shaw. 2015. A Conspiracy of Fishes, or, How We Learned to Stop Worrying about #GamerGate and Embrace Hegemonic Masculinity. *Journal of Broadcasting & Electronic Media* 59 (1): 208–220.

Chess, Shira, Mia Consalvo, Nina Huntemann, Adrienne Shaw, Carol Stabile, and Jenny Stromer-Galley. 2014. GamerGate and Academia. *International Communication Association Newsletter* 42 (9). http://www.icahdq.org/member-snewsletter/NOV14_ART0009.asp.

DiGRA. 2014. Digital Games Research Association. www.digra.org.

Ellis, Carolyn, Tony Adams, and Arthur Bochner. 2011. Autoethnography: An Overview. *Historical Social Research* 12 (1): 273–290.

Frank, Jenn. 2014. How to Attack a Woman Who Works in Video Gaming. *The Guardian*, September 1. http://www.theguardian.com/technology/2014/sep/01/how-to-attack-a-woman-who-works-in-video-games.

Griffin, Rachel Alicia. 2012. I AM an Angry Black Woman: Black Feminist Autoethnography, Voice, and Resistance. *Women's Studies in Communication* 35 (2): 138–157.

Guiller, Jane, and Alan Durndell. 2006. 'I Totally Agree With You': Gender Interactions in Educational Online Discussion Groups. *Journal of Computer Assisted Learning* 22 (5): 368–381.

Hern, Alex. 2014. Feminist Games Critic Cancels Talk After Terror Threat. *The Guardian*, October 15. http://www.theguardian.com/technology/2014/oct/15/anita-sarkeesian-feminist-games-critic-cancels-talk.

Herring, Susan. 1994. Politeness in Computer Culture: Why Women Thank and Men Flame. In *Cultural Performances: Proceedings of the Third Berkeley Women and Language Conference*, ed. M. Bucholtz, A. Liang, and L. Sutton, 279–294. Berkeley, CA: Berkeley Women and Language Group.

Herring, Susan C. 1999. The Rhetorical Dynamics of Gender Harassment On-line. *The Information Society* 15 (3): 151–167.

Jenson, Jennifer, and Suzanne De Castell. 2010. Gender, Simulation, and Gaming: Research Review and Redirections. *Simulation & Gaming* 41 (1): 51–71.

Johnston, Casey. 2014. Intel Issues #GamerGate Apology, Still Not Advertising at Gamasutra [Updated]. *Ars Technica*, October 6. http://arstechnica.com/gaming/2014/10/intel-folds-under-gamergate-pressure-pulls-ads-from-gamasutra/.

Lorde, Audre. 2009. Poet as Teacher—Human as Poet—Teacher as Human. In *I am Your Sister: Collected and Unpublished Writings of Audre Lorde*, ed. R.P. Byrd, J.B. Cole, and B. Guy-Sheftall, 182–183. New York: Oxford University Press.

Martey, Rosa Mikeal, and Jennifer Stromer-Galley. 2007. The Digital Dollhouse: Context and Social Norms in *The Sims Online*. *Games and Culture* 2 (4): 314–334.

Massanari, Adrienne. 2017. #Gamergate and the Fappening: How Reddit's Algorithm, Governance, and Culture Support Toxic Technocultures. *New Media & Society* 19 (3): 329–346.

Salter, Anastasia, and Bridget Blodgett. 2012. Hypermasculinity & Dickwolves: The Contentious Role of Women in the New Gaming Public. *Journal of Broadcasting & Electronic Media* 56 (3): 401–416.

Taylor, T.L. 2006. *Play Between Worlds: Exploring Online Game Culture.* Cambridge, MA: MIT Press.

Terlecki, Melissa, Jennifer Brown, Lindsey Harner-Steciw, John Irvin-Hannum, Nora Marchetto-Ryan, Linda Ruhl, and Jennifer Wiggins. 2011. Sex Differences and Similarities in Video Game Experience, Preferences, and Self-Efficacy: Implications for the Gaming Industry. *Current Psychology* 30 (1): 22–33.

# 14

# Women Agents and Double-Agents: Theorizing Feminine Gaze in Video Games

Stephanie C. Jennings

Ada Wong's chapter in *Resident Evil 6* (*RE6*) (Capcom 2012) opens with a cut-scene. A hulking diving suit descends into the dark waters of the northern Atlantic Ocean. It intercepts a submarine, opens the bulkhead, and boards. As the docking bay drains, a mechanism on the suit activates; the suit begins to open. Ada frees herself from its confines, rising and throwing back her arms. She is naked.

It would be tempting to critique this scene as existing in the service of male gaze. First posited in Laura Mulvey's ([1975] 2009) landmark and widely cited essay "Visual Pleasure and Narrative Cinema," *male gaze* describes the ways in which visual media presume a heterosexual, masculine-identified viewer. According to Mulvey, women's role in visual media is primarily one of erotic satisfaction for male spectators.

Since the publication of Mulvey's essay, male gaze has remained a prevailing— yet contested—analytical framework for feminist criticisms of visual structures, looking practices, and spectatorship in patriarchal systems. In fact, it seems impossible to have any conversation about gazing at visual media without first addressing male gaze. And this scene in *RE6* could be regarded as another piece of evidence among innumerable examples as to why: a normatively attractive woman's bare body is on display with seemingly no other purpose beyond the voyeuristic pleasure of this triple-A video game's heterosexual male players. Ada's introduction is an instance of her sexualization, a penetrating glimpse that

S. C. Jennings (✉)
Rensselaer Polytechnic Institute, Troy, NY, USA

© The Author(s) 2018
K. L. Gray et al. (eds.), *Feminism in Play*, Palgrave Games in Context,
https://doi.org/10.1007/978-3-319-90539-6_14

reduces her body to an image for men's safely distanced sexual gratification. Such is the treatment of women in patriarchal visual culture.

But must we always default to a view of Ada's nudity as a moment of sexual objectification for heterosexual men? In contrast, could we instead understand and talk about players' encounters with video games in ways that refuse the totalization of male gaze? How could we more fully account for the gazing practices of subject positions outside of or in opposition to hegemonic masculinity?

Responding to these concerns, this chapter provides a conceptualization of gazing practices during the playing of video games. Understanding gaze as a gendered performance influenced by intersecting facets of identity, the framework that I propose does not refer to gaze as a characteristic inherent to subjects or to game artifacts, but emphasizes gaze as a praxis that players can adopt, learn, and develop throughout their moments of play. As an example of this approach to gamic gazing, I specifically elaborate on *feminine gaze* to highlight the possible pleasures, desires, and experiences of playing video games from a feminine subject position, resisting or denying the conventions of male gaze.

To account for the specificities of video games as a distinct medium, I acknowledge various levels of gazing in games and examine possible interplays between them. These may include developer-crafted character designs and camera angles; the gazes of in-game characters; and players' active roles in shaping what they gaze upon and how. As bell hooks (1992) wrote, "the ability to manipulate one's gaze in the face of structures of domination that would contain it, opens up the possibility of agency" (116). I take player agency as a starting point, characterizing the playing of video games as agentic experiences.

As a demonstration of feminine gaze, I perform a close reading of Ada's chapter in *RE6*. A femme fatale in a franchise of survival-horror video games, Ada strings together two significant bodies of literature on the gendered dynamics of gazing: those pertaining to the horror genre (Clover 1992) and to the femme fatale (Doane 1991). Previous literature on Ada in *RE6* (Ishii 2014; Platz 2014) has underscored male gaze by criticizing Ada's sexualized appearance as objectifying. However, my analysis points to the ways that Ada and her gaze—and the processes by which players may inhabit and identify with her, and gaze at and through her—can be understood to challenge or subvert these theories.

It is not my intention to establish a unified or holistic framework for describing the multifaceted, intricate elements that converge during moments of play, influencing any given instant of gaze. I will not endeavor to create an exhaustive taxonomy of types of gaze or strategies of looking. Instead, I wish to offer just one possible alternative to certain theories that have traditionally held sway, while also providing a conceptualization of gaze that accounts for the specificities of video game play.

Relations of looking, approaches to gazing, and the processes of identification that they imply are all fragments of broader struggles for subjectivity. With this framework, I hope to provide a toolkit that sheds light on the complex interweaving of levels of gaze, while calling attention to players' strategies for meaning-making throughout their engagement with game structures.

## Contending with the Legacy of Male Gaze

In her article "Femme Doms of Video Games," Maddy Myers (2014) observed that game critics' perpetual use of male gaze as an approach to critique sexualized women characters results in oversimplifications of who might be gazing and how. She emphasized that games criticism needs "a new phrase to describe the complex interlocking of factors that occur when players identify with a character." While game critics have been slow to develop theories of identification that break out from the vast umbrella of male gaze, scholars of film theory have wrestled with the concept since the publication of Mulvey's ([1975] 2009) essay.

One of the most common early critiques of "Visual Pleasure and Narrative Cinema" was its apparent denial of female spectatorship in favor of the all-encompassing male gaze. To answer these concerns, Mulvey ([1981] 1991) issued a response that acknowledged the possibility of female gazing, but that also grimly laid out the ways in which the unconscious of patriarchy and the cinematic apparatus severely restricted active subject positions for women. Building from Mulvey's work, Doane (1991) suggested that it was "quite tempting to foreclose entirely the possibility of female spectatorship," since so much of the history of cinema was understandable only in masculine terms. Doane pointed out that any attempt that women might make to appropriate the gaze for their own would simply remain locked within the same patriarchal, masculine logic.

Many feminist film scholars disagreed. Modleski ([1988] 2009), for instance, asserted the potentials of female spectatorship, directly contradicting Mulvey's analysis. Others insisted that the perpetual invocations of male gaze and its associated attributes were actually reinforcing the male/active–female/passive binary rather than challenging or complicating patriarchal notions of gender and spectatorship (Clover 1992; Tasker 1993; Freeland [1996] 2009). Over time, theories of female gaze emerged (Gamman 1989), some of which characterized female spectatorship as either an appropriation (Cooper 2000; Keller and Gibson 2014) or a deconstruction (Sherwin 2008) of male gaze. In some ways, then, these concepts of female gaze have run risks of bordering the pitfalls against which Doane warned, as they still operate with reference to male gaze and the masculine terms of filmic mechanics.

Moreover, theories of gaze—whether pertaining to male or female gaze— have frequently failed to consider intersectionality, the idea that identity categories such as gender, race, class, sexuality, and ability do not act independently of each other, but intersect as axes in systems of oppression. Consequently, as hooks (1992) points out, when many feminist theories speak about "women's gaze" as an abstraction, they speak specifically about *white* women. In addition, they tend to presuppose a heterosexual female subject and they lack considerations of other axes of oppression such as class, sexuality, and ethnicity. As such, some theories of female gaze have recognized the importance of intersectionality, but have contributed little toward understanding its relation to gaze, leaving the task to future research.

While male gaze is and continues to be an important way to examine representations in the visual landscapes of patriarchal culture, its monolithic presence appears to have stifled any proliferation of theories of gazing practices for those who do not occupy subject positions of hegemonic masculinity. To allow for feminine subject positions, feminist film theory has responded with theories of female gaze—yet these have had their flaws, and crucially, they specifically concern *spectatorship*, not gameplay. Thus, game studies require its own theories of gaze both to understand how gaze in gameplay functions differently from that of filmic spectatorship and to reconceptualize gendered gazing in gaming environments.

## Toward a Theory of Feminine Gaze in Video Games

First, it's necessary to ask what it means to gaze in the first place. But answering that question isn't as simple as declaring the obvious "to look." More than looking, *gazing* is part of struggles for subject positions, informed and shaped by the subject's visual encounters. It is reception and perception, knowledge-acquisition, and meaning-making. It is fragmented, partial, fluid, and dynamic. It is also inventive and performative, informed by identity, identification, and experience. Gaze is also situation- and medium-dependent. Gazing is not the same process when one moves from a photograph to a film to a video game.

Modleski ([1988] 2009) asked whether one could "say that spectatorship and 'narrativity' are themselves 'feminine' (to the male psyche) in that they place the spectator in a passive position and in a submissive relation to the text?" (733). While this question complicates the active–passive dichotomy for film spectators, it still serves to maintain the gender binary by suggesting that all spectators assume a passive-feminine position during their engagement with film. And while this notion might be said to function for film, it certainly does not for video games. Video game players take on active roles in their acts of play. For instance, Galloway (2006) wrote that players take part in determining their vision in video games, arguing, "The camera position in many games is not restricted. The player is the one who controls the camera position, by looking, by moving, by scrolling, and so on" (64).

Looking in video games is not a passive response, even in those circumstances—such as during a cut-scene—when players are not in direct control of the camera or their character's line of vision. Gamic gazing is exploring, interrogating, searching, examining, reacting, creating, shaping, and structuring. One could characterize these gamic qualities by proposing a point similar to Modleski's: if players are active and agentic during their experiences of play, then they must all be in a masculine subject position in relation to the text. But rather than viewing agency during gameplay as an appropriation of male gaze or a masculine position, I conceptualize gameplay as an open, agentic potentiality for expressions and performances of femininity.

Gazing and agency in video games are not limited to active camera positioning or movement through space; they also include playful interpretation and textual invention. But to this point, a great deal of scholarship on gaze and vision in video games still seems to assume a one-to-one transference of meaning—a constant, even, and largely uncontested flow of power—between the intention of structured designs and players' reception and response to them. Even with acknowledgments of players' active roles, such scholarship seems to imply that players are acting, gazing, and constructing subject positions in ways that the game anticipates and determines.

For instance, Arsenault, Côté, and Larochelle (2015) proposed a framework for analyzing visual representation in video games that includes an extensive, unified vocabulary of visual design. As a part of this framework, they posited the concept of ergodic animage, "the meeting point and mediating factor between the player's agency and the game's visual representation of its internal state" (91). However, their understanding of this meeting point leans heavily on the rule-based mediation between the game and the player rather than on an understanding of players' agency as an appropriative, interpretive strategy.

As another example, Ishii's (2014) analysis of players' responses to female Chinese and Japanese video game characters deals expressly with gaze. She draws upon hooks' (1992) oppositional gaze as a way of explaining instances of players critiquing the sexist and racist representation of women. But, although she claims that "players' interactions with stereotypes are highly dependent on the type of gaze they adopt" (96), she does not explain how exactly players go about adopting other types of gazes, what types of gaze might be available, and how these other gazes may function. Moreover, her use of oppositional gaze deals with the ways that players may find character representation objectionable, and not with how players may be gazing during and throughout their play.

Although game structures and rules shape and influence players' gaze, they also cannot fully determine the gazing practices that players may adopt. Gaze is located in no one place when players engage with games. It is a confluence and clashing of manifold layers: designs, rules, player-embodied characters, non-playable characters, player camera control, player action, and player interpretation. And all of these factors are also shot through with a player's individual subjectivity and dispositions—their identities and identifications, their outlooks, and their actions and reactions. While some players may enact and embrace developer-intended playstyles, others may not. Some players may adopt resistant strategies, gazing in unexpected ways during moments of play. In these cases, much as hooks (1992) writes of oppositional gaze, "We do more than resist. We create alternative texts that are not solely reactions" (128). Thus, gazing in video games can be an inventive process—a process of creating visual texts of the player's own.

I propose a theory that views gazing in video games as a constellation of practices and perceptions that crisscross and fluctuate when players engage with games and identify with particular subject positions and characters. Feminine gaze is one such instance of gazing as a praxis that players can take on and learn as they play. It is a strategy of subject construction, a process of identification where character construction and player-selfhood tangle, a way of looking.

I use the term *feminine gaze* rather than "female gaze" for a number of reasons. By terming this type of gaze feminine, I aim to call attention to the fact that this example of gamic gaze is not reducible to sex difference or to some abstraction of womanhood that ultimately serves to further privilege white women. Feminine gaze is equipped and mobilized through performances of femininity—and these performances are suffused with intricate facets of identification. It is fluid and malleable, to be occupied and equipped intersectionally. While the point of this framework is to open subject positions that are not those of hegemonic masculinity—which have typically been ignored, negated, and undertheorized—we must also bear in mind that it is a praxis that is open for players to adopt and develop. For this reason, feminine gaze is available to any gender identification. It is not a subject position that is open to only certain kinds of players, but is an approach to meaning-making that can be learned and honed.

The gendered gaze of gameplay—of which feminine gaze is one example—thus operates in ways that resemble Butler's (1990) understanding of gender as composed of intentional, repeated, performative acts that construct meaning. Feminine gaze is not located exclusively in game design, but in the performance of play as a player's subjectivity intermingles and collides with a video game's representational structures, and as the player takes playful action within the game system. Butler observes that we currently cannot express gender in ways wholly divorced from the binary, but that performative actions can undermine and subvert the maintenance of the binary in ways that allow individuals—and, gradually, cultural expectations of gender—to dismantle the binary's confines. Similarly, feminine gaze views femininity as an identification open to redefinition according to individual and collective performances. Such performances can, then, refute patriarchal gender norms.

To demonstrate the interweaving of identification, textual invention, and subjectivity with the layers of gaze that coalesce and collide during gameplay, let's look more closely at the case of Ada Wong, *RE6*, and the theories of gazing that they bring together, exemplify, and challenge.

## The Active, Gazing Feminine (Double-)Agent: Ada Wong and Resident Evil 6

First appearing in the survival-horror game *Resident Evil 2* (Capcom 1998), Ada Wong is a Chinese-American double-agent who returns throughout the series, yet refuses to reveal her motives, goals, and actions to *Resident Evil* characters and players alike. Calculating, cunning, physically powerful, and assertively sexual, she has frequently been labeled and interpreted as a *femme fatale* by both popular press (Crigger 2007) and academic writers (Platz 2014). Over the course of the series, Ada has both worked for and betrayed the series' primary antagonists; she has taken on one of the games' heroes (Leon Kennedy) as her love interest, frequently coming to his rescue when he is in danger; and she has referenced having employers whose identities she never discloses.

Returning to the scene that opens Ada's chapter with a theory of feminine gaze in hand, we can reconfigure what it could mean for players to gaze at Ada's naked body. While recognizing her sexuality, a player's gaze need not be objectifying; instead, the feminine gazing player may share in the assertion of Ada's sexual freedom and autonomy. Ada knows she is entering hostile territory. But as she casts herself from the diving suit, her nakedness indicates her control over herself, her body, and her sexuality. The scene could be understood as inviting players to revel in her confidence and power over the situation, an experience that could be especially meaningful for women-identifying players who gaze at, identify with, and embody Ada through their play. Of course, players do not have control over Ada or the camera in this scenario, since it is presented as a cut-scene. Nevertheless, the scene foregrounds players' imminent adoption of Ada's role.

Following the cut-scene, players adopt (a limited) control of the camera and Ada as their playable character, commencing her invasion of the submarine. Fully clothed, Ada's appearance remains strongly sexual: she sports black leather pants, boots, and gloves, as well as a tight-fitting, bright red blouse. The game's third-person camera both enables and restricts player control, at times angling or moving in ways that the player cannot change. Some such camera angles emphasize the eroticism of Ada's attire, body, and movements. Ishii (2014) noted that her "sexualized outfit is also accentuated by certain postures she assumes during the game. Often, Ada must crawl through tunnels and passageways during which the camera focuses on her buttocks" (87).

Regardless of the level of influence that players exert on the camera at any given time, their embodiment of Ada consists of a persistent negotiation between representation and play, between designed structures and agency. To play *RE6* as Ada means to gaze with, through, and at her. On the one hand, imposed camera angles and Ada's sexualized appearance might implicate an objectifying gaze. But on the other, Ada's gaze—and the player's with and through her—is active, intrusive, and probing. Her agency is simultaneously representational, technical, and playful as players take on her role and make sense of it.

Carr (2002) observed similar tensions between the layers of representation and the agency of play in her experiences of playing as Lara Croft:

> Lara is watched, while she is being driven. Her physicality and gender invite objectification, yet she operates as perpetrating and penetrative subject within the narrative. This duality involves a certain delegation of agency between on- and off-screen positions. (175)

However, Carr arrives at the conclusion that the narrative and representation of Lara's active subjecthood ultimately serves as an appeal to the interests of a heterosexual, masculine audience:

> The more elaborated, fixed or otherwise legitimised her 'story' is, the more it seems that a desiring and specifically male consumer is being imagined, addressed and constructed, and the more untenable any neutral participation by players outside this particular demographic seemingly becomes. (178)

Rather than an empowering opportunity to take on an active feminine role, this agentic setup is perhaps instead a way to pacify the anxieties that heterosexual men may experience when playing as and identifying with a sexualized woman. Lara's exaggerated sexuality and agency serve masculine pleasures. In this way, Carr argued, the objectifying gaze that the game design anticipates and fosters would constrain the potentials for players to experience their embodiment of Lara as a transgressive gender performance.

But what I contend is that feminine gaze may operate as a reframing of Ada's sexualization to generate a meaningful experience of play—especially for women-identifying players. Gazing through, with, and at Ada as a woman—or as a practiced feminine gazer—proliferates opportunities for experiencing her chapter as a transgressive gender performance that effectively critiques and condemns traditional patriarchal power structures. What interests me are the ways that players may concurrently build on and appropriate designed representations, mechanics, and structures in the processes of identification and play.

Ada and *RE6* also illustrate the intersectional potentials of feminine gaze, while demonstrating the sticky negotiations of representation and play. It is significant that Ada is one of the few multiracial characters in the franchise, but it is unfortunate that the games do little to develop and, in fact, largely whitewash her Chinese-American identity. As with most details of her past and personal background, Ada divulges nothing to other *Resident Evil* characters or to players about her racial identity. Consequently, the game only codes Ada's race according to her physical appearance and through settings in the United States and China that appear to implicate her cultural heritage. Ishii (2014) suggests one potential remedy:

> If the *RE* games incorporated information on Ada Wong's family or personal history, her culture may establish her race more effectively than her physical appearance. An expansion of a character's persona and a reduction in the emphasis on her appearance is an initial step in breaking down structures that perpetuate gender and racial stereotypes within video games. (95)

Even so, Ada's representation enters into a history of sexualized Asian American women in the femme fatale archetype. Shimizu (2007) notes these roles necessitate redefinitions of racialized sexuality: a balancing act that recognizes such representations as simultaneously oppressive and empowering. Invariably, she writes, the Asian American femme fatale "attracts with soft, unthreatening, and servile femininity while concealing her hard, dangerous, and domineering nature" (61). While this may describe Ada's actions in *RE2*, her femininity in subsequent appearances can hardly be described as soft, unthreatening, or servile. In some ways, this resists racialized tropes and offers players a transgressive opportunity; yet, Ada's appearance nevertheless invokes oppressive conventions of racialized sexualization.

Considerations of Ada's race underscore the complexities of processes of identification at work in instants of gamic gazing. Playing *through* Ada is a facet of feminine gaze that refers not to—though existing concurrent with— subject positions of gazing *at* Ada or *alongside* her, but to the adoption and embodiment of her intersectional identity. To play through Ada is to embody her role as a multiracial, able-bodied, woman-identifying femme fatale within the diegesis of *RE6*. Yet, feminine gaze also implicates the collision and suffusion of a character's subjectivity with that of the player's. With this in mind, Ada's racial representation highlights a tension similar to the gendered constraints that Carr (2002) outlined. Ada's whitewashed, sexualized representation could, therefore, be understood as a safe point of access for the colonizing gazes of white players. Ada's Asian American identity may lend itself to this interpretation, given the historical positioning of Asian Americans as assimilated "model minorities" according to white American discourses (Wu 2014). However, Ada's racial identity may serve to challenge players' own racial identities, necessitating that they engage in her subversive performance of racialized, gendered agency. For women-identifying Asian American players, playing through Ada may provide an outlet of playful empowerment, in which they may bring their own identity to bear.

While players may create their own texts, meanings, and experiences in *RE6* in transgressive ways, they do not do so wholly outside of the influences of these racial, gendered representations. Some players may fill and enrich their embodiment of Ada with their own racial identifications, finding import in her multiracial identity. Some players learn to take on a critical gaze that they may carry through their play. And some players may learn through Ada, adopting her feminine gaze as a critical praxis. But the intersectional possibilities of feminine gaze reemphasize the crucial aspects of representation—and the needs for improvements in diverse representation—even as they provide opportunities to subvert the marginalizing conventions of game design.

Narratively, the central conflict of *RE6* pivots on a man's efforts to tame and possess Ada's sexuality for himself, through the obliteration of the agency, autonomy, and selfhood of both Ada and a prodigy geneticist named Carla Radames. Ada's investigation of the submarine starts her down a path of clues—laid for her by Carla—that reveals Carla's metamorphosis into a clone of Ada at the hands of Derek Simmons. Fifteen years prior to the events of *RE6*, Ada had rejected Simmons' sexual advances and left his employment, breaking off all contact with him. Unable to possess Ada on his own terms, Simmons committed himself to creating an Ada of his own. To accomplish this, he took the route of a standard *Resident Evil* villain: turning to a pharmaceutical corporation to conduct biological and genetic research that would allow him to get his way. He decided to clone Ada, and tricked his assistant Carla into the procedure.

For a while, Carla took on the role of Ada just as she had been created to do, no longer knowing of herself as anyone else. But despite Simmons' efforts to obliterate Carla's selfhood, a part of her remained. As her awareness of that fact grew, she came to hate both Simmons and Ada. She committed herself to destroying Simmons and the rest of the world with him, intentionally framing Ada for her actions. In pursuit of this goal, she used her own extensive resources to found a new pharmaceutical corporation and to create the monsters and bio-organic weapons (BOWs) of *RE6*.

Due to the game's design and narrative structure, only Ada discovers and retains the crucial pieces of information that explain the game's core plot. While the protagonists of the other three chapters—and players with them, prior to their completion of Ada's chapter—are left to confuse Carla with Ada, Ada pursues and gains access to the knowledge of these details and histories. Her chapter centers on her pursuit of Carla and, following Carla's death at Ada's hands, her effort to eradicate evidence of the clone's existence.

Thus, as femme fatale, Ada represents a sort of "epistemological trauma" (Doane 1991, 1) to both characters within the narrative and to players. She aggressively seeks out, investigates, and uncovers knowledge, but also limits access to and expunges it. Not only does she refuse to disclose her discoveries to other characters, but she also does not grant players the opportunity to discover the full extent of her awareness. According to Doane, this transformation of the femme fatale into an enigma lends a sort of power to her. However,

> Her power is of a peculiar sort insofar as it is usually not subject to her conscious will, hence appearing to blur the opposition between passivity and activity. She is an ambivalent figure because she is not the subject of power but its *carrier*. (2)

But Ada, I believe, subverts this understanding of the power of the femme fatale by consistently exerting her power and expressing her agency throughout the unfolding of her chapter. Moreover, playing as Ada, actively gazing through her agentic role, and having access—albeit limited—to her knowledge establishes the possibility of experiencing the game as a condemnation of patriarchy and its treatment of women. The game's narrative can be understood as Ada's reclamation and proclamation of her subjectivity against oppressive forces that have sought to wrest it from her. Hence, Ada need not be viewed as a reproduction of unconscious patriarchal fears that have traditionally composed the figure of the femme fatale; she can be played as a critique of them, a force that sets out to strike back and destroy them. The game's conflict is resolved through Ada's—and players'—neutralization of these patriarchal forces. She acknowledges the systemic effects of male gaze and challenges it: she controls her sexuality, exults in it, asserts it. In this way, she formulates, exercises, and retains an active feminine gaze in which players may share and through which they may learn how to gaze.

As Platz (2014) noted, "Ada possesses the power of the gaze. She is the only femme fatale to have a continuous point of view that the player must experience the gaze through" (119). Throughout the events of her campaign, players discover Ada's involvement in and influence over the game's other three chapters, often taking the shape of rescuing the other protagonists, who are not always aware of her presence. In these situations, Ada's gaze—and the player's through hers—is regularly focused through the sights of a long-distance weapon as she aims to dispatch a threatening BOW. Such rescue scenarios occur most frequently for her love interest, Leon, with whom Ada regularly inverts and neutralizes the trope of the damsel in distress.

Traditionally, as Platz (2014) and Doane (1991) explain, the agency and gaze of femme fatales is ultimately punished in order to nullify the threat that they pose to patriarchal masculinity and heterosexuality. Often, this punishment comes in the form of situating the femme fatale as a monster that must be killed.

Intersecting with the literature on femme fatales is also scholarship on women's gaze and monstrosity in the horror genre. In her essay "When the woman looks," Williams (1984) wrote on the ways that horror punishes women for trying to establish agentic gazing subject positions. She argued that women in horror films gaze at threatening monsters and see the monstrosity of their own bodies and sexuality reflected back at them. The monster of the horror film is, therefore, a mirror "held up to her by patriarchy" (31) that serves to punish her for the threat that her mysterious and secretive sexuality represents for hegemonic masculinity. She concluded:

What we need to see is that in fact the sexual 'freedom' of such films, the titillating attention given to the expression of women's desires, is directly proportional to the violence perpetrated against women. The horror film may be a rare example of a genre that permits the expression of women's sexual potency and desire and that associates this desire with the autonomous act of looking, but it does so in these more recent examples only to punish her for this very act, only to demonstrate how monstrous female desire can be. (32–33)

Ada, Carla, and *RE6* simultaneously adhere to and complicate these theories. Ada herself is neither made monster nor punished. Carla, however, is. Simmons has made Carla monstrous by forcibly destroying her selfhood and appropriating Ada's identity to turn her into the pliant object of his sexual desire. In this way, *RE6* appears to perfectly follow Williams' argument by transforming Ada into a monster and holding a mirror up to her. Carla sinks further into her monstrosity after injecting herself with a virus when she is nearly killed by one of Simmons' associates. In her mutated form, she attacks Ada, claiming herself as the real Ada Wong. Ultimately, Ada kills her. We cannot lose sight of the fact that Ada's assertion of her gaze, agency, and sexuality come about at Carla's expense.

Notably, a similar situation happens to Simmons at the end of Ada's chapter: Simmons injects himself with the same virus and mutates into a BOW. Thus, the mirroring effect finally turns itself back toward patriarchy, revealing that the true source of monstrosity and its ascription to femininity lies in hegemonic masculinity. Working together, Ada, Leon, and Helena are able to dispatch Simmons—with Ada landing the finishing blow.

## Conclusion

The concluding scene of Ada's chapter shows her destroying Carla's research and evidence of her existence as Ada's clone. As the laboratory is engulfed in flames, Ada receives a call for a new job from her unrevealed employers. She leaves the scene unpunished, unscathed, triumphant—though, nevertheless, visibly shaken by what she has encountered. Still, despite the trauma that she has endured, Ada retains her indomitable selfhood as she strides from the room to take on her next contract.

Ada's chapter demonstrates the possibilities of feminine gaze. Players learn to take on feminine gaze by playing as Ada—they engage in a praxis that they can adopt through their identification with Ada. Moreover, the game invites players to play with femininity through their embodiment of Ada, subverting and challenging traditional gender roles and conceptualizations of gaze along with her. With a theory of feminine gaze, we can cast aside patriarchal definitions of agency as masculine, moving toward feminine forms of agentic gaze and play.

# Bibliography

Arsenault, Dominic, Pierre-Marc Côté, and Audrey Larochelle. 2015. The Game FAVR: A Framework for the Analysis of Visual Representation in Video Games. *Loading...* 9 (14): 88–123 http://journals.sfu.ca/loading/index.php/loading/article/view/155.

Butler, Judith. 1990. *Gender Trouble.* New York, NY: Routledge.

Capcom. 1998. *Resident Evil 2.* Playstation. Capcom.

———. 2012. *Resident Evil 6.* Multiple-platform. Capcom.

Carr, Diane. 2002. Playing with Lara. In *Screenplay: Cinema/Videogames/Interfaces,* ed. Geoff King and Tanya Krzywinska, 171–180. London: Wallflower Press.

Clover, Carol. 1992. *Men, Women, and Chain Saws: Gender in the Modern Horror Film.* Princeton, NJ: Princeton University Press.

Cooper, Brenda. 2000. 'Chick Flicks' as Feminist Texts: The Appropriation of the Male Gaze in Thelma & Louise. *Women's Studies in Communication* 23 (3): 277–306.

Crigger, Lara. 2007. Resident Evil's Second Sex. *The Escapist,* May 8. http://www.escapistmagazine.com/articles/view/video-games/issues/issue_96/536-Resident-Evil-s-Second-Sex.

Doane, Mary Ann. 1991. *Femme Fatales: Feminism, Film Theory, Psychoanalysis.* New York, NY: Routledge.

Freeland, Cynthia A. 1996/2009. Feminist Frameworks for Horror Films. In *Film Theory and Criticism,* ed. Leo Braudy and Marshall Cohen, 7th ed., 627–648. New York, NY: Oxford University Press.

Galloway, Alexander. 2006. *Gaming: Essays on Algorithmic Culture.* Minneapolis, MN: University of Minnesota Press.

Gamman, Lorraine. 1989. Watching the Detectives: The Enigma of the Female Gaze. In *The Female Gaze,* ed. Lorraine Gamman and Margaret Marshment, 8–26. Seattle, WA: Real Comet Press.

hooks, bell. 1992. *Black Looks.* Boston, MA: South End Press.

Ishii, Sara. 2014. "Unless She Had Implants, She Must Be Chinese": A Feminist Analysis of Players' Responses to Representations of Chinese and Japanese Female Video Game Characters. *Loading...* 8 (3): 81–99.

Keller, Alyse, and Katie L. Gibson. 2014. Appropriating the Male Gaze in the Hunger Games: The Rhetoric of a Resistant Female Vantage Point. *Texas Speech Communication Journal* 38 (1): 21–30.

Modleski, Tania. 1988/2009. The Master's Dollhouse: *Rear Window*. In *Film Theory and Criticism*, ed. Leo Braudy and Marshall Cohen, 7th ed., 723–735. New York, NY: Oxford University Press.

Mulvey, Laura. 1975/2009. Visual Pleasure and Narrative Cinema. In *Film Theory and Criticism*, ed. Leo Braudy and Marshall Cohen, 7th ed., 711–722. New York, NY: Oxford University Press.

———. 1981/1991. Afterthoughts on 'Visual Pleasure and Narrative Cinema' Inspired by King Vidor's *Duel in the Sun* (1946). In *Feminist Film Theory*, ed. Sue Thornham, 122–130. New York, NY: New York University Press.

Myers, Maddy. 2014. Femme Doms of Video Games: Bayonetta Doesn't Care if She's Not Your Kink. *Paste Magazine*, October 30. http://www.pastemagazine.com/articles/2014/10/femme-doms-of-videogames-bayonetta-doesnt-care-if.html.

Platz, Jenny. 2014. The Woman in the Red Dress: Sexuality, Femme Fatales, the Gaze, and Ada Wong. In *Unraveling Resident Evil: Essays on the Complex Universe of the Games and Films*, ed. Nadine Farghaly, 117–134. Jefferson, NC: McFarland.

Sherwin, Miranda. 2008. Deconstructing the Male Gaze: Masochism, Female Spectatorship, and the Femme Fatale in *Fatal Attraction, Body of Evidence,* and *Basic Instinct. Journal of Popular Film and Television* 35 (4): 174–182.

Shimizu, Celine Parreñas. 2007. *The Hypersexuality of Race: Performing Asian/American Women on Screen and Scene*. Durham, NC: Duke University Press.

Tasker, Yvonne. 1993. *Spectacular Bodies: Gender, Genre, and the Action Film*. New York, NY: Routledge.

Williams, Linda. 1984. When the Woman Looks. In *The Dread of Difference: Gender and the Horror Film*, ed. Barry Keith Grant, 15–34. Austin, TX: University of Texas Press.

Wu, Ellen. 2014. *The Color of Success: Asian Americans and the Origins of the Model Minority*. Princeton, NJ: Princeton University Press.

# 15

# Feminism and Gameplay Performance

## Emma Westecott

*Feminism begins with a keen awareness of exclusion from male cultural, social,
sexual, political, and intellectual discourse. It is a critique of prevailing social
conditions that formulate women's position as outside of dominant male discourse
(Dolan 1991, 3)*

The call to diversify representational practices in digital games is common across much mainstream media and provides one backdrop for the rise of feminist activism. Feminism is an important political driver for the ongoing expansion and inclusivity of game culture writ large. At its simplest feminism is concerned with working towards equal rights for women and other marginalized groups and has long been concerned with the re-inscription of dominant power ideologies over time.

Now that technology is pervasive, impacting many aspects of most people's day-to-day lives, the utopian visions of the last century for the potential of technology to disturb the power dynamics of Western society seem rather naive. Yet it is important to note the significant re-figuration of social and cultural norms enabled via the domestication of digital technology. Any development of this scale comes with the necessity for widespread critical engagement to understand the dynamics in play, and to '… move forward, we need to understand that technology as such is neither inherently patriarchal nor unambiguously liberating' (Wajcman 2010, 148). What perhaps is more

E. Westecott (✉)
Ontario College of Art & Design, Toronto, ON, Canada

© The Author(s) 2018
K. L. Gray et al. (eds.), *Feminism in Play*, Palgrave Games in Context,
https://doi.org/10.1007/978-3-319-90539-6_15

pressing is how rapidly technology becomes invisible in day-to-day use and how a growing technological dependency is accepted as simply 'the way things are'. It is this acceptance that allows for the erasure of marginalized groups from the histories of technological evolution.

Historically feminism has been spoken about in terms of waves, yet in the current environment of rapid technological change that collapses time and space, in which differing ideologies co-exist, it is difficult to hold fast to these generational focal points. It is the recognition of affinities, and the building of alliances, and coalitions that allow feminists to acknowledge the multitude of individual and collective identities held by women worldwide. Women do not have common experiences but can recognize and unite around shared interests and objectives. Whilst acknowledging individual feminist positions is critical to make explicit personal biases, it remains the case that feminism can only move forward via these coalitions. Given the ongoing inequity experienced by minorities over time perhaps it might be productive to conceive of feminism as a form of iterative software design problem, one that recurs at least once a generation as new challenges and opportunities arise?

## The Politics of Pleasure

Whilst this chapter argues for the ongoing dilation of game development and culture beyond the increasingly fossilized formats of mainstream entertainment, it does so by prioritizing the pleasures inherent to gameplay. Engaging politically motivated activity in game cultures should grow from a purposeful playfulness in approach, playfulness is a much more potent force than direct conflict and offers an important means of engagement. For example, women's access to leisure time (when games are played) is often limited by the other activities she must attend to first. As a site of explicit gender play, in which the player can adopt different identities and gain a sense of personal power, gameplay offers potential as a liberating tool in and of itself. Opening games up to new players and new makers is not just a commercial drive but is a political imperative.

Whether it be in the 'personal games movement' or the 'games for change' setting, games that are made outside of the mainstream sector allow for wider experimentation in theme, form, and structure than those within the 'for profit' space. These expanded contexts of game-making provide distinctive gameplay performances for the player. Rather than the anxiety of shooting zombies when I play *Hush* (Antonisse and Johnson 2007) I experience the anxiety of avoiding detection. Rather than the adrenaline of fast movement within an action adventure I experience the lack of choice on offer in *Dys4ia* (Anthropy 2012).

Rather than the exhilaration of beating a level I experience the realization that there is always collateral damage in *September 12th* (Newsgaming/Frasca 2003). This diversity of experience provides the player with a range of pleasures holding potential for critical engagement with a wider set of social and political issues.

Feminist scholars have long argued that all representational form is political, that there is no objectivity as every artefact made by human hand expresses the values of its maker. This runs directly counter to the presentation of games as 'just entertainment' prevalent in the commercial sector. Regardless of any discussion of artistic merit, games are a representational form with expressive capacity in terms of the gameplay action on offer.

# Feminist Games?

It is possible to trace common trajectories across feminist engagement in the representational arts as a way of identifying, acknowledging, and adopting prior successes as feminist engagement in digital game form gathers momentum. For example, practices of distanciation and personalization are common to other areas of the arts engaged in feminist activity. The history, approaches, and activities of feminist theatre and performance scholars indicate one possible trajectory for the emerging field of feminist game studies. The blend of distinct interests, critical engagement, and theoretical approaches that engage both political activism and creative work whilst remaining fundamentally interdisciplinary can act as inspiration for ongoing feminist activity.

## Approaches to a feminist text

One definitional challenge for feminism lies in how creative output is included in feminist discourse, what is it about a piece that lets it be described as feminist? How is feminist work identified as such without reiterating the multiple judgements and exclusions evident in culture more broadly? This is a question central to the feminist project, without celebrating and making visible feminist creative practice, distinguishable by the political intent of the creator, it is not possible to work against the erasure of women from history. Yet the process of categorization implicit to this process in and of itself risks reproducing exclusionary practices. Elizabeth Grosz's essay *Feminism after the Death of the Author* (1995) sustains a response to this challenge with the intent of allowing an approach that moves beyond self-limiting frameworks. Grosz suggests an alternate approach to feminist texts as taking place in consideration of:

1. The relations between a text and prevailing norms must be explored, to be feminist '… it must render the patriarchal or phallocentric presumptions governing its contexts and commitments visible.
2. Texts retain a trace of their production, so a feminist text must problematize the standard masculinist ways in which the author occupies the position of enunciation.
3. A feminist text must help facilitate the production of new … discursive spaces, new styles, modes of analysis and argument, new genres and forms—that contest the limits and constraints currently at work in the regulation of textual production and reception.' (Grosz 1995, 23).

Whilst not necessarily self-identifying as feminist many of the game projects referenced in this chapter meet at least some of Grosz's criteria and, as such, offer a range of approaches to making feminist games.

## Feminist Interventions in Game Form

Game-making is, of course, not the only strategy available to a feminist player or maker invested in taking direct action in game form outside of the gameplay experience itself. Staged performances in multi-player games, modding, and machinima are established ways that players can, and often do, take active part in creating their own game experience. Each of these practices are evidenced in art game settings more generally as well as across wider player and fan-based communities. Whilst an in-depth exploration of these forms is outside the scope of this chapter, a brief investigation of explicitly feminist activity in these spaces is useful. The tradition of staged performances in multi-player games is rich, with artists like Joseph DeLappe's[1] (2006) game performance work functioning as activism interested in critiquing and drawing attention to a moral void on display in many gaming contexts. One of his most well-known projects, *dead-in-iraq* (2006), involves creating an id tagged 'dead-in-iraq' in America's Army (a FPS designed as a recruiting game) and typing in the names of all of America's military casualties from the war in Iraq. Artist Angela Washko's[2] *The Council on Gender Sensitivity and Behavioral Awareness in World of Warcraft* (2012) in which she responds to the often-misogynistic adopted common language evidenced in the MMORPG by engaging players within the game in discussions on the definition of feminism. She does this in artist spaces, and posts the results of her conversations online, as videos and transcripts.

Modding is a much older practice and refers to the use of game engines (often provided with a released game, or free-to-download), as a tool either to create new levels or to produce patches that modify existing games. Some of the earliest feminist activity in game modding can be traced to Anne-Marie Schleiner,[3] whose mutation.fem[4] curated a series of skins, patches,[5] and wads for the *Marathon* (Bungie Software 1994), *Doom* and *Quake* series that created female variations of male player characters for play within these games and whose Velvet-Strike (2002) offers a collection of spray paints to create graffiti in *Counter-Strike* (1999). There is a long tradition of gender hacks of 8-bit classics for the NES-ROM, see Weil's (2013) discussion for more background on how modders re-make existing games to other ends. Together with mods like *Hey Baby* (LadyKillas 2010) first-person shooter that plays with conventions of who the protagonist is, it is possible to observe at least traces of feminist activity in game modding experiments. In machinima (a film-making practice that involves recording gameplay action), Vandagriff and Nitsche's (2009) exploration of women's machinima outlines themes, technologies, and expressive focus developed in the films of a handful of female makers.

There remain scant examples of feminist art games. Perhaps one of the first feminist art games, entitled *All New Gen* (1993/4), was made by VNS Matrix, an Australian collective who authored the *Cyberfeminist Manifesto* (1991) that appropriated the language and narratives of cyberpunk to feminist ends. The next significant feminist activity in game-making can be traced to the artistic, theoretical and activist work of Anne-Marie Schleiner. Her ongoing body of work engages politically motivated interventions in game culture, including game art mods, that: '... can be seen as critical frameworks, and when used in the context of artistic practice, become environments in which player-participants can make meaning' (Flanagan 2005, 160). Flanagan's thesis work connects her exploration of critical play practices—later developed for her monograph *Critical Play* (2009)—to digital game design approaches via '... turn-of-the-millennium "cyberfeminist" practices...' (120) and whilst pointing to problems in the cyberfeminist project as '... unrealistic in the face of real discrimination and social imbalances.' (Wilding 1997, quoted in Flanagan 2005, 122) nevertheless proposes a design framework based on her research into critical play practices. The process of game-making described in Flanagan's thesis moves through refined iterative cycles that re-work the iconography of existing game genres (arcade and first-person shooters) and refine and balance game mechanics to orient towards more gender inclusive play design frameworks. Flanagan's important work engages feminist art and play practices in her development of a framework for socially activist game design. Yet whilst Flanagan's schema of re-skinning, unplaying, and re-writing can be applied to feminist art, a review of feminist approaches more generally yields signs of a wider expressive toolkit. The use of parody, irony, and other forms of humour pervade feminist activity, whilst techniques such as distanciation, embodied role play, and personal storytelling can be traced across multiple strands of feminist expression.

Many of these same thematic categories can be seen emerging on the periphery of the indie games community. Two thousand and thirteen saw the birth of the self-titled 'personal games movement' (Keogh 2013) in which a group of North American game-makers cohered around game-making as a form of personal expression. The 'personal' provides an emphasis on using game design as a way of expressing something personal and meaningful to the maker. Many of the rapidly growing scene's output are small, free-to-play, individually made games distributed for free online that gather significant social network attention via the thriving indie games festival circuit. Whilst the games that self-identify this way are diverse in content, style, and theme, they share both a certain expressive interest and a mutually supportive network that amplifies impact and a viral approach growing in international reach. Many of the makers in this community identify as queer and regard this identification as central to their game design practice. This community has been facilitated by easy access to game-making tools and often engage non-traditional game tools like Twine[6] (a tool for building Interactive Fiction rather than games per se) as one means to make their games. Many more traditional game-makers question the status of these experiences as games at all, but perhaps it is a marker of the growing maturity of game form that the naming of an experience as a game is sufficient for it to find a place in games culture more broadly.

## Feminism in Theatre

Feminist theatre and performance orients around an integrated view on theory, practice and activism in its approach to destabilizing dominant approaches and norms, offering a useful model for any similarly directed activity with games. A feminist approach involves the desire to effect change in the status quo. The benefit of looking at models from more established representational form is that a body of feminist work has been identified, made visible and investigated, whereas in the early twenty-first century there are few game-makers who self-identify as feminist or whose practice can be seen to serve feminist agendas. By looking at the successes and failures of past feminist projects, it becomes possible to conceive of a range of approaches that may be useful for a feminist approach to games.

Arising from histories of exclusion, feminist activists and scholars have responded in a range of ways, specifically in theatre, for example, by revisiting the 'traditional history' of the stage to challenge the patriarchal values of the canonical, to discover the hidden histories of women theatre makers, and to look in 'other' places for women's performance, whether in the street or the home. Elaine Aston's foreword in Sue-Ellen Case's introduction to feminism and theatre argues that: 'The quest for a feminist aesthetics is where feminism and theatre joined forces; is where different feminist positions as political standpoints formed the basis for theatre-making and writing.' (Case 2008, xii).

For example, techniques derived from a Brechtian-influenced feminist approach involve the performer (or in the apparatus of games, the player character) expressing her awareness of being watched. Dolan expands on Brecht to '… suggest a triangular relationship between the actor, character and spectator…' (Dolan 1991, 45), thereby disturbing the voyeurism inherent to a spectatorial position. This suggested 'triangle' provides three separate subject positions that have the potential to disturb the power dynamics evident in systems of representation. Game performance conflates the role of actor and that of spectator to the player. In third-person games, for example, the player's relationship to the player character fleshes out the unfolding game drama. Player action on a pre-fabricated game body pushes the game forward and Dolan's suggested 'triangle' can be achieved via the designed actions on offer to the player. Specifically, when a player character acknowledges the presence of the player she is reminded that she is an active spectator with agency, however limited.

In traditional theatre, gender is often more exaggerated than in real life. Indeed, theatre has often been a home, and a safe space, for gender play whether on stage or beyond, this is not the case in game culture. The representation of gender in digital games fits this sense of exaggeration, yet it does so within a remarkably narrow range of options. Built by teams of individuals distributed across production locations, it is not much of a surprise that player characters can often feel disjointed or void of emotion. Game action is often prioritized over more fluid and detailed approaches to other aspects of game development, including how gender is represented.

# Gameplay Performance

Within the context of gameplay as a performance form, digital games offer the player an opportunity to play with gender identities that are different from those they may experience in real life. The apparatus of games offers a range of engagement via the game camera used: from the intimacy of first person, to the multiple identifications of third person, the experience of performing gender in games varies in different contexts. Some titles offer, albeit constrained, customization options that allow the player some agency over how she appears in game. Game representation provides a range of potential pleasures by allowing for a type of 'computer cross dressing' (Stone 1991). It is important here to note that all player characters are fictional constructs built collaboratively by a team of developers to fit heroic archetypes for gameplay. Regardless of the gender of the player or the gender of the player character, this engagement involves cross-dressing. The norms that have built up in commercial development unnecessarily constrain the range of choices on offer to players. The call here is for an increase in the range of representational approaches (both in image and gameplay) to player characters to provide an associated increase in the range of experience on offer.

Performance can be seen across a wide range of game contexts: in artistic engagement with game form, with gender hacks, for example, as well as in more mundane gameplay encounters and the making of games themselves. The player, her identity as gamer, and her gameplay experience are all subject to the inscription of gender. The interactions between these multiple subject positions have not always been either recognized or explored. Female players are often either ignored by designers because they have historically played whatever is available or provided with casual, or worse 'pink'ed, games based on research that collapses access to leisure time or literacy with gender preference. Now that the gamer identity carries social capital, it can be seen as exhibiting a range of exclusionary tactics and with multiple visible examples of abuse evident online, women and girls are, understandably, increasingly hesitant about self-identifying in this way. Even when women and girls are directly represented as the protagonist in games, game developers remain remarkably averse to portraying powerful, dressed, playable and nuanced role models that resonate with game mechanics in an integrated manner.

# A Performance Approach

Performance studies can be understood as expanding the contexts and application of dramatic theory and praxis beyond the space of theatre, yet there remains an umbilical connection to the spaces and practices of theatre that is useful to a discussion of feminist approaches that may prove productive to a closer investigation of gender in games.

Performance theory remains influenced by feminism in the same way that performance offers a site for feminist expression. The generational bonds between the growth of performance studies and the maturing of feminism are tightly interwoven politically, theoretically, practically, and expressively. In an era increasingly taking up the metaphor of performance as a way of being-in-the-world, it is somewhat inevitable that the lens of performance be cast across a wide range of fields.

# Performance and Performativity

Separate from the increased theoretical use of performance approaches across discipline is the field of performativity. Theories of performativity insist that all social realities are constructed and it is in the areas of gender, race, and identity that these theories have been most productively taken up. Judith Butler's (1988) work on gender has been significant to this in building a cohesive approach to understanding the ways in which gender is created. Butler's analysis of gender has been widely influential and centres on the view that gender is performative, specifically the sense that the categories of sex, gender, and sexuality are created by dominant cultural and social mechanisms via the repetition of stylized acts over time. It is relatively straightforward to extrapolate Butler's notion of repetition as essential to gender creation to the repetitive actions of gameplay that create the identity category 'gamer'. It is in the performative context of the repetitive action of gameplay that gamers are created. It is my contention however that the identity construct 'gamer' is often distinguishable from the actual experience of real players. It is this real gameplay experience, this performance, that offers a player both alternate points of view and achievement of proficiencies that hold potential to disturb existent social and cultural norms.

McKenzie's close reading of Butler discusses at length her transformation of performativity from a site of resistance to '... a dominant and punitive form of power' (McKenzie 2001, 220). The 'misreading' of Butler's approach to gender as volitional resulted in a more defined separation of performance and performativity in her later work. As performance experience, digital gameplay offers the opportunity to act 'as' another, whilst the performative identity 'gamer' remains subject to a reductively narrow view of a mainstream market. For those interested in viewing gameplay as both intrinsically performance and extrinsically performative, it is perhaps too easy to see the connections between repeatable and allowable actions as also a core component of the game experience. The process of repetition is central to gameplay to support skill acquisition, and functions both outside and inside the game world, that is, players repeat actions on controllers in front of the game screen and their movements are mirrored on screen as the main way of engaging in a game.

The construction of a 'gamer' identity accessible by traditionally excluded groups' figures in many discussions in feminist game studies (Taylor 2008). There are equivalent numbers of women and men playing games, although many do not necessarily identify as 'gamer'. Interestingly, there is a growing community of players who identify as 'gaymers' (Shaw 2012) publicly connecting their sexuality with their identification as a gamer. Game developers are by majority men (according to an International Game Developers Association (IGDA) study in 2014, 76% of the industry are male). Initiatives from feminist game studies that aim at working against this ongoing imbalance have included creating women-only groups of players and game-makers to build both game-making and play communities that work to '... perform and make visible an identity typically hidden: woman as gamer ... this in turn legitimizes that behavior, and that identity, for women' (Taylor 2008, 61).

The application of approaches drawn from feminist performance can be seen as a productive way to deepen the dialogue around gender and games. Regardless of the disconnect between Butler's (1993) view of gender as performative and feminism's engagement with the performance of gender on stage and screen— gender is performed. The performative frame of gameplay and the machinery of the game industry constructs the identity 'gamer', whilst the performance of gameplay itself allows the player to perform 'as-if' she was the player character. In line with Nakamura's notion of 'identity tourism' (1995) or even Ferreday and Lock's sense of 'identity travelling' (2007), the player adopts the role of protagonist in game via the agency and dramatic context provided by the game she is playing. This involves a spectrum of possibility for identification, and in line with historical approaches to acting styles, often the player is not even expected to identify with her player to drive it forward through the game.

The growth of feminist theatre practices over the past 30 years has been marked by significant experimentation in form, address, and content. Some of this experimentation worked against more traditional narrative frameworks for staged drama and beyond the context of theatre to the wider setting of performance art. Feminism, gender, and queer theory have been taken up across a range of expressive forms but have, as yet, not reached the commercial game industry. It might be argued that in the pursuit of mainstream success that games have not had to engage a diversity of form for multiple market-places. It remains to be seen whether trends continue to open up development settings and delivery platforms to result in a more open and inclusive indus-try. One important approach that has succeeded in supporting diversity lies in the ability of feminists, or indeed any group excluded from privilege, to build and sustain communities of interest, and practice. Groups that invest time, effort, and energy to building communities to provide safer spaces for those normally excluded from full participation can actively engage that commu-nity in inclusive practices.

## Learning from Art Practices

There is a tradition of feminist work in the field of technology and perfor-mance if not in games per se. Laura Bissell's PhD thesis (Bissell 2011) pro-vides an excellent overview of the spaces, approaches, and projects that explore a feminist praxis for technologized performance form. Surveying work as diverse as Char Davies' (1995) *Osmose* and Brenda Laurel's *Placeholder* (Strickland and Laurel 1992) to Avatar Body Collision, subRosa and Julia Bardsley, Bissell draws on digital performance to explore feminist work in this area. The female body is an important component of this, connecting projects to a longer tradition of feminist performance art. Bissell's thesis, much in the same way as Flanagan's (2005), highlights game art by women to explicate and explore individual approaches. In this view, it is possible to acknowledge that artistic performance acts as one intervention that critiques the status quo, generates new knowledge, and creates opportunities for new form.

Digital game performance is mediated by both the technology of its delivery and via the gaming screen that provides feedback. Games can be approached as mediated performance, a view growing in popularity in contemporary games studies. In many digital games, the medium used is both highly sensorial as well as multi-modal (using interactivity, animation, images, sound, etc., together in varying configurations) to generate gameplay experience for the player.

Wark (2006) traces a history of feminism and performance art in North America by discussing the ways in which women artists continue to use per-formance as an art practice. Performance art is a very specific context that situates artistic work in an embodied and direct encounter between a per-former and her audience.

The connections between feminism and performance art can be traced to the amorphous status of performance as artistic material itself, as a new set of practices being taken up in the visual arts more generally. Performance art remained fluid enough to be open to engagement by a wider community than that traditionally found in the visual arts. Wark (2006) discusses in some detail the appeal for feminists inherent to performance as an art form as

1. Allowing feminists to disrupt dominant narratives building alternate approaches to narrative and autobiography as '... one of the most definitive characters of feminist performance as a whole.' (Wark 59)
2. Centring on the 'enactment of agency' (Wark 59) thus indicating a possibility for affecting change
3. By featuring a living body, performance allows women to 'assert themselves as the active and self-determining agents of their own narratives' (Wark 60)
4. Intersecting the personal with the performative '... blur the distinctions between author and agent, subject and object. The tension and distancing between acting and lived experience allow the performer to stand beside herself ... to "show the show"' (Wark 60)
5. Allowing for cathartic experiences on behalf of the performers, '... performance provided a way to articulate and focus their anger into a formation of political consciousness.' (Wark 88).

Although Butler (1990) herself is uncomfortable with any association with performance form itself (e.g. theatre and dance), her theories have been nonetheless widely taken up by performance theorists from the nineties onwards. Whilst scholars such as Aston (2005) acknowledge Butler's distinction between the presentation of gender performativity in everyday life and the representation of gender on stage as the result of specific choices she argues for the potential of performance to make visible the ways that gender is coded more generally. Theatre practitioners suggest that by performing 'performingness' on stage and screen that gender can be de-naturalized and shown as the fabrication that it is, 'as a resistant mode of "doing" rather than "writing" it [performance] offers the possibility of new "ways of seeing"' (Aston 2005, 16). The possible critique of gender implied by this call needs to acknowledge the specificity of the representational frame, in Aston's case theatre, as an artificial place and time within which to operate and the significance of the director in staging events that work towards these goals. When a player controls her player character to drive the game forward, her agency is constrained by the rules, norms, and structures of the specific game she is playing.

Queer theory (in which Butler is a founding figure) has created a space in which to discuss cross-gender identifications. For example, Mercer (1991) talks about holding 'two contradictory identifications at one and the same time' and the idea of multiple identifications can be seen as having always been part of the female experience of viewing. The idea of the split subject has grown in parallel with the rise of computational technology over the past quarter century as the ways that we engage each other through digital communication has fundamentally shifted. More specifically through the lens of queer theory, gender identification (although not necessarily gender itself) can be viewed as a fluid process that pivots on an individual's particular context, personal preference, and perspective allowing for queer readings of heteronormative texts. Feminists have long argued for approaches to reading against the dominant meanings inscribed in representational form and whilst this does not exclude the need for a more equitable approach to representation more generally, it does develop a practice of active engagement in meaning-making practices. The active nature of games creates a particularly potent site for the creation of 'unstable signifying practices'. When I play as a woman controlling a male hero, it is an act of enforced gender-bending, yet as I progress I feel empowered, the sense of achievement of having succeeded in a particular challenge makes me feel powerful. I have access to the pleasures of games both ungendered (infinite lives, scaffolded skill acquisition, the visceral pleasures of multi-modal feedback) and gendered (physical strength, character tropes, narrative framing). Even further 'queer representations ... offer wider opportunities for viewing/identification than those associated with the more stereotypical representations' (Evans and Gamman 1995, 36); the argument here being that the overuse of exaggerated stereotypes constrains the range of ways in which identification can take place, whereas gender ambiguity offers a wide set of possible readings for the future gamer.

Beyond the activity of feminists in theatre, performance art has offered a productive setting for feminist work since the seventies. Performance can occur in a wide range of spaces and places: from the popular to the refined, from the domestic to the public and from the personal to the professional, performance acts occur in almost any setting. Richard Schechner—a founding father of performance studies—was keen to expand the bounds of what performance could be and the general climate in North America in the late sixties and seventies provided fertile ground for the convergent practices of performance, feminism, and art that challenged and re-configured institutional boundaries and definitions. Perhaps games have reached sufficient critical mass to explore a history of feminist performance art to unfold practices that expand game form.

## Notes

1. http://www.delappe.net.
2. http://angelawashko.com.
3. http://www.opensorcery.net.
4. http://www.opensorcery.net/mutation/.
5. Patches are software releases to update a game or its data, to improve, or fix it.
6. http://twinery.org.

## Bibliography

Anthropy, Anna. 2012. *Dys4ia*. Adobe Flash [Computer Game]. Accessed December 19, 2014. http://www.newgrounds.com/portal/view/591565.

Antonisse, J., and Johnson, D. 2007. *Hush*. Mac OS X/Windows. [Computer Game]. Accessed December 19, 2014. http://valuesatplay.org/play-games.

Aston, Elaine. 2005. *Feminist Theatre Practice: A Handbook*. London: Routledge.

Bissell, Laura. 2011. *The Female Body, Technology and Performance: Performing a Feminist Praxis*. PhD dissertation, University of Glasgow, 2011. [Online]. Accessed December 15, 2014. http://theses.gla.ac.uk/2474/.

Bungie Software. 1994. *Marathon*. Mac OS. [Computer Game].

Butler, Judith. 1988. Performative Acts and Gender Constitution: An Essay in Phenomenology and Feminist Theory. *Theatre Journal* 40 (4): 519–531.

———. 1990. *Gender Trouble: Feminism and the Subversion of Identity*. New York and London: Routledge.

———. 1993. Critically Queer. *GLQ: A Journal of Lesbian and Gay Studies* 1 (1): 17–32.

Case, Sue-Ellen. 2008. *Feminism and Theatre*. New York: Palgrave Macmillan.

Davies, Char. 1995. *Osmose*. [VR Installation], Documentation. Accessed December 19, 2014. http://www.immersence.com/osmose/.

Delappe, Joseph. 2006. *Dead-in-iraq*. [Game Performance] Documentation. Accessed December 19, 2014. http://www.delappe.net/project/dead-in-iraq/.

Dolan, Jill. 1991. *The Feminist Spectator as Critic*. Ann Arbor: The University of Michigan Press.

Evans, Caroline, and Lorraine Gamman. 1995. The Gaze Revisited, or Reviewing Queer Viewing. In *A Queer Romance: Lesbians, Gay Men and Popular Culture*, ed. Paul Burston and Colin Richardson, 13–56. New York: Routledge.

Ferreday, Debra, and Simon Lock. 2007. Computer Cross-Dressing: Queering the Virtual Subject. In *Queer Online: Media, Technology, and Sexuality*, ed. Kate O'Riodan and David Phillips, 155–174. New York: Peter Lang.

Flanagan, Mary. 2005. *Playculture: Developing a Feminist Game Design*. PhD Dissertation, University of The Arts London.

————. 2009. *Critical Play: Radical Game Design*. Cambridge: The MIT Press.

Grosz, E. 1995. Space, Time and Perversion, New York: Routledge.

Keogh, Brendon. 2013. Just Making Things and Being Alive About It: The Queer Games Scene. *Polygon*. Accessed December 19, 2014. http://www.polygon.com/features/2013/5/24/4341042/thequeer-games-scene.

LadyKillas Inc. 2010. *Hey Baby Game*. Trailer [Computer Game]. Accessed December 19, 2014. http://www.heybabygame.com/info.php.

Matrix, V.N.S. 1991. *A Cyberfeminist Manifesto for the 21st Century*. [Game Manifesto] Documentation. Accessed December 20, 2014. http://transmediale.de/content/cyberfeminist-manifesto-21stcentury.

————. 1993/4. *All New Gen*. CD-ROM. [Computer Game] Documentation. Accessed December 19, 2014. http://www.medienkunstnetz.de/works/all-new-gen/#reiter.

McKenzie, Jon. 2001. *Perform or Else: From Discipline to Performance*. London: Routledge.

Mercer, Kobena. 1991. Skin Head Sex Thing: Racial Difference and the Homoerotic Imaginary. In *How Do I Look?: Queer Film and Video*, ed. Bad Object Choices, 1–23. Seattle, WA: Bay Press.

Nakamura, Lisa. 1995. Race in/for Cyberspace: Identity Tourism and Racial Passing on the Internet. *Works and Days* 25 (26): 13.

Newsgaming/Frasca, Gonzalo. 2003. *September 12th*. Web. [Computer Game]. Accessed December 19, 2014. http://www.gamesforchange.org/play/september-12th-a-toy-world/.

Schechner, Richard. 2002. *Performance Studies: An Introduction*. New York: Routledge.

Shaw, Adrienne. 2012. Do you Identify as a Gamer? Gender, Race, Sexuality, and Gamer Identity. *New Media & Society* 14 (1): 28–44.

Stone, Allucquere Rosanne. 1991. Will the Real Body Please Stand Up? In *Cyberspace: First Steps*, ed. Michael Benedikt, 81–118. Cambridge, MA: MIT Press.

Strickland, Rachel, and Laurel, Brenda. 1992. *Placeholder*. [VR Installation]. Documentation. Accessed December 19, 2014. http://tauzero.com/Brenda_Laurel/Placeholder/Placeholder.html.

Taylor, T.L. 2008. Becoming a Player: Networks, Structures, and Imagined Futures. In *Beyond Barbie and Mortal Kombat*, ed. Yasmin B. Kafai, Carrie Heeter, Jill Denner, and Jennifer Y. Sun, 51–66. Cambridge, MA: MIT Press.

Vandagriff, Jenifer, and Michael Nitsche. 2009. Women Creating Machinima. *Digital Creativity* 20 (4): 277–290.

Wajcman, Judy. 2010. Feminist Theories of Technology. *Cambridge Journal of Economics* 34 (1): 143–152.

Wark, Jayne. 2006. *Radical Gestures: Feminism and Performance Art in North America*. McGill-Queen's Press-MQUP.

Washko, Angela. 2012. *The Council on Gender Sensitivity and Behavioral Awareness in World of Warcraft*. [Game performance] Documentation. Accessed December 19, 2014. http://angelawashko.com/home.html.

Weil, Rachel. 2013. NES ROM Hacks and Discourses on Gender Anxieties. Accessed December 20, 2014. http://rachelsimoneweil.wordpress.com/2013/03/23/nes-rom-hacks-and-discourses-ongender-anxieties/.

# Index[1]

---

[1] Note: Page numbers followed by 'n' refer to notes.

© The Author(s) 2018
K. L. Gray et al. (eds.), *Feminism in Play*, Palgrave Games in Context,
https://doi.org/10.1007/978-3-319-90539-6

Made in the USA
Columbia, SC
01 November 2018